MUSICAL LEICESTER

Max Wade-Matthews

MUSICAL LEICESTER

Max Wade-Matthews

Heart of Albion Press

MUSICAL LEICESTER

Max Wade-Matthews

Heart of Albion Press
ISBN 1 872883 51 6

© Text and illustrations (except where otherwise credited) copyright Max Wade-Matthews 1998.

The moral right of the author has been asserted.

All rights reserved. No part of this book may be reproduced in any form or by any means without prior written permission from Heart of Albion Press, except for brief passages quoted in reviews.

British Library Cataloguing in Publication Data
A catalogue record for this book is available from the British Library.

Printed in England by Intype London Ltd

Heart of Albion Press
2 Cross Hill Close, Wymeswold,

𝄞 DEDICATION 𝄞

For Tom - may his life be full of harmony.

Front cover: Christmas Eve, Highcross Market, Leicester in the sixteenth century. A painting from about 1900 by Henry Reynolds Steer (1858–1928). By kind permission of Leicester City Museums.

This imaginative painting shows the Leicester Town Waits playing by the High Cross. It is anachronistic as the High Cross was demolished in 1773 but the Waits did not change from stringed to wind instruments until 1819.

𝄞 PROGRAMME 𝄞

Foreword by Neil Crutchley

Introduction

1: PRELUDE   1

    The Waits   1
    The Theatre and Guildhall   2
    Benefit concerts   5
    William Hanbury   6
    The Great Meeting   7
    The Leicester Infirmary   8
    Militia bands   11
    Local musical venues   12
    The first Subscription Concerts   14
    Beethoven - a first for Leicester   15
    The Piano   16

2: CON MOTO   21
    The Assembly Room   21
    Dancing academies   24
    Mr Ray   24
    Henry Bland   25
    George Partington   26
    Frederick Freak   28
    Monsieur d'Egville   28
    Charles Smart   29
    Teachers of music   29

3: ANDANTE   32
    Subscription concerts   33
    Charles Jarvis   35
    Mary Linwood   36
    Charles Guynemer   37
    Music at the theatre and local inns   38
    The Leicester Choral Society   41

4: MUSIC SHOPS	43
Samuel Deacon	43
Mary Ann Deacon	44
Charles Mavius	46
William Bithrey	48
Thomas Sternberg	48
Popular music	49
William Moore	50
William Burden	51
A.T. Pole	51
James Herbert Marshall	51
5: THE 1827 MUSIC FESTIVAL	57
Preliminary plans	58
Thomas Greatorex	61
Finalising arrangements	62
The doors open	69
6: ALLEGRO MA NON TROPPO	76
The New Hall	76
The Musical Society	78
Subscription concerts	80
Bands	85
Concerts for the people	87
The Mechanics' Institute	91
William Gardiner	93
7: VIVACE	97
The opening of the Temperance Hall	97
Popular music at the Hall	99
Furnishings in the Temperance Hall	101
The Temperance Hall organ	102
Jenny Lind	102
Picco	103
Family combinations and minstrel troupes	104
Minstrel troupes	107
Local bands of minstrels	110
British music	111
European music	112
The Floral Hall	113

8: THE NICHOLSON FAMILY — 114
- Henry Nicholson — 114
- Henry Nicholson junior — 117
- Local talent unfairly neglected — 122
- Henry Nicholson attains national recognition — 123
- Alfred Nicholson — 127
- Valentine Nicholson — 129

9: CANTABILE — 130
- The Royal Opera House — 131
- Charity concerts — 135

10: A CAPELLA — 140
- Nineteenth century organists and choirmasters — 140
- George Augustus Löhr — 141
- Löhr's three sons — 143
- Edwin John Crow — 143
- Joseph T. Stone — 144
- Henry Bramley Ellis — 144
- Mary Scott — 147
- John Morland — 147
- Charles Hancock — 148
- Hancock's pupils — 151
- Nonconformist chapels — 152
- Ranshall Rowe — 152
- The Rowlett family — 152
- The Wykes family — 153
- Organ builders — 154
- Stephen Taylor's musical sons — 155
- Joshua Porritt — 157
- Campanology — 157

11: ALLA MARCIA — 162
- John Alfred Smith — 162
- Open air band concerts — 165
- Sunday band concerts — 169
- Francis Ptacek — 171
- Local bands — 175
- The Police Band — 175
- Other brass bands — 177
- Band concerts — 179
- Visiting bands — 180
- The Leicester Commemoration Exhibition — 181

12: TUTTI	182
The Harmonic Society	182
The Madrigal Society	183
The New Choral Society	183
The Orchestral Union	186
The New Musical Society	186
The Philharmonic Society	191
Sidney P. Waddington	194
Colin McAlpin	195
Lucy Downing	195
Other local societies	196
13: CODA	197
Concerts	197
Societies	200
The Municipal Orchestra	201
Lawrence Wright	203
Into the twentieth century	204
CODETTA 1	
New Philharmonic Society members 1866	205
CODETTA 2	
Philharmonic Society members 1897	206
CODETTA 3	
Favourite local musician competition 1891	207
END NOTES	208
BIBLIOGRAPHY	226
INDEX	230

♪ ACKNOWLEDGEMENTS ♪

This book would not have been possible without the help and advice of many people, too many to mention here. However, special thanks are due to Mr Neil Crutchley who proof-read the final draft and supplied the Foreword; Mrs Gabrielle Brown (granddaughter of Henry Bramley Ellis), Mrs Pam Baker-Clare (great-granddaughter of William Thorpe Briggs); Mr Harold Nicholson (great-grandson of Henry Nicholson); Mr Harry Skelson M.B.E. (Hon Secretary Leicestershire Yeomanry Association); and the invaluable assistance of the staff of the Leicestershire Record Office.

FOREWORD

By Neil Crutchley
Music Critic and Features Writer
Leicester Mercury

Only now, at the end of the twentieth century, do we have a comprehensive study of music in Leicester in the preceding two hundred years. A work like this is long overdue and should prove to be of interest to scholar and layman alike.

Twentieth century Leicester has had a rich and varied musical life. Amateur music making of all kinds, from theatre to church and orchestra, has flourished. So too has professional music: helped of course by the building of the De Montfort Hall in 1912.

However, many of the seeds for these activities were sown in the last century.

It is fascinating to read of the names and personalities of those days: the splendid William Gardiner, responsible for the first English performance of a work by Beethoven; the Nicholson dynasty whose tireless efforts to bring the best music to Leicester make most impresarios seem tame by comparison; the organists and rival organ builders Taylor and Porritt (whose names and instruments are familiar to all local organists to this day); the singers, conductors, choirmasters and bellringers are all chronicled along with the halls, churches and salons, many of which are long gone, in what adds up to a splendid document of musical and social history.

Present and future generations of music lovers will find much to enjoy as will musicians and historians. Max Wade-Matthews has shed light on a darkened room with this enjoyable, informative and well illustrated volume and for that I, for one, am grateful.

🎼 NOTES 🎼

Currency is kept to pre-decimalization units.
Twelve old pence = one shilling = five new pence.
Twenty shillings = one pound.
Twenty-one shillings = one guinea = 105 new pence.

All topographical references are contemporary with the event described. Where the name has been changed the present nomenclature is added. When not otherwise stated places are in Leicester.

🎼 INTRODUCTION 🎼

The main period covered by this book is the nineteenth century – a period when the population of Leicester increased from just under seventeen thousand in 1801 to over two hundred and eleven thousand in 1901.

With small halls and audiences made up almost solely of the middle and upper classes, the only way concerts could be held in the eighteenth and the first decades of the nineteenth century was on the subscription principle. In this way promoters of concerts knew just what money was available and thus were able to hire the finest performers they could afford. Not until the middle of the nineteenth century, when large halls were opened such as the Temperance Hall in Leicester, was there a change from subscriptions to the selling of tickets at reasonable prices.

During the second half of the century musical societies, once the preserve of the middle classes, began to welcome working-class members who, with more free time and education, were eager to get first-hand experience of the music of the great composers such as Handel and Mendlessohn. By the end of Victoria's reign, as well as the Leicester Philharmonic Society there were many smaller musical societies in the town, both secular and church-based.

Another change was the increase in the number of professional musicians as the century progressed. In 1801 the only professionals in the town were a handful of teachers whereas one hundred years later not only were there many more teachers but also professional performers. As a sign of the changing times, just before Christmas 1898, in an attempt to get a pay rise, the musicians of the local theatres demonstrated outside the Theatre Royal by playing the *Dead March*, a protest like this would have been unheard of in 1801!

Chapter 1

𝄞 PRELUDE 𝄞

The eighteenth century opened with few indigenous professional musicians in England - the performers being mainly French, Italian or German. Concerts as we know them today were unknown with musical performances restricted to the homes of the nobility. As the standard of living gradually rose, so did the mercantile class whose new opulence stimulated a desire for novelty in all forms of artistic expression, including music. It was, however, still music by the upper classes for the upper classes. That this was so is aptly illustrated by the comment in *The Englishman's Journal* of 1738 that everybody knew that Handel's 'entertainments are calculated for the Quality only and that people of moderate fortunes cannot pretend to them'. This arrogant conception of music slowly died out and, by 1775, the love of music had become so wide-spread that even 'common servants' could be met with who pretended 'as much judgement of an opera tune as my Lady Duchess.'[1]

The Waits

The first professional musicians in Leicester were the waits who, dressed in scarlet gowns, perambulated the town playing their instruments. Round the neck of each of the master waits, who each had an apprentice, hung a silver chain on which the badge of the borough was affixed, an insignia so valuable that two securities had to be given to answer for its safe return in case of death or dismissal. In 1729 the salary of these musical peripatetics was six pounds thirteen shillings and fourpence. However, by May 1781, partly as a result of corporation savings, and partly by a decease in the waits' duties, this salary had fallen, by more than half, to three pounds a year.

The waits' work was not always of the standard expected for, in September 1797, they were reprimanded for neglect of duty and threatened with dismissal if they did not improve and become more reliable.[2] One of their busiest times was Christmas when, starting

The Badge of the Leicester Waits. (Kelly's The Great Mace of Leicester)

early in the morning, 'with strains and welcomings which belonged to the night', they gently woke the sleeping town with 'music that seemed to have commenced in their dreams.'[3]

Though the town waits were officially disbanded in January 1836, it seems as if they kept together for, in early November of each year, up to 1876, they applied to the mayor for permission to play in the town during the Christmas season. Examples of the tunes played by the musicians at this time of the year include the now forgotten 'Meet Me By Moonlight Alone', 'Oft In The Stilly Night' and 'On This Cold Flinty Rock'.[4]

In December 1842 a 'Constant Reader', who was concerned with the 'nocturnal nuisance' of the waits, reminded the editor of the *Leicester Chronicle* of a letter, which had been written a few months earlier by William Gardiner, concerning the singing of ballads in the streets by 'Every poor wretch who is blest with a stout pair of lungs'. Gardiner's distaste of indigenous English music had been highlighted at the the close of the letter in which he praised the example set by the 'itinerant foreigners' who gave 'agreeable music with their portable pianofortes and voices,' whereas the native English singers helped 'to degrade us as a musical people.' The 'Constant Reader' concluded his letter with the wry observation that in the case of the waits it was often distance that led enchantment to the sound.[5]

The Theatre and Guildhall

In the spring of 1750, almost forty years after Thomas Hickford had opened the first room to be devoted to formal concerts in London, local wine merchant, John Bass, erected the first theatre-cum-assembly room in Leicester, a town with a population of about nine thousand. Facing Humberstone Gate, near the site of the present Clock Tower, the building consisted of a large upper room supported on columns, beneath which lay a large open space from where the coal from the Swanington and Coleorton mines was delivered to the local dealers. Previously the only buildings in Leicester large enough for public concerts and assemblies had been the Guildhall and the Exchange, while the Castle Great Hall was occasionally used for grand balls.[6]

The Guildhall was built about 1380 (dendrochronology shows that the timber was felled in 1370) for the Leicester Corpus Christi Gild, which had been founded in 1343. The members, who had a chapel in nearby St Martin's Church, afforded each other financial and practical help in times of need, as well as providing the funds for masses to be said for the souls of deceased members. By 1494 the town corporation was using the timber-framed building for its meetings, purchasing it outright, after the Reformation, in 1563. As well as town meetings the hall was also used by itinerant players, indeed it is quite possible that Shakespeare himself may have performed here.

The earliest extant reference to a public ball in Leicester, as against an event taking place in a country house, occurs in 1722 when there were two in the space of a few weeks - leading one to suspect that there had

Leicester Guildhall, as it appeared in the mid-nineteenth century.
(Robert Read's Modern Leicester)

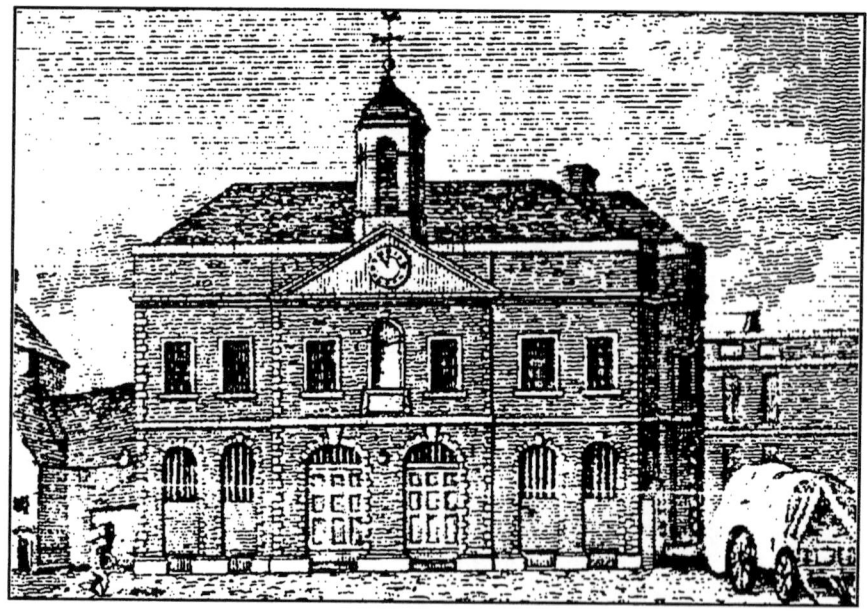

The Exchange, roughly on the site of the present Market Exchange, was erected in 1748 at the cost of about four thousand pounds. It was demolished and replaced in 1851. (Nichols)

been others, the details of which being now lost. Indeed, earlier in the year the corporation had found it necessary to control the letting of the town hall, by passing the order that the mayor should not let it 'to any players for any shows whatever, nor to any dancing masters for balls without the consent of the Common Hall'.[7]

The two recorded events of 1722 took place in the November. The first was on the sixteenth when Mr Tyrrell, a dancing master, had permission to use the town hall on the conditions that he set 'nothing but forms and chairs upon the ground' and that he made good 'any damage that may happen'. The second, on the twenty-eighth, seems to have been a much grander affair, taking place in the castle with one Thomas Hodgson as master of ceremonies. The card of notification included the advice that there would be no admittance after 4 pm. The Guildhall was also the venue for the annual Race Night balls which, in the first half of the eighteenth century, were under the direction of the town's various dancing masters such as Hudson, Tyrrell, Unwin or Langton.[8]

Benefit Concerts

In 1759 there were two benefit concerts, tickets two shillings and sixpence each, held in the Assembly Room on behalf of local musicians John and Henry Valentine. The first, in March, included a harpsichord solo by John Philpot; a bassoon concerto by Scamerdine; Geminian's *Sixth Concerto* and Carelli's *Twelfth Concerto*.

The Valentines lived in a large house, next to the Cap and Stocking public house near the East Gate, which was demolished in 1808 to make way for road widening. Their grandfather, Henry, had been appointed organist at St Martin's in 1701, a post which was later filled by their uncle Mark who, in 1748, was discharged after several unspecified charges had been levied against him.

As far as can be ascertained the Valentines were the only professional musicians in the town at this time. Apart from the mainly German and Italian, professionals based in London, Edinburgh and Dublin there were very few, if we exclude the organists of the major churches, full-time practical musicians in the country until the beginning of the nineteenth century.

The second benefit concert of 1759, held in June, was on behalf of William Boulton who had been appointed organist of St Martin's some three years earlier. No doubt with memories of Mark Valentine, Boulton's appointment had been made on the condition that 'he behaves well'. The intermediate organist, Dr Musgrave Heighton, had been organist at Hull (1717-20), Dublin (1725-28) and Great Yarmouth (1733-46) before coming to Leicester in 1748. In 1756 he left Leicester for a post at Dundee, where he died in 1764 aged eighty-four.[9]

In the late 1750s, due to the danger of a possible French invasion, militias all over the country were embodied. It was one of these exercises, in 1759, that brought the Suffolk Militia, under their general, the Duke of Grafton, to Leicester. The Corporation held numerous balls and functions for the officers including one in the Exchange. Reputed to have been the most expensive feast ever given by the Corporation, we are told that all those who attended, including the Duke and the Mayor, were 'levelled with the mighty power of wine'.[10] Although the best part of these balls consisted of country dances and quadrilles, they usually commenced with three or four stately minuets, a dance introduced in the mid-seventeenth century which transformed men into courtiers while the ladies, who had previously played a subservient part in the dance, obtained equal rights, their hooped skirts ensuring, however, that they never offended the morality of the age by coming into close contact with their partner.

William Hanbury

William Hanbury was born in September 1725 in Bedworth, Warwickshire. In 1749, the newly-ordained William, who had matriculated at Magdalen Hall, Oxford, was appointed vicar at Church Langton. Very interested in botany, Hanbury set out a number of tree plantations and within a few years had amassed a small fortune from these horticultural activities. The money so raised was put into his charity trust fund.

On the occasion of the establishment of the trust, on the weekend of the twenty-sixth and twenty-seventh September 1759, Hanbury held a rather ambitious music festival in the village. The music on the Saturday was of the nature of a church service with no admission fee, but with a collection being taken at the doors. The Sunday programme, admission one guinea, was a grand performance of the *Messiah*, composed some seventeen years earlier. This, the first recorded performance of the work in a rural parish church, was so popular that the doors had to be barricaded to prevent overcrowding.

In June 1762 Hanbury arranged an 'oratorio season for the Nobility and Gentry' in Leicester. Held in St Martin's Church, the three days of music, led by Dr William Hayes of the University of Oxford, included the *Messiah*, *Judas Maccabaeus* and *Samson*. Tickets for the performances were five shillings each and were available from either the Three Cranes, Gallowtree Gate, or John Gregory, the publisher of the *Leicester Journal*.

On the evening of each day there was a 'performance of a familiar nature' and a ball in the Assembly Room. This event not only resulted in profits of over one hundred pounds, which Hanbury put towards his charity, but also brought the performers to the attention of people from surrounding towns, such as Nottingham and Derby who asked that similar performances be arranged in their own localities.[11]

The Great Meeting

The Great Meeting in Bond Street is believed to have been the first chapel in Leicester to introduce musical instruments into its services. Erected in 1708, part of the nearby mediæval town walls were used in the foundations of this the first substantial brick building in the town. It is still standing, albeit with a 'new' nineteenth century porch.

In 1760 Thomas Gardiner, one of the town's leading hosiers, amateur flute and cello player, and choirmaster of the Great Meeting, persuaded the Elders to replace the precentor's tuning fork, with which he used to find the note to begin the singing, with a bass viol to accompany the voices. Although bassoons and oboes were in common use in country churches this was the first instrument of its kind to be introduced into one of the town's dissenting meeting houses. At first the new viol, which was supplied by the famous stringed instrument maker Barak Norman, was censured as approaching too near the 'ceremonies of the Church', but the demand for music in the chapel was such that, in 1802, the congregation paid thirty-five pounds for a new organ built by Jonathan Ohrmann, who had taken over the firm started by the noted organ builder John Snetzler, who had died in 1785. The chapel's choir, which had been in existence since the 1760s and was one of the finest in the town, celebrated the event by an oratorio. However, bad weather prevented many from attending the excellent performance.[12]

In 1774 some of the members of the Great Meeting's and St Margaret's choirs formed St Margaret's Catch Club. The invitation to one of these free concerts, held in the Haymarket Assembly Room, included the following verse:

> *To our musical choir long life and prosperity:*
> *May it flourish with US, and so on to prosperity.*
> *May Concord and Harmony ever abound,*
> *And Divisions here only in MUSIC be found.*

In 1792, the chapel held a concert in aid of their charity day school, the oldest such institution in the town. The concert, which featured a pair of kettledrums, had an orchestra so large that 'it nearly ascended to the roof'. Indeed, such was the interest in the event that many were left standing outside on the pavement.[13]

The Leicester Infirmary

In September 1771, the opening of the new Leicester Infirmary was celebrated by a musical service in St Martin's, in which the choir of St Margaret's sung parts of Handel's *Messiah* and *Coronation Anthem*. In the evening, under the direction of Joseph Cradock, a grand concert was held in the Haymarket Assembly Room. Cradock, a former High Sheriff of the County, was a lover of the arts who lived in the newly-built Gumley Hall. The music for the occasion was lent by Cradock's friend, David Garrick, the renowned actor and manager of the Drury Lane Theatre.

Among those who took part in this prestigious concert were John Fisher (violin), Johann Fischer (oboe), Joseph Vernon (tenor), Samuel Champness (bass) and Haydn's niece, Mary Barthélmon (soprano). The concert, which was conducted by Cradock and the Reverend Jenner, also included the music of the band of the 'Blues', whose Colonel, the Marquis of Granby, was the Duke of Rutland's son. The event raised nearly one hundred pounds for the worthy institution.[14]

For several years afterwards the Infirmary held an annual concert and ball which brought the best musicians from the metropolis to the town. Among those who appeared in Leicester were the celebrated violinist Felice Giardini; James Cervetto, cellist; Thomas Norris, a popular tenor whose career was blighted though drink; Frederica Weichell, soprano; Mr Sharpe; Mr King; Mr Adcock; and thirteen year old Miss Greatorex, organist of St Martin's, who played the harpsichord.[15] For the anniversary meeting in 1774 Cradock wrote *Here Shall Soft Charity Repair*, an ode which was put to music by William Boyce, Master of the King's Musick. The melodramatic verse enjoyed wide popularity and is known to have been performed as least as far away as Bangor.[16]

The orchestra, the largest assembly of musicians that had ever appeared in Leicestershire, was led by Giardini and included the Earl of Sandwich, First Lord of the Admiralty, who exhibited his prowess on the kettledrums.

On the first evening there was a grand concert in Leicester Castle at which Giardini appeared dressed in a green and gold coat richly adorned with lace and with three large buttons on the sleeves. On the morning of the second day, in St Martin's, where a temporary gallery

HERE SHALL SOFT CHARITY REPAIR

Lo! on a thorny bed of care
The trembling victim lies;
Deep sunk his eye balls with despair,
What friendly hand his want supplies?
Deplore his fate to woes consign'd
Deplore the fate of human kind.
Forbear to murmur at Heav'n's high degree
Nor swell the bulk of human misery.
Think not in vain the pitying tear
To thoughtless man was giv'n;
Sweet as the moon its dews appear,
A balmy increase in the sight of Heaven.
Here shall soft Charity repair
And break the bonds of grief
Down the flinty couch of care
Man to man must bring relief.[17]

The Leicester Infirmary c.1800.
Opened in 1771, the infirmary was often the beneficiary of concerts which were held in the town. (Nichols)

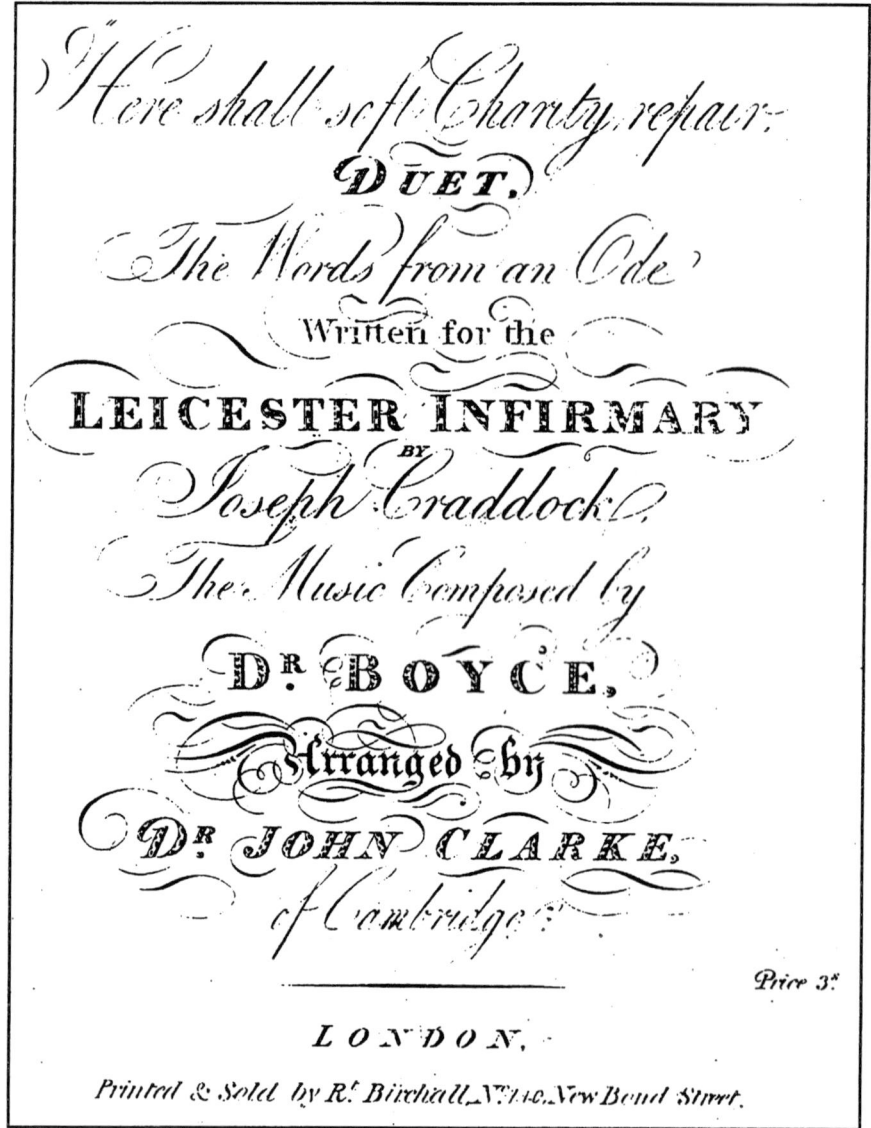

The title page of 'The Infirmary Ode' which was sung at the 1774 Infirmary Anniversary Concert. (Leicestershire Record Office)

had been erected in the nave to accommodate the orchestra, Handel's *Jephtha* was performed for the first time in Leicester.

This concert also saw the formal opening of the church's new organ, which had been specially tuned so that it could be played with an orchestra. Played on this occasion by Joah Bates, the instrument had been built by John Snetzler at the cost of six hundred and twelve pounds, the arrangement being that he took five hundred pounds in cash and the old instrument in part-exchange.

Snetzler's first organ in this country had been built for Handel and used during the first performance of *Messiah* in Dublin, in April 1742. Handel is believed to have composed the music for his oratorio at Gopsall Hall, Leicestershire, the home of his friend Charles Jennens who selected the words for the work. Unfortunately, in spite of the wealth of musical talent that had been hired for the occasion, the meeting made a financial loss of over four hundred pounds.[18]

In 1785 Thomas Gardiner arranged a concert in aid of the Infirmary. With the assistance of Mr Frudd, a dancing master who played violin, a selection from the *Messiah* was performed in St Martin's Church. The principal vocalist at this concert was Gertrude Mara (née Schmeling 1749-1833) who had arrived in England from Germany a few months previously. Although an inferior actress, her voice was noted for its beauty of tone and wide range of nearly three octaves. Known for exhibiting a high-handedness, so typical of prima donnas of her day, while performing in Leicester for no charge, she did ask that her hairdresser's fee of twenty-six guineas might be paid![19]

Militia Bands

A few months earlier the officers of the militia had entertained the town to a tea party in the Bath Gardens where a band, stationed on a pleasure boat on the river, 'discoursed sweet music with charming effect.' Four years later, in 1778, it was decided that the militia should have its own band and to this end six promising musicians were sent to London to be given tuition on various instruments, including clarinets and oboes. Although we are not told the full list of instruments used by the Leicestershire band do know that the usual line up of instruments in military bands of the period was a combination of oboes, bassoons, and French horns. It is interesting that the only instrument which records mention by name is the clarinet, which, although in common use in Prussian and French bands, did not come into universal use in British military bands until the 1790s.

In June the band helped to cheer the men on their nine-day march to Liverpool, where they embarked for Ireland. There they remained until 1783 when they returned home,'having performed no one feat of arms, or achieved one earthly good'.[20]

Local Musical Venues

On the three nights of the annual races, which were held near the present Aylestone Road, there was singing, and country dancing to a band in the Vauxhall Gardens, near the present West Bridge. The Gardens were rather grandly named after the Vauxhall Gardens in London which had been holding alfresco musical entertainments since 1732. When, in 1796, the Leicester gardens closed, to make way for wharves on the newly-built canal, the festivities transferred to the Bowling Green in St Peter's Lane.

Tickets for these events, which concluded with a firework display, cost as much as one shilling and sixpence [7.5p], thereby preventing many of the poorer inhabitants from attending, for whom the price of admission was well over a day's pay.[21]

Some of the larger inns of the town, such as the Three Crowns, on the corner of Granby and Horsefair Streets, held music meetings, where groups of singers met for singing the humorous catches and joyful glees which were so popular in the late eighteenth century. Almost all these catches are now forgotten with the exception of one known by everybody whose first language is English - 'Three Blind Mice'. An example of the catches sung in the eighteenth century is 'Old Thomas Day'. Written by Dr Harrington, the effect of the song was heightened by the singers being attired as three old women in nightcaps.[22]

On his frequent visits to Gumley Hall Joah Bates, the founder of the Concerts of Ancient Music in London in 1776, would join the incumbent of St Margaret's, the Reverend Robert Burnaby (violin), and William Tilley (cello) at musical meetings in the Three Cranes,

Opposite 'Old Thomas Day'. Written by Dr Harrington, this is an example of the popular catches of the eighteenth century.
(*William Gardiner's* Music and Friends)

Prelude 13

Gallowtree Gate, where they entertained themselves and the inn's patrons.[23]

One local publican, Mr Martin, the landlord of the Blackamoor Lady, near the Castle, even made his own double bass. However, it could not have been a very practical instrument, for it was so big that a hole had to be cut in the ceiling and it could only be tuned by going upstairs to the room above![24]

The First Subscription Concerts in Leicester

Although subscription concerts had been held in provincial centres since the 1730s - Newcastle holding a series in 1736 and Manchester in 1744 - it was not until the 1760s that they began to take root. Although there had been individual subscription concerts held in the town, such as that arranged by John and Henry Valentine in 1762, the

The Three Crowns c.1820.
Demolished in 1864, the inn was often the venue for informal musical meetings in the eighteenth and early nineteenth centuries.
(Leicestershire Record Office)

first series of concerts in Leicester, held in the Guildhall, was organised by John Brooke in 1785.

Brooke, a tall, wealthy man with refined manners, had a house which was more like a museum of fine arts than a home, containing books, engravings, pictures and musical instruments. Each of his well supported fortnightly concerts, annual subscription fifteen shillings, terminated, as was the custom of the day, with a ball of country dances and minuets. For the first time the more conservative of the dissenting families were able to attend musical events, objecting as they did to the more worldly card and dancing assemblies which were held in the town.

The orchestra for these concerts consisted of the Reverend Robert Burnaby, his son Thomas, William Tilley, John Brooke (cello), William Hodges, Robert Coleman, Henry Carrick, Thomas Gardiner and his son William who, no doubt influenced by the Earl of Sandwich whom he had admired on that instrument some eleven years earlier, played the kettledrums. Also taking part in this first season of subscription concerts was the Valentine family: Ann (organist at St Margaret's), Fanny (singer), John (violin), Henry and Robert junior.[25]

Beethoven - A first for Leicester and England

In 1794 Leicester was the first town in England to enjoy the music of Beethoven. The previous year, in the general flight from Bonn at the approach of the French Republican troops, the Abbe Döbler, chaplain to the Elector of Cologne, accompanied Mrs Frances Bowater, the daughter of the Earl of Faversham and estranged wife of a Warwickshire man, to Hamburg. While at the Hanseatic port the Abbe was declared an emigre, so Mrs Bowater, who owned Old Dalby Hall, invited him to accompany her to Leicester. Döbler soon integrated himself into the musical life of the town, making friends with the Valentines and William Gardiner. Amongst the music which Döbler brought over in his luggage was a copy of Beethoven's *Violin Trio in E flat*, which he, Gardiner, and a member of the Valentine family played one evening at the Bowater house - three years before the work was published in London.[26]

Gardiner's admiration for Beethoven's music was well-known. In August 1845 he was invited by Caroline de Bellville, the only female Beethoven ever taught and who had married the English violinist Antonio Oury, to the unveiling of the statue of the famous musician in

Bonn. Dr Walter, of that town's university, spotted Gardiner in the crowd and called him to the podium where he was introduced as the man who had introduced the music of Beethoven to England. Then, much to Gardiner's astonishment, he was invited to sign the parchment which recorded the date and facts of the inauguration which was to be soldered up in a lead box and deposited in the base of the statue. The only place on the parchment which would accommodate Gardiner's signature was under the names of Victoria and Albert. As he often related, this was the proudest day of his life.[27]

William Gardiner's love of music had been with him since childhood. As a six year old he had sung a solo at the wedding of one of his father's friends. While a child he learnt to play the piano and viola and, inspired by the return of the Militia from the American wars, in his early teens wrote a march and a quickstep for the band. Presented to the bandmaster, with no indication of the identity of the composer, young William's heart filled with pride as the band played his compositions in the Market Place.

At about the same time, under the name Paxton, he wrote a hymn tune for the Great Meeting choir which soon became a great favourite with the congregation. Gardiner, a member of the town's Adelphi Philosophical Society, continued to write and his arrangements were sung all over the country - in 1821 his trio 'The Lord Will Comfort Zion' was performed at a provincial festival, at which the programme notes attributed the work to Haydn! Gardiner also arranged secular words to music such as Shakespeare's 'Take, O take those Lips away' which was published, about 1790, in London. The sheet music, price one shilling, named the composer as 'W. G. of Lester'.

Gardiner was also a devotee of the music of Haydn. In 1804 he had his hosiery factory make six pairs of cotton stockings in which were worked various quotations from Haydn's music. These he sent to the impresario Johann Salomon, who some twenty years earlier had introduced the music of Haydn to the English public, with the request that he present them to the Austrian composer on his (Salomon's) forthcoming visit to Vienna. Somehow the parcel of stockings got lost and 'the god of science' never received them.[28]

Prelude

'Take, O Take those Lips away' by 'W.G. of Lester'. This copy, which is preserved in the Leicestershire Record Office, has a pencil inscription by Gardiner, 'I wrote this, I suppose, at 1790'.

The Piano

As the eighteenth century drew to a close pianos were finding their place in the homes of the well-to-do. The piano had been first introduced into an English concert hall in May 1767 when Charles Dibdin accompanied a song sung at Covent Garden. The following year, on 2 June 1768, the great Bach's son Johann Christian, who had been living in London since 1762, played the first public solo, a concerto of his own composition, on the 'new instrument called Forte Piano'.

One of the most remarkable musical visitors to Leicester in the eighteenth century was six year old William Crotch who played a concert in the Exchange in 1782. Born in Norwich, the son of a carpenter, he was a child prodigy without parallel in the history of music. By the time he was two he was able to pick out tunes on an organ, which his father had built. A year later he gave his first public concert prior to his mother taking him on a series of concert tours throughout the country. By the time he was four he was able to transpose into any key and had played before King George III.

At the time there were only two or three pianos in Leicester including that in the Gardiner household made by Johannes Pohlmann. Pohlmann, one of the first makers of pianos in England, had moved to London from Germany in 1767, and it was on this instrument that Crotch played. As well as the piano Crotch also played violin, which he did standing on a chair so as to be seen by his audience. His aural faculty for detecting faulty intonation was such that at one point in the concert, young as he was, Crotch stopped the musicians to tell William Tilley that he had played a section incorrectly. In 1822 Crotch was

William Crotch (1775-1847). Six year old William Crotch performed in Leicester in 1782. (Grove's Dictionary)

appointed the principal of the newly-established Royal Academy of Music.[29]

The harpsichord finally disappeared from the concert platform in 1795, when it was used for the rehearsal of a birthday ode for the king - it was, however, replaced by a piano at the actual performance. The older type of instrument did, however, linger on in musical households partly due to a conservative distrust of the newfangled invention and partly due to the high price asked for the early models. In 1797 James Harrison commenced his *Piano-Forte Magazine*, which sold for half-a-crown. Each issue included a note, signed by Harrison, promising a new piano to any reader who purchased the entire two hundred and fifty numbers, and produced two hundred and fifty signed certificates.

Pianoforte by Johannes Pohlmann, 1773.
This is a similar piano to that which was in the Gardiner household.
(Victoria and Albert Museum)

By the end of the century public music-making had become more and more frequent. Although concerts, both in London and the provinces, had become public rather than events held in the homes of the nobility, they were, due to the high price of subscriptions, still positively middle class. Opera, however, remained confined to the capital, and did so until the mid-nineteenth century. Purpose-built concert halls were erected in London (Carlisle House, Soho Square, 1764; the Pantheon, Oxford Street, 1772; and the Hanover Square Rooms, 1775) as well as in some of the major provincial centres such as Bath, which, due to its spa, was the centre of fashion.

Leicester, musically speaking, at the turn of the century was still just an average town with no regular concert season. Birmingham, Chester and York, on the other hand, all held triennial music festivals. Music in Leicester seems to have been on an ad hoc basis with concerts put together more for the satisfaction of the players than for the edification of the auditors, such as the afore mentioned performance of Beethoven's trio in 1794. However, as we shall see, as the nineteenth century progressed so did musical life in the town until it became one of the most thriving provincial musical centres in the country.

Chapter 2

♪ CON MOTO ♪

The Assembly Room

In 1791 the gentry of the county proposed to build a new hotel and assembly room in Leicester (from which Hotel Street was named). However, with the high increase in taxation and the introduction of income tax at two shillings in the pound, made necessary by the wars with France, which by 1797 had cost the country some nineteen million pounds, the plan had to be shelved. It was to be another seven years before economic conditions were such that it again became possible to reconsider the proposal and launch an appeal for funds.

The Hotel Assembly Rooms. Built in 1800 the rooms were the venue for the balls which were a feature of early nineteenth century Leicester.
(Max Wade-Matthews)

In spite of strenuous efforts, the building, designed by local architect John Johnson, and built on the site of the former cockpit, could not attract a purchaser. It was, therefore decided to subdivide the ground floor and let the rooms to various concerns, such as bookseller Thomas Combe, and use the first floor as the Assembly Room.[1]

The first known event in the Assembly Room, which was the centre of public entertainment until the erection of the New Hall, in 1832, was a card and dancing assembly which took place in February 1801. The following July, the room was the venue for a well-attended concert of music by Handel and Haydn, at which just over thirty-nine pounds was raised for the Infirmary. The organisers of the evening were Dr Thomas Arnold, who ran a hospital for the mentally ill; local banker John Mansfield; Henry Carter; and the Reverend Thomas Burnaby, who had succeeded his father as vicar of St Margaret's.[2]

Although tickets for individual balls and assemblies were available for people living outside the town, they were not on sale to 'resident gentlemen', who were expected to purchase a season ticket costing one guinea. As well as the six-monthly Town and County Subscription

The Bell Hotel, Humberstone Gate.
In the second quarter of the nineteenth century, under the management of Henri l'Hermitte and Arthur Boyer, the kitchens of the Bell supplied the food for many of the balls held in the Assembly Rooms. (Nichols)

Balls the Assembly Room was also the venue for benefit balls, such as those in 1814 for the inhabitants of Germany who were suffering from the effects of the Napoleonic wars. Another, in 1817, was in aid of The Ladies Fund for the Relief of the Poor, while in 1818 the Infirmary was the beneficiary. In September of each year there was also a ball on the last evening of Race Week, as well as when the militia were in town.[3]

Advertisement from the Leicester Chronicle for the February 1845 Leicester Ball.

With the transfer of concerts to the newly-opened Wellington Street Rooms in 1832, events in the Assembly Room were mainly restricted to balls. In February 1835 the local Conservatives held such a ball to celebrate the return of the two Tory MPs, Thomas Gladstone (brother of William who became prime minister) and Edward Gouldburn (a sergeant at law who had been borough recorder). The festivities continued until the early hours, with some of the guests not getting home till five the following morning.

The Assembly Room was also the venue for the annual Hunt Ball for which tickets cost a massive twelve shillings and sixpence each. The three hundred or so who attended these events would dance into the early hours to the music of either Henry Nicholson's band or that of the Leamington-based Weipart. As well as dancing, the revellers would revive themelves with food provided by the Bell Hotel, Humberstone Gate.[4]

Other annual balls held in the Assembly Room included the Licensed Victuallers Association (January); the Freemasons (February); the Yeomanry (September); and, in December, the Anniversary Ball for the benefit of the County Lunatic Asylum (now the Fielding-Johnson building of the University).

In January 1858, the Room was the venue for a public ball to celebrate the marriage of the Princess Royal and Prince Frederick of Prussia, while the following January there was a special event to raise funds to decorate and refurbish the building. Minor events also continued to take place in the Guildhall, as in February 1851, when the Nicholson and Weston band introduced 'La Gorlitza', a dance which was described as 'extremely pretty'.[5]

Dancing Academies

The new dances of the early nineteenth century were inseparable from the changes in fashion. Up till about 1810 the well-dressed woman was still holding her bosom high with tightly laced up corsets. She kept warm with several petticoats, over which she wore a simple dress. Then, in the spirit of Wordsworthian romance, ladies discarded their corsets and petticoats and replaced them by one simple dress cut low over the bosom. With the rejection of petticoats women of fashion began to wear knickers, an item of apparel which up till then had only been worn by professional dancers. Men's fashions also changed with, in 1814, George 'Beau' Brummel's introduction of the wearing of trousers in the place of breeches.

By 1800 the minuet was almost obsolete. The changes in fashion encouraged the more proletarian dances, such as the waltz and polka, to creep into the balls of the upper classes. The waltz, which appeared in Vienna about 1780, and introduced into England about 1805, was thought particularly decadent because, unlike the more formal stately figure of the minuet, the partners came into close contact with each other.

Mr Ray

As the nineteenth century opened, with a population of about seventeen thousand, there were three 'professors of dancing' in Leicester. Mr Ray, with premises in New Street, who taught at various schools in the town, was the longest established and was well known for his balls. which were one of Leicester's annual highlights with the usual drab appearance of the town enlivened by the many carriages which transported the gaily dressed well-to-do to the Assembly Rooms. It was said that the elegance of manners and deportment, which formed the principal characteristic of the Georgian Age, were never more conspicuous than at the ball of 1817. Regarded by many as one of Ray's best, after the dancing display by his pupils everybody was invited to join 'the mazy dance' which continued till the early hours.[7]

As well as public balls Ray also held exhibitions in the local schools. One such event, in June 1807, at Mary Linwood's 'Priory School', in

Belgrave Gate, included the dancing of three of Miss Linwood's nieces and Thomas Paget, a young man who, as the nineteenth century progressed, was to make a name for himself as an Honorary Fellow of the Royal College of Surgeons.[8]

> Get all the ladies that you can;
> And let each lady have a man;
> Let them, in a circle placed,
> Take their partners round the waist;
> Then by slow degrees advance
> Till the walk becomes a dance,
> Then the twirling face to face,
> Without variety or grace,
> Round and round and never stopping,
> Now and then a little hopping
> When you're wrong to make things worst,
> If one couple so perverse,
> Should in the figure be perplexed
> Let 'em be knocked down by the next.
> "Quicker now" the ladies cry
> They rise they twirl, they swing they fly
> Puffing, blowing, jostling, squeezing,
> Very odd but very pleasing -
> Till every lady plainly shows
> (Whatever else they may disclose)
> Reserve is not among her faults, -
> Reader, thus it is to waltz.[6]

Henry Bland

In January 1827, on Ray's retirement, Henry Bland, who lived in Charles Street, took over the New Street Academy. Bland, who also taught fencing, continued Ray's tradition of annual balls, for which admission was five shillings. With a rising population and more and more of the *nouveaux riches* interested in learning new dances, business was such that Bland had to begin to open his academy on two evenings a week.[9] Two of these new dances were the Galop, which was introduced into London in 1829, and the Muzurka, introduced into England in January 1833.

Typical of Bland's balls was that of June 1836. The Duke of Rutland's band, led by Samuel Weston, started the evening with Rossini's overture to *Tancredi*. This was followed by dances which had been specially arranged by Henry Nicholson. These included the Duke of Devonshire's 'much admired' Muzurka, Quadrilles, Galopedes and a *pas de deux* by 'Master Jones' and Bland's daughter Angelina, who, as she got older, helped her father by playing the piano at his classes.[10]

Dancing the Polka.
(Illustrated London News April 1844)

One or two times a year Bland visited London and Paris, to learn the new continental dances, such as the Redewa Waltz, the Muzurka, the German Polka and 'the graceful Polonaise' which were coming into fashion. In the 1840s the polka, which made its appearance in London in 1844, was looked down upon as Rock 'n' Roll was in the 1950s, being described 'as if an individual has a hole in his pocket and was futilely trying to shake a shilling down the leg of his trousers.'

In March 1849 Bland danced away from his home in New Street leaving many of his creditors unpaid. Although the local rumour was that he had gone to America he had in reality moved back to his home at 1 Cadogan Square, London where, a few months later, he was declared bankrupt.[11]

George Partington

The second dancing master in the town at the turn of the century was George Partington who had been an assistant to Mr Wilson of 42 Haydn Square London. A native of Melton Mowbray, where he was already established as a dance teacher, Partington opened a school for the 'tuition of young ladies and gentlemen' at Hextall's Long Room at the Bowling Green. In 1808 the rise in popularity of dancing among the growing numbers of the new middle classes, led Partington, as well as having academies in Leicester and Melton, to begin operating at Lutterworth, Burbidge, Hinckley and Enderby. In 1809 he moved his Leicester school from the Bowling Green to the large room in the former Haymarket Assembly Room.[12]

As well as teaching the older country dances, which were coming back into fashion, Partington often made trips to the London Opera House to learn the ever-increasing numbers of new dances which were in vogue and which he demonstrated at his annual balls. Tickets for these events were three shillings and sixpence - half a workman's weekly pay. By 1814 he had moved again, this time to the White Hart Inn, Humberstone Gate, where he remained until 1817 when he relocated a few yards up the road to the George Inn. Two years later he moved again, this time to the large room over Benjamin Payne's Auction Mart in Hotel Street.[13]

Dancing the Polka.
(Illustrated London News *April 1844)*

By 1820 Partington was holding lessons at the newly-built Bowling Green, St Peter's Lane. The complex, consisting of gardens and a cafe, had been laid out to replace the Vauxhall Gardens in Bath Lane, which had been converted to wharves, and the omnipresent public house, to serve the new canal which had been built to facilitate the transportation of goods to London as well as the local trade with Loughborough. Owed by Mr Hextall the Bowling Green was also the venue for summer concerts which usually concluded with a firework display. The autumn events commenced with the pyrotechnics after which the company would repair to the Bowling Green Hall for singing and dancing.[14]

Partington stayed here until 1825 when, on his return from Paris, where he had been under the instruction of the French dancing master Eugene Coulon, the academy moved back to the White Hart Inn. Here he remained until 1833 when he relocated to Barlow's Commercial Room in the Market Place. Ever on the move, the following year he was giving lessons at Mrs Heggs's, South Gate Street, next door to the New Inn. Finally, in 1835, the year he retired, he was holding his classes in the Saracen's Head. George Partington died in June 1857, and was buried in Welford Road Cemetery where a headstone was erected to the memory of 'George Partington, Gentleman'.[15]

Frederick Freak

In 1801 Frederick Freak opened a dancing academy in St James Square, roughly on the site of the present Municipal Building. By 1808, with his daughter assisting him, he was holding lessons from his home in New Street. Soon after this date Freak moved back to Northampton. In the winter of 1815 his son, also named Frederick and who had been trained by the London Opera House ballet masters Des Hayes and Brigirand, moved to Leicester to open an academy for 'Fashionable Dancing' in a room at Johnson's Jewellers in the Market Place. His first home in the town was in St Nicholas Street, but by 1818 he had moved to Granby Place, holding his dancing and fencing lessons in Barlow's Market Place Commercial Room and annual balls in the Assembly Room. In 1830 he was living in Charles Street and, a year later, in New Walk. Early in 1832 Freak handed over his academy to Monsieur Vedy who had been at the London Opera House for the previous nine years. Vedy's stay in the town was not long for he seems to have left about two years later.[16]

Monsieur d'Egville

In 1814 Monsieur d'Egville from the London Opera House, who was already established in Hinckley, announced his intention of visiting Leicester with a view to giving private quadrille dance tuition. Based in the George Inn, d'Egville, who only gave lessons to gentlemen, charged one guinea a quarter for his services. In 1823 two new dancing academies briefly opened in the town, one by Miss Robertson, and the other by Mr Teray, who, while 'totally disapproving of dumb bells', taught the most fashionable dances with a 'particular regard to elegance of carriage and deportment'.[17]

Charles Smart

Charles Smart, from Stamford was appointed music master at the newly-built Stoneygate School in 1846. He came to Leicester from Stamford in 1846. He was a smartly-dressed, short, agile man with long, dark hair, who accompanied himself on the violin as he danced. His first home in the town was 16 London Road. However, two years later he moved to a house in New Walk which had previously belonged to Samuel Viccars, one time mayor of the town. In 1852, assisted by his daughter Caroline, he was operating from a house on the corner of York Street and Welford Road.

A popular man, he was often the recipient of gifts from his pupils such as in 1852, when they presented him with a silver cup and his wife, Sabrina, with a butter cooler and two butter knives. During the 1856 annual ball he was presented with a silver snuff box, while the following year he received a golden chain.[18]

In March 1862 Smart, who had inherited his father's debts, had to file for bankruptcy. At his hearing, the following May, he explained that that he had been unable to discharge the debts as he and his family had been ill. His creditors accepted his defence and he was discharged and able to recommence his classes. In an age before air conditioning the extreme heat of the hot summer of 1864 caused Smart, along with the other dance teachers of the town, to postpone the start of the Autumn term. Smart died in December 1869 at the relatively young age of forty-two, his business being continued by Londoner Morris Barnett who was based at 5 St Martin's East.[19]

Teachers of Music

With the ever-increasing trend among the middle classes to own their own piano came the need for tuition which was met by a growing number of teachers. In 1782, according to William Gardiner, there were only two teachers of the piano in Leicester, while, in 1803 only a Mr Holmes was offering to give lessons on piano, cello and violin. Over the next twenty years, with the population nearly doubling from seventeen thousand in 1801 to thirty-one thousand in 1821, other teachers such as Ebenezer Jones and John Ella were brought to the attention of music loving Lestrians. It was not, however, until the second decade of the century that music teachers began to be regular advertisers in local newspapers and listed in town directories.

'The Dancing Academy' as portrayed by George Cruikshank in 1837. (Charles Dickens Sketches by Boz)

In 1815 Jones, a pupil of François Fèmy and leader of the Leamington and Birmingham Quadrille Bands, opened for business as a piano tuner and teacher of piano, violin and cello. At first he could only be contacted at Mr Smith's, a cabinet maker with a shop in the Market Place, but by 1826 he had set up home in Oxford Street. In March 1849 he provided the music for a quadrille party held by Mr and Miss

Freer at the Three Crowns Assembly Room, an event which carried on till six o'clock the following morning.[20]

Wider fame came to Leicester-born John Ella. The son of a confectioner in the Market Place, Ella was born in 1802. Graduating from the Royal Academy of Music, he made his first appearance as a professional performer, at the Drury Lane Theatre in 1821. After further study in Paris Ella joined the orchestras of the London Philharmonic, the King's Ancient, and the Italian Opera. In 1845 he founded the London Musical Union, a society which gave concerts of chamber music. These early events, held in Ella's home, were exclusive high class social gatherings, admittance to which being only gained by personal introduction. By 1856 the annual series of eight afternoon concerts were moved to the Hanover Square Rooms and the following year to St James's Hall. Totally blind for the last years of his life, John Ella died in October 1888.[21]

By the 1830s the piano was coming into the drawing rooms of the well-to-do and there were often advertisements in the local newspapers from people who either no longer needed a piano or who had purchased a newer model. Always at a good discount from the new price, less wealthy people would purchase a second-hand instrument rather than buy a new bottom of the range piano. An example was that offered for sale in 1834 by King & Co, tea dealers of Gallowtree Gate, who were asking forty-eight guineas, as against the new price of sixty-five guineas. The cost of sheet music was also coming down and in 1833 John Davis, bookseller of the Market Place was announcing that he had just received fifty numbers of the National Music Library for the piano which were on sale at 1½d each.[22]

Chapter 3

𝄞 ANDANTE 𝄞

Throughout England the later half of the eighteenth century was a period of enlightenment and growth. As the nineteenth century dawned, music began to be dominated by the bourgeoisie as opposed to royalty - a move no doubt in some way caused by the aftermath of the French Revolution. In Leicester, a town without resident gentry, music was promoted by the growing numbers of affluent manufacturers.

As we shall see until almost 1850 it was to be music by the middle classes for the middle classes, the poorer section of society not being able to afford the high prices asked for tickets, which in many cases were over a week's pay. Not until 1844, when Henry Nicholson began to promote his 'Concerts for the People', was, at long last, the working man able to afford to attend concerts and enjoy the music that had been for so long denied him.

In 1803 St Martin's Church held a performance of the *Messiah*. Amongst the nearly two hundred performers, taking part were Miss Tennant; Mr Smith (from the King's Chapel Windsor), Mr Lindley (cello), Mr Holmes (leader), Mr Boyce, Mr Meredith, Miss Leanders, Mr Hyde (trumpet), Mr Taylor, Mr Pierson, Richard Blagrove (from the Liverpool Music Hall) Mr Ward, and Mr Mather (an organist from Sheffield).[1]

Attended by the 'most distinguished families in the county', in October 1815, St Martin's was again the venue for a music festival which, as well as the perennial *Messiah*, included music by Haydn, Mozart and Beethoven. On the Thursday evening there was a concert and ball in the Assembly Room for which tickets, available from Edward Quilter, a solicitor of Gallowtree Gate, cost four shillings each. In order to encourage patronage on this cold autumn evening, the church advised that it was being heated by stoves in the nave.[2]

In August 1826 St Mary de Castro produced the *Messiah* under the direction of Mr Watson of Covent Garden. Other people booked for this event included Miss Travis, Miss Graddon, Miss Hughes, Master Barker, Messrs J. and H. Watson, Mr Robinson, Mr Tinney and the renowned John Braham. In December 1827 the same church was the venue for a concert of sacred music by Mr Topliff, organist, and his pupil Master Benson whom Braham had described as 'the first boy singer in the Kingdom'.[3]

Subscription Concerts

In 1802 a series of subscription concerts was arranged by the members of the newly-established Leicester Music Society. Although the subscription for the ten concerts was fixed at one guinea with single tickets priced at four shillings each, this series could not have been successful, for it was to be another ten years before the exercise was repeated.[4]

The forward march of nineteenth century musical life in England began in 1813 with the founding of the London Philharmonic Society, whose main aim was to perform the great orchestral works of the day. Music in Leicester also had a rebirth at this time. In the winter of 1812-13 a new series of six subscription concerts, under the stewardship of the High Sheriff Charles Loraine Smith of Enderby Hall, the Reverend Thomas Burnaby, and Dr John Freer, was so successful that the Music Society was able to give the subscribers an extra concert. Some of the single ladies of the town, it would seem, attended these concerts only for the ensuing ball, their minds being more on the dance, or rather their possible partners, than on the music of the concert.[5]

One of the musicians who took part in these concerts was Richard Blagrove, who had been born in Nottingham. In 1813, after serving an apprenticeship at Broadwood's piano factory in London, he relocated to Leicester where he opened a music shop in Gallowtree Gate. Within a year he moved his home and shop to Highcross Street where, in a house opposite the Stamp Office, he sold music and musical instruments as well as tuning and repairing them. His sojourn in Leicester was not long and within two years he returned to London where he took up a professional career as an instrumentalist.[6]

Under the stewardship of Colonel Crump of Allexton Hall, the Reverend Burnaby and George Bellairs, the 1813-14 season of concerts, opened in the Assembly Room on the fourth of November. Subscriptions for the six concerts cost one guinea for gentlemen and fifteen shillings for ladies, with non-subscribers having to pay six or four shillings for the individual evening concerts which begun at nine and ended at midnight. The January concert, which included the usual mixture of Handel and Haydn, had the added attractions of Dr Clarke singing 'In Peace Love Turn'd the Shepherds Reed' and Richard Blagrove playing a violin concerto by the Italian violinist and composer Ivan Jarnovic.[7]

The August 1814 concert was graced by the presence of the violinist François Fèmy, whose father, Ambrose, on one of his business trips to Leicester, had met William Gardiner at the Angel Inn. During the course of their conversation Gardiner had found out that Fèmy senior played the violin and that his son Henri, who was in business with his father, played the cello, while the other son, François, had studied violin under the famous virtuoso Luigi Cherubini.

Amongst the local musicians who performed at the concert were Elizabeth Austin and John Norton, whose trumpet solo 'The Echo Concerto' was considered an unparalleled performance. The following October the versatile Norton announced his intention of giving lessons on the flute, trumpet and 'other wind instruments now in use'. Five years later, in 1819, he was teaching the 'proper method of double tonguing'. About 1820 he joined the orchestra of the Theatre Royal, Drury Lane, from where he commenced selling instruments by mail order. In 1838 he emigrated to New York, dying in Philadelphia in January 1868 aged about eighty.[8]

The 1814–15 musical season begun in October with a grand concert of vocal and instrumental music, tickets for which cost five shillings each and were available from Thomas Combe's bookshop. This event, which included the Fèmy brothers (François taking the top stand as leader), John Norton and Elizabeth Austin, was followed by a new series of subscription concerts with subscriptions increased to twenty-five shillings for gentlemen and a guinea for ladies, with non-subscribers paying seven shillings for a single ticket. This price increase was due to the inflation which had been caused by the eight hundred and thirty million pounds which England had spent in withstanding Napoleon's ambitions in Europe. Stewarded by Sir Frederick Fowke, the Reverend Thomas Burnaby and Thomas Peach, a wine merchant, who had been mayor of the town in 1801, in an age before street lighting it was announced that the concerts would take place on the Thursday nearest the full moon.[9]

This season of concerts was well-attended and, although not engaging any of the big names from London, it was agreed that the local musicians provided music of the 'first description', which proved a 'graceful treat to the scientific ear of the musical amateur'. Indeed so impressed was the *Leicester Journal* that it contended that the music reflected infinite credit to the performers and was 'certainly not surpassed by any out of the Metropolis'.

Those who provided the graceful treat during the season included John Norton (trumpet), Miss Hewitt (piano), Norton's two sons Paul and William (clarinets), Mr Spray (second violin), Mr Smalley (flute), Mr Clarke (trombone), Mr Marshall and Samuel Deacon (basses), Mr Lilly and Mr Turner (horns), John Waldrom (bassoon) and Mr Nichols (serpent).

The serpent, so called from its shape, had originally been developed to strengthen the sound of church choirs. In the mid-eighteenth century it was adapted by military bands where it was gradually replaced during the first half of the nineteenth century by the bass of the saxhorn family of instruments.[10]

Charles Jarvis

Another local man who took part in these concerts was Charles Jarvis who, as a boy, had been proposed by Lord Maynard to study under François Barthélmon. As it turned out the French violinist did not take pupils, but was prepared to send the young Charles, who had not received any rudimentary education, to his chaplain, Dr Hey, at Passingham to be taught to read and write. His period of tuition did not last long and Charles was soon sent back to Leicester where William Gardiner, who felt sorry for him, gave him a piano - an instrument on which Jarvis soon distinguished himself. A no mean performer on the drums, Jarvis was also in demand as a singer both by the Leicester Music Society and as a member of a trio of glee singers (the other two were Mr Stanhope and Mr Nicholson).[11]

Charles Jarvis died in 1822, leaving his widow and nine children unprovided for. However, such was his popularity that a subscription was raised for the benefit of the family. Local musicians, including John Ella, Miss Hewitt (organist), Joseph Maffre (clarinet) and John

Waldrom, augmented the fund by giving a concert of sacred music which raised a further forty-five pounds.

In 1828 Jarvis's daughter Sarah, who gave singing and piano lessons, left Leicester to marry John Inman of Wolverhampton. However, she was still in demand by her Leicester friends and the following June returned to sing at a concert in the Exchange, for which tickets were five shillings each.[12]

Mary Linwood

In 1827 Joseph Maffre, a composer and violin teacher who lived in St Peter's Lane, wrote and arranged for the piano a set of quadrilles dedicated to the renowned Leicester artist Mary Linwood. The following year Maffre published a Military March which he had written for piano with flute or violin accompaniment.[13]

Mary Linwood, born in Birmingham, had moved to Leicester with her family in 1780. She commenced needlework when she was thirteen, holding her first exhibition in the London in 1798. Her home town also had several opportunities to view her work, such as in January 1817 when her needlework was exhibited in the Exchange. The last person in the town to use a sedan-chair, it was said that Leicester and Miss Linwood were synonymous. Indeed, Mrs Fielding-Johnson, writing in *Glimpses of Ancient Leicester* tells us that such was her popularity that many people passing through the town would frequently miss their coaches in order to see some of her work.

Her very varied output ranged from a banner she made for the newly enrolled Leicester Infantry Volunteers in 1794 to her largest work, 'Judgement upon Cain'

Mary Linwood (1755–1845).
In 1827 Mary Linwood was honoured with having a set of piano quadrilles, composed by the local musician Joseph Maffre, dedicated to her.
(Leicestershire Record Office)

which took ten years to complete. Presented to most of the crowned heads of Europe she was one of the very few English people to visit France during the Napoleonic Wars. Ever ready to help the town's institutions an exhibition of her work in 1813, in aid of the Infirmary, raised over one hundred and fifty pounds.

Charles Guynemer

The singers of the 1814-15 season were Elizabeth Austin, Charles Jarvis, his daughter Sarah, Mr Smalley and Mr Nicholson. At the concerts Austin 'evinced considerable talent and promised to become a singer of eminence' while Smalley's flute playing was considered 'the finest style of excellence'. Two years later Smalley, along with two other Leicester musicians, John Waldrom and John Norton, established a wide reputation by taking part in the 1817 Birmingham Music Festival.[14]

The March concert introduced to the town Charles Guynemer, a violinist from the Paris Conservatory, who delighted his audience with his own composition, *A British Fantasia*, which was a selection of British airs. Formerly employed by the French Government to collect taxes from the Belgium brewers, Guynemer had been made redundant by the fall of Bonaparte and the capture of Paris. Deciding to seek his fortune in England, he chose Leicester as a base, due to its central position in the country, armed with letters of introduction to Thomas Pares (banker and former MP for Borough) from the Marquis of Exeter, whom he had met in Paris; and to William Gardiner, from the pianist Mazio Clementi.[15]

During his sojourn in the town Guynemer and his wife lived in High Street and made their living by teaching Music, Dancing, Drawing and French. In 1816, the Frenchman published two books of dances arranged for the piano and the harp. Guynemer introduced to Leicester Mr Balliot, the leader of the Concert Spiritual, a man whose enthusiasm was infectious and 'whose stay in the town caused such a carnival of music that had never before taken place in a county town'. Even though he moved to London in 1817 Guynemer did not forget Leicester and returned many times, as in January 1826 when he led the orchestra at a concert arranged by Sarah Jarvis in the Theatre, which included the famed tenor John Braham. Guynemer, who also organised the music at the town's new Roman Catholic Holy Cross Church in New Walk, returned to Leicester for a few months in 1830 when he recommenced his dancing classes.[16]

In March 1816 there was a rumour circulating the town that the concerts were to be discontinued and assemblies introduced in their place. Many were dismayed at this and one anonymous correspondent to the *Journal* proudly proclaimed that the Leicester musicians were the equal, if not better, than anywhere else in the country and that the town ought to be prepared to support them. The committee tried to carry on but by 1818, as the numbers of subscribers fell, they were left in debt and the concerts came to an end. One of the last, in March 1818, which as well as including Guynemer as leader; Mrs Salman, the principal singer at the King's Concerts; also introduced Richard Blagrove's five year old son Henry, who delighted the audience with a violin solo.[17]

Music at the Theatre and Local Inns

Although not adapted for musical productions, the Theatre was often used for concerts during the first three decades of the nineteenth century. Built in 1799 and opened in 1800, it was demolished in 1836 and a new one, designed in Grecian style by William Parsons, opened under the management of James Monroe in September 1836.[18]

Examples of musical events which took place in the old Theatre during these thirty years include Charles Incledon of the Theatre Royal Covent Garden who, in June 1802, gave a concert of serio-comic songs. In October 1803, John Braham and Nancy Storace appeared in the comic operas 'The Cabinet', 'The Duenna', 'No song no supper' and 'My Grandmother'. The following year Daniel Auber's opera *Gustav III* had a four night run. A Frenchman who spent his early years living and working as a clerk in London, Auber returned to his native land, as an established composer, in 1823. A man who never attended performances of his own works, Auber died in 1871.[19]

John Braham (1774–1856) From an 1802 etching by Robert Dighton.

One of the occasional visitors to the Theatre in the late 1820s was C. Bland of Covent Garden. In March 1828, he sung at a benefit concert to raise money for Elizabeth Sharpe, a harpist and singer in the household of Lady Halford at Wistow Hall, to further her musical education in London. Thirteen months later Bland gave a concert of songs which had been arranged specially by William Gardiner.[20]

In December 1824, the Hewitt sisters promoted a concert at the Theatre. The two Hewitt sisters, with their father John, ran a music school for children aged seven to fourteen and a piano shop in South Gate Street. The Hewitt's taught piano by the Logierian System of Musical Education. This was a technique developed by Johann Bernhard Logier (1777–1846), a German piano teacher, who had anticipated the growing demand for tuition. Pupils were taught together in a class of up to a dozen which meant that lessons were cheaper than they would have been on a one-to-one basis. The system had a major disadvantage in that it taught the children to play a number of pieces without instilling any knowledge of harmony or theory. Logier also invented the 'Chiroplast', a laterally sliding frame for the hands which was fitted above the keyboard, to develop the hand muscles.

As well as the two sisters on piano the concert included Miss Melville (a pupil of Rossini) Sarah Jarvis, Miss Russell, Mr Morris, Isaac Handscomb, C. McKoskell on harp and Elizabeth Sharpe. Led by John Ella from the Philharmonic Kings Ancient and Italian Opera, tickets for the concert were from one shilling and sixpence to five shillings each. So successful was the evening that the sisters had to repeat the event the following year. This concert, which included Beethoven's *Men of Prometheus*, featured the sisters' piano playing; Mr Marshall, a cellist from Warwick; and local violinist Joseph Maffre who led the band.[21]

In the 1820s as well as the piano the guitar was also popular, Leicester boasting at least two teachers of the instrument - Miss Russell and Mr Poletti. The latter, who also taught Italian, lived in Church Gate and charged one guinea for six lessons. In December 1826 Miss Russell promoted a concert in the Theatre to raise money to pay for her period of tuition in London. Local amateurs such as Sarah Jarvis, Elizabeth Sharpe, Mr Wykes, Handscomb, McKoskell and Charles Mavius, performed along with guest musicians, such as Guynemer, who led the orchestra; Signor Begre from the Italian Opera; and François Fèmy, who was now a member of the Russian Czar's

The monument to the blind musician Edward Mammatt (1807–1860) in St Helen's church, Ashby de la Zouch.

orchestra. After this successful concert, which included music by Weber, Rossini and Beethoven, the general feeling in the town was that it was strange that such concerts were not more frequent.[22]

In December 1829 Miss Russell promoted a concert performed entirely by local musicians. One of those taking part was Edward Mammatt who had only heard the music for the first time the day before, having been engaged at the last minute when Charles Mavius, who had originally been booked to play the piano, found himself unable to attend. Blind since he was six, twenty-two year old Mammatt, the organist at St Helen's Church, Ashby de la Zouch, also lectured on anatomy, astronomy, geology and electricity. Miss Russell made her London début in November 1830, but did not forsake her Leicester friends, as she returned to her Dover Street home for a few weeks each year to give singing lessons.[23]

Musical events also took place at Robert Barlow's Market Place Commercial Rooms where, in 1830, the five members of the Rainer Family from Tullerthal, Austria, appeared in concert. A month later the rooms hosted two lectures on music by a Mr Adams in which he included 'a large number of curious experiments', the nature of which is not now known.

The George Inn, Humberstone Gate. The George, demolished in 1969 to make way for the Haymarket Shopping Centre, had a music room which occasionally played host to visiting singers. (Leicester Illustrated)

Musical events were also held at some of the larger inns of the town such as the George Inn, Humberstone Gate, when in 1815, for 'positively for one night only' it was host to 'the celebrated musical phenomenon' The Master and Miss Smiths who displayed their 'wonderful powers in the harmonic art.' In January 1844 the Bell was the venue for the annual Tradesman's Ball, when 200 guests paid six shillings each to dance to the waltzes and country music of Samuel Weston's Quadrille Band, before tucking in to the cold supper which was served to revive the dancers.[24]

The Leicester Choral Society

In 1827 the Choral Society, which had been founded by William Gardiner to cultivate sacred music, gave a performance in St Margaret's Church to raise funds for new music. At this time printed music was so expensive that it was one of the reasons why music was so little studied in England. Gardiner himself contended that it would be only when sheet music became cheaper that England would have some chance of becoming a musical country.[25]

So popular was the Society that even its fortnightly practices, held in St Margaret's Church, attracted an audience who paid either a guinea or ten shillings and sixpence for a subscription ticket. At first some people took advantage of the rehearsals being held in the church and just walked in without paying. This left the Society little choice but to make it clear that no one without a ticket was to be allowed entry.[26]

In February 1829 a selection of sacred music was performed in St Margaret's Church, in aid of the Society's funds. The tickets were available from Deacon's and Mavius's shops, at two shillings and sixpence for gentlemen and one shilling and sixpence for ladies, the programmes costing threepence extra. As the concert was to take place in mid-winter the Society felt the need to reassure potential concert-goers that fires were to be made in all the stoves early in the morning thereby ensuring that all areas of the church would be warm. With over two hundred in the orchestra, the concert was obviously a success for it was repeated two months later with admission being increased to three shillings and sixpence. The Society made such a name for itself that it was invited to perform in Stamford as well as to sing the Easter Day service at St Mary de Castro.[27]

Not all ecclesiastical choirs were so harmonious. In 1841, a unique case came before the Leicester magistrates. A Mr Perkins was charged with 'singing out of tune and disturbing the congregation' at Kibworth Chapel. For some reason, not recorded, Perkins had offended some of his fellow choristers who had endeavoured to have him expelled from the choir. To get his revenge Perkins, when the choir commenced singing, began to sing a different tune! The result of the case was that he was discharged with costs awarded against him.

As the century progressed, with the social musical barriers falling, new purpose-built halls were erected in the town to house public concerts and other musical events. The founding of movements such as the Mechanics' Institute, made music become less and less the preserve of the upper classes with the skilled artisans beginning to develop a taste for serious music. It was to be these men who would be the backbone of many of the local music societies which were to spring up in the 1830s and 40s.

Chapter 4

𝄞 MUSIC SHOPS 𝄞

Samuel Deacon

As the nineteenth century dawned the main, if not the only, music shop in Leicester was that of John Deacon. A long-established watchmaker, goldsmith and jeweller, Deacon's father, Samuel, was the minister of Friar Lane Baptist Church. John Deacon, who also hired out instruments as well as attending customers' homes to tune their own pianos, also gave piano lessons and played double bass. By 1807 he had built up such a fine stock that he was able to claim that his selection was just as comprehensive as any in London.[1]

In 1814 Deacon's twenty-six year old son Samuel announced that he planned to open a 'New Musical Repository' in Gallowtree Gate, while his brother Frederick was to take charge of the family's Market Place ironmongery and jewellery business. Samuel's new shop sold a wide variety of musical instruments including, in 1826, a six octave three-unisoned self-acting cabinet piano by Clementi which, as well as being played in the normal way, could also, by means of a mechanism, perform a number of popular tunes including an air with variations from Gellmek. One of Deacon's clients was the Leicester Corporation which, in 1819, purchased a set of musical instruments, to the value of thirty-nine pounds and nine shillings. These were for the use of the town waits, who were changing over from stringed to wind instruments.[2]

Making frequent trips to London to bring back the latest models in pianos, in 1820, Deacon announced that, as well as having a good quantity of new and second-hand pianos for sale, he was entering the art world, offering to do 'profile likenesses in a superior style of finishing from seven shillings and sixpence to a guinea'. In 1823, no doubt feeling the competition of the new music shops which were opening in the town, he was offering his customers a twelve month guarantee plus free tuning for a year. In 1825 Frederick resigned the ironmongery side of the business to a Mr Griffin but continued the watch and clock making enterprise at his brother's music shop. In 1826 he sold off all his stock and moved to Battersea, London.[3]

In December 1830, at a concert held in the George Inn Assembly Room, Deacon introduced his improved Patent Piano. Said to be one of the finest instruments ever introduced into a concert room, it produced not only a fuller volume of tone but also remained in tune much longer than the conventional piano. Deacon's principle was that the wires were fixed in such a way as to supersede the then usual method of twisting thereby rendering them less liable to break, either from changes in the atmosphere or playing upon them, however hard the keys were struck. Deacon was so sure of his handiwork that he claimed that the strings could bear a tension of a third to a fourth above concert pitch without breaking. Indeed he promised to take back any piano within six months if it did not give satisfaction. In November 1830, while in Brighton, Deacon was honoured to exhibit one of his new pianos to the King and Queen, who, it would seem, were so impressed that they purchased one, for by 1834 Deacon was proudly proclaiming his establishment as 'By Appointment'.[4]

In 1849, Deacon was appointed the Leicester agent for the British Music Society's publications, and, in 1852, that for Geoff Luff & Sons. The latter had just introduced the Royal Albert Cottage Piano which, along with superiority of touch and increased durability, was claimed to be able to achieve a greater and more equalized power of tone over all other pianos.[5]

Mary Ann Deacon

On Samuel's death in 1867 his daughters, Mary Ann, Elizabeth, Adelaide and Lucy, all fine musicians in their own right, carried on the Hotel Street family business until about 1884 when they retired to Cotswold House, De Montfort Square.[6]

Born in 1822, Mary Ann, was from an early age an accomplished pianist, who served as organist at St Mary de Castro (1845–65) and the Bond Street Chapel (1866–1876). One of the most kindly ladies to be found in the town, from the establishment of the Leicester Philharmonic Society in 1858 she was Henry Nicholson's accompanist and deputy conductor. One of the Society members was later to recall that sometimes, when conducting practices in the absence of Nicholson, she would go among the singers trying to pick out those who were not singing or whose intonation was faulty, and, in an excess of enthusiastic zeal, drop her music book on the head of any offending chorister.

In the spring of 1855 Mary Ann's sister Lucy, who had been studying the music, language and literature of Germany, returned home and as well as helping her sisters in the shop, soon established herself as a teacher of German.[7]

In November 1864 the 'elite of the town' attended Mary Deacon's grand concert which, as well as the one hundred and fifty strong chorus of the New Philharmonic Society under George Löhr, included Miss Stabbach from the Leipzig Gewandhaus, Frances Gill, Lucy Deacon, Henry Lazarus, Henry and Alfred Nicholson, and the celebrated baritone Charles Santley, who was making his last appearance in England before leaving the country for the winter. Also on the programme was Anna Maria Clowes, who had come to Leicester from Newport, Monmouthshire in 1862. A piano and singing teacher based at Westbourne House, 10 New Walk, Clowes was also an alto soloist and harpist who helped out at many concerts during the second half of the nineteenth century.[8]

Mary Ann Deacon (1822–1903) One of the foremost musicians in nineteenth century Leicester. (Wyvern 8 May 1896)

In November 1866 Handel's *Israel in Egypt* was produced by the Philharmonic Society as a testimonial on behalf of Mary Ann Deacon whose popularity, coupled with the interest in the first performance in Leicester of the work, ensured that the tickets sold out almost as soon as they were put on sale, with more seats having to be installed in the hall.[9]

In May 1896, the Temperance Hall hosted another grand testimonial concert on Deacon's behalf. Conducted by Henry Ellis, Henry Nicholson and Charles Hancock, at the close of the programme, which included Schubert's *Rosamunde*, Beethoven's *Figaro* and 'The Long Day Closes', Miss Deacon was presented with bouquets as she was 'recalled again and again by her beloved public'. When, the following October the mayor, Edward Wood, presented Deacon with a 'splendid portrait of herself' and the sum of three hundred pounds that had been raised at the testimonial, the popular lady returned the money with a deed of trust stating that it should be invested and the interest applied annually 'for ever' as a prize for pianoforte playing and singing alternately. Called the 'Deacon Prize' it was competed for by boys and girls, fifteen years and younger, and resident in Leicester.[10]

The winner of the thirty-nine young pianists who took part in the first competition in June 1898 was Cecilia Gertrude Lester. The following year the first singing competition test piece, 'I Know that my Redeemer Liveth', caused concern amongst the musicians of the town, as to how girls aged between thirteen and fifteen could be expected to sing it with any degree of credit.

Miss Deacon died in 1903. Her death inspired local lawyer, Arthur Talbot to pen these words.[11]

> *Silence for us, but somewhere in the Light,*
> *A voice to swell the glorious waves of sound*
> *That ripple through the Ether infinite*
> *Where ever-widening harmonies abound.*

One of the more notable winners of the Deacon Prize was Benjamin Burrows who in May 1906, age fourteen, won the first prize with seventy-two marks out of a possible eighty. The son of a music teacher, Burrows went on to become one of Leicester's foremost musicians. Born at 21 College Street in October 1891, Burrows's organ tutor was Henry Ellis on whose death in 1910 Burrows succeeded as organist at St Mary de Castro. By 1912 he had become a Fellow of the Royal College of Organists, taking his Bachelor of Music in 1913 and, in 1921, his Doctorate. In 1923 he resigned from his post at St Mary de Castro and after a rest of six years took over from Victor Thomas as organist at Victoria Road Baptist Church. Although originally an organ tutor he later taught theory and music appreciation, both at Leicester's University College and by correspondence. Benjamin Burrows died in 1966.

Charles Mavius

In 1821 Charles Mavius, who had been born in Bedford but now living in Kettering, moved to Leicester. By November 1822 he was selling pianos and teaching pupils from his shop in Gallowtree Gate from

Charles Mavius, musical instrument dealer advertisement from Thomas Combe's 1827 Leicester Directory.

where he made frequent visits to London to get more pianos and sheet music. Mavius was also host to Samuel Adams, the representative from Broadwood & Sons, Great Pulteney Street, London, who made quarterly visits to the town to tune and regulate his firm's instruments.[12]

Between 1824 and 1826 Mavius moved three times: first to Market Street, then Church Gate, and, by October 1826, to the Gallowtree Gate shop recently vacated by Thomas Sternberg. As well as stocking a supply of 'superior harps', in 1828 he had a special carriage constructed with large springs for the 'conveyance of pianofortes with safety'. When we consider the state of the roads in the 1820s this special conveyance must have proved a godsend both to Mavius and his customers. Dealing in new as well as second-hand instruments, in 1829 he was offering for sale a six octave horizontal grand piano by Broadwood & Sons which was priced at thirty guineas, while for those of lesser means his second-hand pianos were available from eight to twenty guineas.[13] At a time when a working man might expect to earn about eight shillings a week pianos at this period were obviously the preserve of the middle classes.

As well as selling music and being in demand as an organist and pianist, Mavius also tried his hand as a composer and arranger. In 1826 he published his 'Leicester Quadrilles', the sheet music for which, arranged for the piano, cost four shillings. In August 1848 Mavius moved from his Gallowtree Gate shop to a new one in the Market Place, next to Cort, Law & Co., from where, as well as new and second-hand pianos, he also sold harps, especially those built by Erat & Co. In 1851 Mavius, who died in 1855, was still living in the Market Place with his forty-nine year old Leicester-born wife Harriet, his three sons: Charles age twenty-six, a dentist; Frederick age twenty, a banker's clerk; and George, age twelve. His daughter, aged twenty-three, described as a Professor of Music, was also living at home.[14]

William Bithrey

In 1852 Mavius retired and sold the goodwill of his piano tuning business to William Silvester Bithrey who had worked for him since 1846 and was now starting out in business for himself. In 1860, with business expanding, Bithrey, who had moved three times over the previous ten years, took over the books of Charles Bernard of Leamington who was retiring for health reasons. One of the villages Bithrey visited in the course of his work was Great Glen, the road to which (the present Church Road) he complained was often impassible 'without the risk of being drowned.' Not a man to stay in one place long, in 1867, he was based at 88 Hastings Street, in 1875 Wellington Street and by 1881 in East Street.[15]

Thomas Sternberg

In 1823 Thomas Sternberg, who lived in Abington Street, Northampton, with a shop in that town's Sheep Street, relocated to Leicester where, with his sister Frances, he opened for business in Gallowtree Gate. In October 1825 Frances, who gave piano, singing and Italian lessons from a room in the Gallowtree Gate shop, married a Mr Cuffley who lived in New Walk. By this time Thomas and Frances had been joined by their sister Sophia, who taught harp and piano, and had come to render assistance to her siblings as they had more pupils than they could cope with on their own. A few months later Sophia also married a local man, Alex Viner, a liquor merchant who lived in King Street. In 1826 Sternberg moved to the Bazaar, Humberstone Gate, and seems to have left Leicester during the next twelve months.[16]

Popular Music

Much of the sheet music sold in the first three decades of the nineteenth century, such as the patriotically entitled 'Our King is a true British Sailor', 'Our Queen is the Wife of a Sailor' and 'England the home of the World', all by one Captain Mitford, is now lost. The first of these songs was compared to those of Charles Dibdin (1745–1814), the writer of many songs and musical plays, most of which being pathetic pieces about the sea. The one most well-known today, thanks to Henry Wood's *Sea Songs*, played every year at the Last Night of the Proms, is 'Tom Bowling', the subject of which being supposed to be based on Dibden's own brother. Dibdin's personal knowledge of the sea was an aborted trip to India in 1788 when his vessel was driven into Torbay by a violent storm. He abandoned the trip and returned to London. In a xenophobic age in which Britannia ruled the waves, some song writers, such as Dibdin, were actually commissioned by the Government to write such jingoistic songs.[17]

One of the new songs of 1826, which has stood the test of time is Charles Horn's *Cherry Ripe*. On sale at Deacon's shop, who described it as 'a very pretty ballad', the song enjoyed big sales both in London and the provinces. Accused of plagiarising the tune (the words were by the seventeenth century poet Robert Heyrick) from fellow song writer Thomas Attwood's 'Let me Die', Horn successfully defended himself in court by singing the two songs to the jury.

Sheet music in the early part of the century was relatively very expensive, the average price being two shillings. On occasions, however, the *Leicester Chronicle* had special sales of new music at half price.[18]

Other small music businesses in the town during the 1820s and 30s included Frederick Dobney from Northampton who had a shop in Belgrave Gate from where he sold both new and second-hand instruments as well as sheet music. Dobney also taught violin and cello for which he charged one pound a quarter or one shilling and sixpence a lesson.

William Eames had a piano shop in Humberstone Road, while Mrs Hackett, who sold pianos, first from St Nicholas Street and then from 11 Belvoir Street, became in 1848 the first shopkeeper in Leicester to sell the concertina, an instrument which had been invented by Charles Whetstone in 1829. In 1834 local shops were selling the full score of Auber's *Gustav III* which was currently playing at Covent Garden and which the *Leicester Journal* pronounced as a 'hit', an early use of the word in that context.[19]

Between 1841 and 1851 the town's population increased from fifty to sixty thousand and more music shops were opened, including that of William James Windram, an auctioneer, who opened a piano warehouse in Belvoir Street in 1852. Sheet music was also on sale from Fieldwick's Granby Street book shop, which had first opened in 1839 and was by 1855 the sole Leicester agent for Wooley & Co's pianos. Other booksellers who went into the sheet music business were John and Thomas Spencer, of the Market Place, who sold music at a large discount from the published price, as indeed did Samuel Deacon who gave a massive fifty percent discount 'if paid for when purchased'.[20]

Smaller music shops of the town in the mid-nineteenth century included that of Samuel Brown, a cabinet maker in High Street who, in 1864, advertised for sale a cottage piano with 'handsome truss legs and all the latest improvements' at fifteen pounds;[21] Benjamin Harbot, a piano and music dealer of East Bond Street; William Thomas Holland of 35 New Bond Street; and Market Place piano dealer Alfred Austin who closed down in 1881. Alexander Laurence, based at 2 King Street, was an organ and harmonium maker who took over William Petch's piano tuning business in 1867. Before coming to the town Laurence had spent fifteen years as a tuner with Broadwood in London and is said to have built the piano which won a silver medal at the 1862 London Exhibition. By 1890, he had established his 'Midland Steam Pianoforte Works' at Ayleston.

William Moore

One of the first local musical instrument manufacturers who comes to our notice is William Moore of Syston, whose death in 1819 necessitated the sale of his effects which included tools for making bass viols, violins and wind instruments. Other early nineteenth century makers were William Coltman of Red Cross Street; E. Keny, a harp, piano and flute maker, of Melton Street, Nottingham, who had spent some time in London and occasionally visited Leicester to repair and tune; and George Ward of Halford Street, who from 1825 combined piano tuning and repairing with restoring old pictures.[22]

William Burden

William Chester Burden, who lived at 'The Retreat', Lansdown Road, had a shop at 35 Granby Street from where he sold pianos costing from twenty-four guineas. Sole agent in Leicester for the Estey Organ, by 1878 Burden had opened a showroom in Ashwell Street and a workshop in East Street. He also wrote songs such as 'That's just how married life should be' which, adapted to the French melody 'Voulez Vous Danser', was considered the best humorous song published for years. In 1881 Burden also had two melodies 'The Bonnie Scottish Maid' and 'The Sailor's Dream' published by local musician A. T. Pole.[23]

A. T. Pole

Pole had established his business, at 90 Granby Street, in 1874. Described as a manufacturer and importer of 'musical instruments of every description from a whistle to a church organ', as well as music by Burden, Pole was also the publisher of 'The Chinese Garden March' by Thomas Henry Spiers of 30 Gopsall Street, the local representative of the London College of Music; 'Alice' and 'Une Fête Rustique' by J. W. Lowe of Leicester. Appointed choirmaster and organist at St Nicholas's in 1880 Pole was also the local representative for the College of Violinists.[24] Pole's father, James, who died in 1868, had been a popular harpist, while his brother Thomas sold music from 'Handel House', 72 Northampton Square.

James Herbert Marshall

The first of many shops owned by James Herbert Marshall, a former Guardsman and commercial traveller for a firm of piano manufacturers, was built opposite the skating rink on the corner of Rutland Street and Humberstone Gate. The grand opening of 'Marshall's Midland Musical Depot' (the name board can still be seen over the windows) was celebrated by a grand concert and sale at which, it was said, no reasonable offer was refused. Marshall took old instruments in part exchange for new ones and such was the level of business that in the winter of 1884 he was forced to hold a clearance sale of second-hand pianos as well as opening a sheet music branch in

Top Left: *James Herbert Marshall (1851–1918) was the foremost musical instrument dealer in Leicester and founder of the Leicester Philharmonic Society. (*Wyvern *11 December 1891)*

Top Right: *Advertisement from the* Wyvern *30 September 1892.*

Bottom: *Marshall's Rutland Street shop. (Max Wade-Matthews)*

Gallowtree Gate. He also manufactured pianos such as his 'Students Model' (twenty guineas) and his 'Acme' (thirty guineas).[25]

Always keeping up to date with new musical trends in 1898 Marshall advertised an 'Armour-clad' damp-proof piano at twenty-two guineas cash or fifteen shillings a month, while two years later he was selling, at three guineas, the recently invented gramophone. No doubt some of the buyers of these 'recording and producing apparatus complete with trumpet and double hearing tubes' would have been members of the Leicester Phonographic Society which had been formed in 1892.[26]

President of the Music Trades Association of Great Britain, in 1900 Marshall expanded his business by opening premises in Regent Street, London. His first customer, so the story goes, was the King of Portugal who purchased an Angelus Orchestral, a devise described as a 'perfect piano player and organ combined' which could be attached to any piano or used separately. A few days later the King of Greece, in company with the Crown Prince of Denmark, visited the shop and purchased a piano for his palace in Athens.[27]

In 1904, Marshall expanded his business in Leicester by taking over the former Victoria Coffee and Cocoa House in Granby Street. Considered one of the finest music shops in the world, the basement was used as a workshop and the ground floor for general music sales. The first floor was used for performances by Marshall's own fourteen piece band which was led by Walter Waddington. Pianos were on display on the second floor while organs were on the third. The top floor was devoted to practise rooms where local teachers could hold private lessons. In celebration of the new use of the building one wag of the town penned:[28]

Victoria, Victoria,
Chiefest of emporia,
For coffee, buns,
And Sally Lunns,
And such like common scornia!
Gloria Victoria,
In escelsia gloria!
What joy to rise
From tarts and pies
To fugues and oratoria!

VICTORIA
ORGANS
MUSIC
GALLERIES
PIANOS
J. HERBERT MARSHALL

Music Shops

Above: *A cartoon of 1909 depicting James Herbert Marshall as a knight, mounted on one of his pianos. As a reference to his political sentiments he is seen brandishing the sword of Tariff Reform. (More-or–Less-Stir)*

Opposite: *Marshall's Victoria Music Depot, Granby Street. Designed by Edward Burgess and built in 1887, for the Leicester Coffee and Cocoa Company, the building, one of Leicester's landmarks, is still standing. (Leicester Guardian 8 October 1904)*

In politics Marshall was a Conservative. A member of the Council, in 1897 he served the town as mayor. Knighted in December 1905, in 1910 Marshall unsuccessfully contested the Market Harborough division. In 1911 he formed a limited company, opening a factory in north London where he produced the Marshall and Rose piano. James Herbert Marshall, who was married to Clara Ann, daughter of Vittore Albini of Garzuo Italy, died in August 1918.

Other shops in the town at this time included that of brass band instructor John Smith, who, in 1869, boasted that his King Street premises had the 'largest and best stock of pianos in the Midlands'. Richard Catlin, Robert Cox and Francis Moore joined forces to run a music shop in the newly built Royal Arcade, while, in 1900, George W. Findley, who had commenced business at 71 High Street, moved to 46 St Nicholas Street. At 18 Gallowtree Gate William Wood, who had taken over William Dodgson's piano tuning business, sold pianos and American organs, allowing payment over three years or a discount for cash.[29]

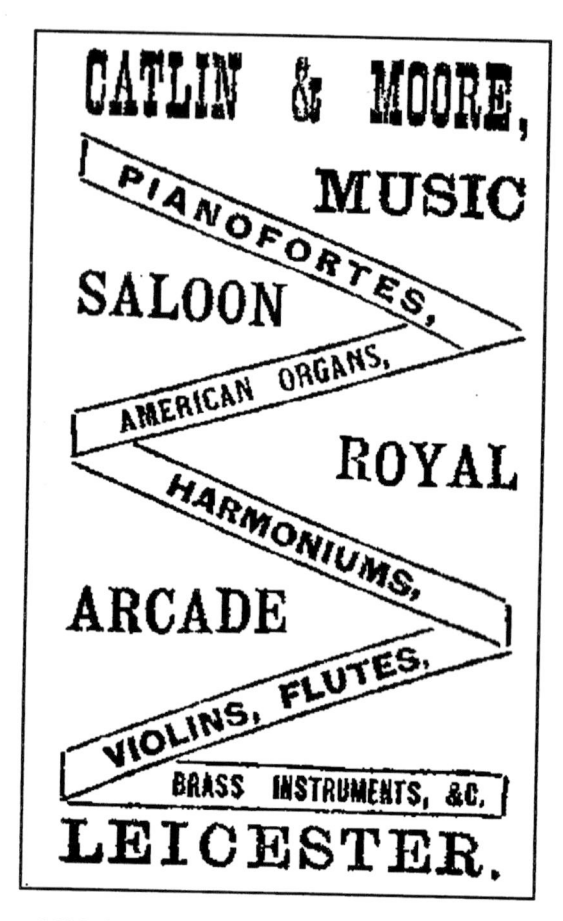

It was one of the effects of the 'Industrial Revolution' which compelled the ordinary people to find their own recreations as cheaply as they could amongst themselves. Some of the more skilful artisans, such as William Findley, turned to making their own musical instruments. Findley, a carpenter and amateur cello player, had a workshop where it was said chairs were made and fiddles mended. A liberal reformer, whose shop was a battle ground for debates as well as a makeshift room for musical quartets, he was said to be able to see a viola in a worn block of rough wood. A well liked man who would not hurt a fly, Findley died in 1901, aged seventy-five, as he was preparing to emigrate to America.[30]

1883 Catlin and Moore advertisement from Leicester Old and New.

Chapter 5

𝄞 THE 1827 MUSIC FESTIVAL 𝄞

One of the phenomena unique to early nineteenth century English society was that of the music festival. Lasting two or three days, they were held in many provincial towns, drawing in the famous musical names of the day to give local people a chance to hear what London audiences were able to enjoy on a regular basis. As we have seen Leicester held two such festivals in 1771 and 1774 and, in July 1803, just over the border in Warwickshire, Nuneaton held a two day event in the course of which there was a 'grand pianoforte concerto by a lady of Leicester.' This may have been Mary Linwood who, according to William Gardiner, was the only lady in Leicester that could read difficult music at sight.[1]

In 1823 and 1825 York held two very successful festivals and, in 1826, under Royal patronage, over two thousand four hundred pounds was raised in Birmingham, a town which had been holding triennial festivals since the 1790s.[2]

During the fifty years since the two festivals of the 1770s Leicester had developed a fine musical community, both professional and amateur, in which 'the captivating art had so fully entered into all public amusements [that] it was considered that Leicester was becoming a town of musical people'.[3] As well as the eleven professional musicians mentioned in Thomas Combe's Town Directory of 1827, there were many talented amateurs in Leicester, of whom William Gardiner was one of the foremost.

So, when in the summer of 1826 Dr John Hill and John Mansfield, local banker and treasurer to the infirmary, came to Gardiner to discuss the possibility of holding a musical festival for the benefit of that institution Gardiner was only too happy to give his full support.

Those mentioned in the 1827 directory were: Samuel Deacon, music warehouse, Gallowtree Gate; Frederick Dobney, musician and broker, Belgrave Gate; John Hewitt, teacher of music, Southgate

Street; Miss Jarvis, teacher of music, York Street; Ebenezer Tristam Jones, musician, Oxford Street; Joseph Maffre, musician, St Peter's Lane; Charles Mavius, Professor of Music and music warehouse, Gallowtree Gate; Henry Nicholson, musician, New Walk; Thomas Sternberg, pianoforte tuner and repairer, New Walk; Miss Valentine, organist, Belgrave Gate; John Waldrom, musician and music seller, Market Street.

Preliminary Plans

A committee of local people was soon formed who met for the first time that October. At this first meeting concern was expressed as to the type of music which was to be performed, for, it was observed, some other provincial festivals had been uninteresting due to the 'eternal repetition of the same round of dull insipid ballads'. Another point discussed was that organizers of festivals were apt to make their evening events too long for people who had sat through a morning concert of 'soul-subduing harmony'.[4] As it turned out the committee

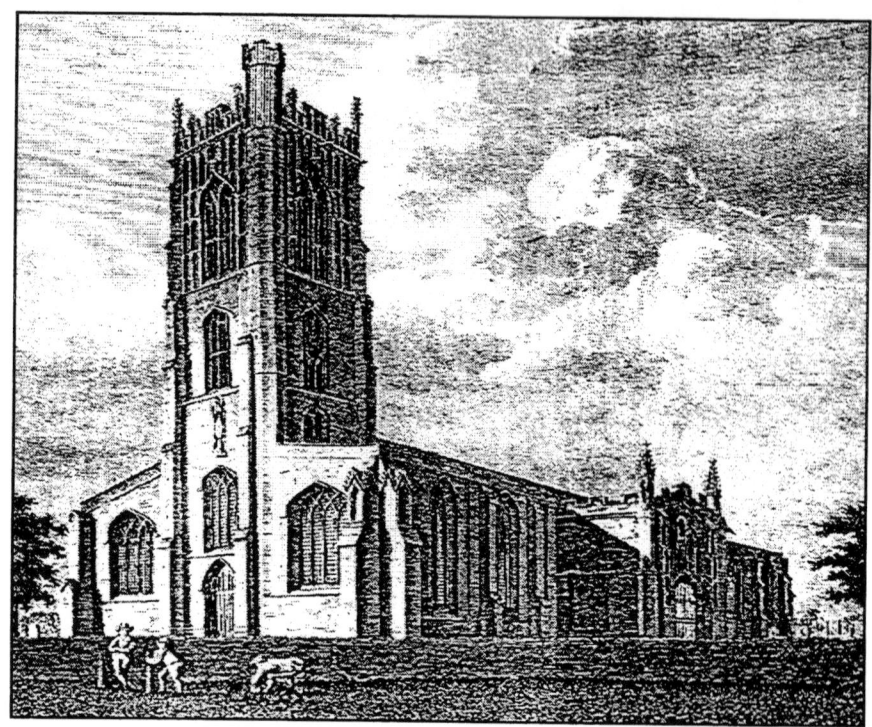

St Margaret's Church c.1800. (Nichols)

had no need to fear, for, as we shall see, Leicester's festival was a success.

The two main issues on the committee's agenda were finding a site for the festival and selecting the musicians to be asked to offer their services. A sub-committee was formed, under the leadership of Gardiner, to inspect the local churches and public halls and ascertain their suitability for the purpose of the Festival.

A few weeks later they reported that they considered the church of St Margaret to be the best suited for the morning concerts of sacred music, for not only was it the largest of the five town churches but it also had the advantage of having better acoustics than the other four. The nave, reported Gardiner, was able to hold about fifteen hundred people while a further three hundred and twenty could be accommodated in a proposed gallery which could be built for an estimated twelve pounds.

As for the evening concerts, which would be of a more secular nature, it was decided that the Assembly Room, Hotel Street, rather than the Theatre would be best suited. The Theatre, so Gardiner argued, was ill-adapted for a musical performance, whereas the Assembly Rooms were ideal and capable of holding an audience of between six and seven hundred.[5]

Gardiner was also given the task of engaging the musicians for the festival. Well-known in musical circles, he was a frequent visitor to London and attended most of the musical meetings which took place round the country. He was soon able to report that a number of first-rate artists had promised their services at fees ranging from ten to one hundred pounds.

Franz Cramer, one of the finest violinists of his day, who had joined the London Opera when he was only seventeen, had been engaged as leader. A frequent performer before King George III, Cramer, by then in his fifties, had been one of the first professors at the recently-formed Royal Academy of Music.

To lead the cello stand Gardiner had engaged Robert Lindley, a Yorkshire man who had been playing since he was five and whose technique was so brilliant that he was able to play first violin parts on his cello. In 1794, aged eighteen, Lindley had the honour of playing before the Prince Regent and now, 1826, he was lead cello with the Italian Opera in London.[6]

Left: *Domenico Dragonetti (1763–1846), one of the principal musicians at the 1827 Leicester Music Festival.* (Illustrated London News *April 1846)*
Right: *John Braham (1774–1856) one of the leading singers at the festival.* (Illustrated London News *March 1852)*

Leading the double bass section was to be the famous Venetian Domenico Dragonetti. Considered to be the world's finest bass player, such was his mastery over his instrument, made especially for him by Stradivari, that while staying at a monastery, he had stood in the corridor one night and with his bass imitated a storm. The result of this nocturnal episode was that the next day the main topic of the monks' conversation was the 'thunder storm' of the previous night. A very eccentric man, Dragonetti was an avid collector of dolls, one of which, a black one, he called his wife. He was very difficult to understand, his speech being a mixture of English, French and Italian dialects.[7]

Among the singers engaged were Henry Phillips and John Braham. Phillips, one of England's foremost bass singers, was to be paid fifty guineas for his services while Braham, one of the country's leading tenors, commanded a fee of one hundred guineas. Born in 1774, Braham had started his life selling pencils round the streets. His fine voice, however, soon got him onto the Covent Garden stage while he was but thirteen years of age. When his voice broke he taught piano until his adult voice developed, making his Drury Lane debut when he was twenty-two. A composer of operas, now forgotten but mentioned by Gardiner in his memoirs, Braham had spent a few years studying in Italy, before returning to England in 1801.[8]

Thomas Greatorex

Not only nationally known musicians were asked to take part in the festival, for Gardiner also drew on the wealth of local talent. Leading the flute desk was Henry Nicholson, while Thomas Greatorex (1758–1831), organist at Westminster Abbey and Professor of the Piano and Organ at the Royal Academy of Music, was booked to play the organ. He had moved with his family from Shottle, Derbyshire to Leicester in 1766. At the 1774 festival in St Martin's he had met the Earl of Sandwich, who invited him to join his household as a music teacher.[9]

From 1781 to 1784 Greatorex was organist at Carlisle Cathedral where his father Anthony was vicar-choral. In 1784 he moved to Newcastle before, two years later, setting off on the Grand Tour to 'perfect his education'. Said to have introduced the music of Handel to the Italians, on his return journey he climbed to the top of the spire of Strasbourg Cathedral. When he had got as far as he could using the conventional steps and ladders, he climbed out of a window and did the rest of the ascent using the crockets.

In 1793, on the retirement of Bates, he was appointed Director of the Ancient Concerts and made a Fellow of the Royal Society. A fine organist, whose playing was likened to Doric Architecture, massive and grand, he was in great demand all over the country playing at almost all the provincial music festivals in the first quarter of the nineteenth century. He also had a lucrative teaching practice and was said to have given eighty-four singing lessons in one week at one guinea a time.[10]

Thomas had two sisters, one of whom died when she was only five years old. A headstone to her memory used to stand in St Martin's churchyard with the pathetic inscription:[11]

> *Here lie the remains of Anthonina Greatorex*
> *who was born Oct 2 1762 and died July 20 1767.*
> *Harmonious soul! took'st thou offence,*
> *At discords here, and fled'st from hence?*

> Or, in thy sacred raptures, hear
> The music of Heaven's warbling sphere?
> Then mounted straight where Angels sing,
> And love does dance on ev'ry string.

Thomas's other sister begun her musical career as a child by accompanying her grandfather, a carpenter by trade, to wakes and fairs at which she danced to his hurdy-gurdy accompaniment. Appointed, on the recommendation of Joseph Cradock, organist of St Martin's in 1774, within a few years she was a performer of eminence and promoter of annual concerts during Assize Week, for which she availed herself of the talents of Bartleman, Harrison, William Knyvett and her brother, 'the most perfect set of English singers that ever joined their voices together', who used to visit Sir Charles Hudson at Wanlip Hall at this time.[12]

Finalising Arrangements

As well as performers the committee also needed patronage and by January 1827 they were able to report that almost all the gentry to whom requests for support had been sent had returned positive replies. An exception was the Bishop of Lichfield, who had replied that he felt it would be better if he gave his charity to his own area rather than to Leicester. Amongst those who did give their support were the Earls of Denbigh, Chesterfield, Cardigan, Ayesford, Harborough and Besborough; Earls Spencer, Ferrars and Howe; the Duke of Rutland and the Bishop of Lincoln.[13]

By the spring of 1827 most of the arrangements had been finalized and the builder, who was to erect the gallery in the church chancel, sent to Birmingham to see how such a gallery had been erected there for the 1826 Festival. Advertisements were placed in the local press asking for offers of accommodation for the many visitors who were expected. In July an order for two hundred printed bills advertising the Festival was placed with Thomas Combe, book seller, printer and librarian, who by now had moved to Gallowtree Gate. Sent to all the main inns in the town and county, as well as giving a list of the patrons and principal performers they also gave an outline of the three-day event announcing that 'encouraged by the very high and distinguished patronage afforded the intended Festival they [the committee] have ventured to engage many performers of the finest musical talent in the Kingdom, both vocal and instrumental.' In August Combe was given the additional task of printing the concert programmes.[14]

Leader, ... Mr. CRAMER.

ACT I.

OVERTURE, Anacreon. .. .. Cherubini.
ARIA, Signor De Begnis, *Largo al Factotum*, Il Barbiere, Rossini.
SCENE, Mrs. Austin, *Entendez Vous*. Le Rossignol, Lebrun,
    Flauto Obligato, Mr. Nicholson.
SONG, Mrs. W. Knyvett, *Bid me not forget thy smile*, Knyvett.
DUETTO, Madame Caradori and Mr. Braham, *Ah se
    puoi così*, (Mosè in Egitto) .. .. .. Rossini.
SONG, Mr. Phillips, *When forc'd from dear Hebe*, Dr. Arne.
TRIO, Messrs. Cramer, Lindley, and Dragonetti, Handel & Martini
SCENA, Madame Pasta, *Tu ch' accendi*, (Il Tancredi) Rossini.
GLEE, *With sighs sweet rose*, ... Callcott.
CANTATA, Mr. Braham, *Alexis*, (Violoncello Obligato,
    Mr. Lindley.) .. .. Pepusch.
SONG, Madame Caradori, *Should he upbraid*, .. Bishop.
DUETTO, Madame Pasta and Mr. Braham, *Amor
    possenti*, ... Rossini.
GRAND FINALE, *Signori, di fuori*, (Figaro) Mozart.

ACT II.

GRAND SINFONIA, No. 1, in C... .. .. Beethoven.
SCENA, Madame Caradori, *A compir già*, (Semiramede)
    Accompanied on the Violin by Mr. F. Cramer, Guglielmi.
SONG, Signor de Begnis, *En revenant*, ... Castelli.
ARIA, Madame Pasta, *Cadde l' iniquo*, ... Nicolini.
CONCERTO, VIOLIN, Mr. Keisewetter, .. Hoffman.
ARIA, Madame Caradori, *Batti Batti*, ... Mozart.
DUETTO, Mr. Braham and Signor de Begnis, (Il Bar-
    biere di Siviglia.) .. .. Rossini.
ARIA, Madame Pasta, *Ah! come rapida*, .. Meyerbeer.
FANTASIA, HORN, Signor Puzzi, ... Puzzi.
SONG, Mrs. Knyvett, *Lo, here the gentle lark*. .. Bishop.
SCENA ED ARIA, Signor De Begnis, (Il Fanatico) Sacchini,
SONG, Mr. Braham, *Blue Bonnets*. .. .. Lee.
OVERTURE, *La Gazza Ladra*, ... Rossini.

*The Programme for the Tuesday evening concert.
(Leicestershire Record Office)*

> ## LEICESTER
> ## MUSICAL FESTIVAL.
>
> August 29, 1827.
>
> THE Committee have great satisfaction in announcing to the Public, that they have been fortunate enough to secure the distinguished services of
>
> ### MADAME CARADORI
>
> Who has most kindly undertaken to sing the principal Songs assigned to Miss PATON and Miss STEPHENS, from the former of whom they have to regret that they received the resignation of her engagement, on account of serious illness, accompanied by the certificate of her physician, Dr. Nevison. The latter is prevented attending by the recent death of her father.
>
> The Committee have also engaged the celebrated
>
> ### SIGNOR DE BEGNIS,
> FOR THE CONCERTS.

Not only was Gardiner involved in the background organisation, but he was also in charge of training the choir of mainly local amateurs, augmented by a few more established singers from the neighbouring towns of Lincoln, Nottingham and Kettering. Gardiner had just formed a Choral Society, which had been instituted for the purpose of cultivating sacred music,[15] and it was with this nucleus that he formed the Festival chorus, the training of which began almost as soon as the idea of the Festival was first mooted. One of his main concerns was to ascertain that all the members of the choir had the same translations of the works to be performed, it being common practice for different publishers to use different translations of the same work. As singers were expected to supply their own music, it was not uncommon in a large choir to find two or more translations being used.

Everything seemed to be going smoothly until a few weeks before the festival when one or two major problems occurred. In early August the committee received a letter from Elizabeth Austin, one of the soprano soloists booked by Gardiner, in which she complained that on receipt of her programme she had noticed that two of the songs promised her had been given to two of the minor vocalists - Mrs King and Catherine Stephens. Not wanting, however, to cause undue problems for these two ladies, who were just embarking on their musical careers, she was prepared to let the changes stand. She also pointed out that the thirty guinea fee which she had accepted was much below that which she normally would have expected, but as it was for a good cause, and that she had deep respect for Gardiner, she had agreed to perform for the figure offered.[16]

Then came the news that two of the main singers had been forced to withdraw - Mary Ann Paton, who had fallen ill, and Catherine Stephens, whose father had died. When Earl Howe, the chief promoter of the Festival, proposed to replace the two ladies by engaging the Italian singer Guiditta Pasta, on the high terms of three hundred guineas, Gardiner told him that it was too great a sum to be laid out on one singer. The Earl, however, replied, 'She will do Sir!' and promised to put one hundred guineas towards the fee himself.[17]

With only ten days to go, Gardiner was able to engage Maria Caradori, a popular singer who had made her London debut four years earlier in Mozart's *Magic Flute* for which she had been paid three hundred pounds. Two years later, in March 1825, she had sung the soprano solo in the first English performance of Beethoven's *Symphony no. 9*. Not too familiar with English sacred music, Caradori was criticized for singing 'in the continental manner'. However, in the evening concerts she was praised as shining 'with scarcely secondary lustre'.[18]

If this were not enough De Beriot, who was to have played a violin concerto, found himself, at the last minute, unable to obtain leave of absence from the Dutch Court where he was solo violinist to King Wilhem. His place was taken by Keisewetter, who, as it turned out, was to make his final appearance at Leicester. Although very ill he did not want to let down the audience and had to be helped to the stand by his fellow musicians. The audience listened to him with intense admiration, as the violinist, 'apparently on the brink of Eternity', produced an effect almost supernatural.[19]

Keisewetter, in spite of being implored not to perform, insisted on playing, but looked so ill that many people feared he might die on the stage. A few days later he left for Norwich, where he was booked to play at another festival, however, on arrival he was deemed too ill to play and had to return home to London, where he died a few days later.[20]

Then there was the question of the extra rehearsals. Three of the London musicians hired by Gardiner: Mackintosh (bassoon), Willman (clarinet) and Harper (trumpet) wrote to the committee explaining that when they had agreed to their fees (twenty guineas each) they

> **LODGINGS**
> **FOR THE**
> **INTENDED MUSICAL FESTIVAL.**
>
> ALL Persons who may be disposed to accommodate Families or Individuals with LODGINGS, at the approaching MUSICAL FESTIVAL, in September next, are requested to send particulars of the accommodation they can furnish, with their Terms, to Mr. COMBE, that they may be laid before the Committee, on or before the 14th of June next.

had not known about the possibility of extra rehearsals, stating that as they were men of honour, they would still come, but hoped that the committee would see their way clear to paying them for the extra work. As the committee minutes are incomplete it is not clear if they were paid anything extra. The *Leicester Chronicle* observed that Mr Harper's trumpet playing was as if by an archangel, and that Mr Willman's clarinet playing could only be described in one word - 'wonderful'.[21]

One of the last problems to be resolved as the festival took final shape was that of Mr Moralt who, on receipt of his programme, had noticed that he was to lead the second violin section, something he had not known when he had agreed to his fifteen guinea fee. He now wanted twenty - a small price to pay for the Director of the German Opera in London.[22]

It was not, however, all set backs. The two music shop owners of Gallowtree Gate both offered their services - Samuel Deacon on double bass and Charles Mavius on violin. A week before the commencement of the Festival Mr Bishop was called in to tune St Margaret's organ, while the local innkeepers put up posters announcing the forthcoming event. Advertisements for the festival were inserted in the main national newspapers *The Times*, *The Morning Post*, and *The Morning Chronicle*, while those who had offered accommodation were asked what rooms they were offering and at what price. Many of those who did offer rooms charged such high rates that some of the visitors to the festival only sat through half a concert and then travelled the long distance home rather than pay

> ## Musical Festival.
>
> F. JACKSON takes leave to call the public attention to his superb and valuable STOCK of JEWELLERY and FANCY ARTICLES, of every description, which, on the present occasion, he has with especial care selected from the very newest and most elegant patterns which can be supplied by the first houses in the respective branches. Cheapside (near the Conduit), Leicester.

the exorbitant rates being asked. There does not seem to be any reference as to what exactly was charged by the Leicester folk but in the previous year's festival at Birmingham the average rates were seven shillings a night in hotels and one to two pounds for private rooms for the duration of the festival.[23]

For those unable to attend the concerts on the three evenings of the festival, there were grand firework displays on the Wharf Street Cricket Ground. The final evening concluded with a masked ball, music provided by a military band, in a specially-built pavilion. Unlike the Thursday evening ball in the Assembly Room, where fancy dress was optional, the cricket ground dancers had to be masked. 'No admittance unmasked' announced the advertisement which also explained that 'the most judicious arrangements will be made to keep order and regularity'. Tickets for the fireworks, which included Six Pointed Stars, Illuminated Crosses and Bengal Lights (one shilling and sixpence, children one shilling) and masked balls (five shillings) were available from the Gallowtree Gate office of Benjamin Payne.[24]

The local shops and businesses also took advantage of the influx of visitors to the town: Clayton's Gallowtree Gate fruit shop brought in a large assortment of pineapples, melons, grapes and filberts. F. Jackson, a jeweller, in Cheapside, offered a 'superb and valuable stock of jewellery and fancy articles of every description'. Cape Hodgkin & Co informed their friends that they had provided for the approaching festival 'a most extensive assortment of goods in linen and woollen drapery, silk mercury etc.' which were promised to be at lower prices than any other establishment.

> ## Mr. C. MAVIUS
> RESPECTFULLY announces, that he has received a large supply of the best editions of all the SONGS, DUETTS, GLEES, &c. &c., that are to be performed at the approaching MUSICAL FESTIVAL. To be had at his
> ## MUSIC AND MUSICAL INSTRUMENT
> WAREHOUSE,
> (Adjoining Messrs. Jackson's),
> ### GALLOWTREE-GATE, LEICESTER.
> Having recently been in London, he is at present able to offer for the approval of his Friends and the Public, a very extensive assortment of HORIZONTAL GRAND, CABINET, COTTAGE, CIRCULAR, and SQUARE PIANO-FORTES, personally selected from the factories of Messrs. Broadwood, Stodart, Clementi, Tonkison, Dettmer, &c. &c., comprising every improvement up to the present period.
> Also, double-action HARPS, GUITARS, VIOLINS, FLUTES, &c. &c., with every article appertaining to Music.
> N.B. Several second-hand Instruments, in excellent condition.
> SUPERIOR PIANO-FORTES, FOR HIRE.
> Aug. 30, 1827.

It goes without saying that the local music emporia were hoping for large orders. Charles Mavius had on sale all the sheet music which was to be performed at the festival, as well as having 'a very extensive assortment of horizontal, grand, cabinet, cottage, circular and square pianofortes'. There was also an art exhibition mounted by William Nedham, a local artist who had a studio in Humberstone Gate.

The town inns were hoping for an increase in business. Many of them, such as the Three Crowns, Granby Street, the George, Haymarket and the Three Cranes, Humberstone Gate, were holding ordinaries on the afternoons of the festival at prices ranging from four to ten shillings a head. When one considers that this was the average weekly pay of the town's artisans these were very expensive dinners![25]

The demand for festival tickets was high. Costing between five shillings and one pound almost all were sold before the opening day.

The Duke of Devonshire alone purchased one hundred pounds worth, however, at the last minute, neither he nor his party were able to attend. Such was the interest shown that by the Tuesday of the first concert tickets were changing hands at up to twelve times their face value.[26]

Most of the musicians arrived in the town on the Sunday before the festival in order to be ready for Monday's main rehearsal, while the principal soloists, such as Guiditta Pasta and John Braham, arrived on the Monday afternoon after a long trip from Ireland.[27]

The Doors Open

By nine o'clock on Tuesday 4 September, the first day of the festival, there was a long queue outside St Margaret's Church waiting for admittance. Such was the traffic that the organizers had arranged a 'one-way system' for the hundred or so coaches that were expected to be bringing the more well-to-do and nobility. The coachmen were instructed to go down Church Gate where they were to form a single file with the horses' heads pointing toward Sanvey Gate, down which they were instructed to go after letting off their passengers by the west door. Those who came on foot were to enter by the south door. Not only were the roads crowded with the festival-goers, but also by the curious town folk who just wanted to see the fashionable ladies who, due to the warm weather, chose to walk to the church rather than get their gowns creased by sitting in their coaches. At nine-thirty the doors opened and the crowds entered.[28]

The three hundred strong orchestra was placed under the tower at the west end, while at the east end, richly bedecked with tulips and carnations, was the specially erected gallery in which the gentry and nobility sat. Among those who graced the concert by their presence were the Duke of Rutland, the Earl of Stamford, Lady Fielding, Earl Ferrars, Earl Howe, Colonel Keck and the town's two Members of Parliament, Charles Otway Cave and Charles Hastings. Indeed, 'never in the memory of any living person, perhaps at no former period, did Leicester contain such an assembly of rank, title, wealth, beauty and fashion as on this occasion'.[29]

To help with the smooth running stewards were appointed and, so that they would be recognisable, they were to wear a light blue ribbon in their lapels. Such was the political feeling of the town at this time, just after the infamous general election when Leicester's Corporation had spent a fortune on ensuring that their candidates won, that one man felt compelled to pen his feelings on the matter in a letter to the *Leicester Chronicle*. He remarked that blue was a political colour and as the festival was a non-political venture, with, it was hoped, people of all political complexions vying with each other to promote the objects of the event, it was an unfortunate choice of colour.[30]

During the first morning's concert, which opened with Vaughan and Phillips singing Cradock's 'Charity Ode', the Reverend Erskine, vicar of St Martin's, preached on behalf of the charity. One of the more liberal-minded clergy in the town, Erskine was to be in the vanguard of the opposition to church rates in the 1830s.

Highlights of the festival included the singing of John Braham who, owing to a severe cold caught on his journey to Leicester from Ireland, had to omit several of his songs due to the impairment of his voice. Indeed, were it not for the disappointment which it would have caused, Braham would have cancelled his whole programme. In spite of this desire to please some of his songs did not meet with wholehearted applause, it being felt that a singer of his stature should not stoop to singing 'popular' songs:

'Mr Braham in his 'Blue Bonnets' was over the border again. We lament that such masterly talents should be so employed, and lowered to the level of a popular ballad - but this kind of singsong is perhaps more to the taste of the unlearned in music.'[31]

This remark, by the unknown author of the 'Account', gives an insight into the minds of the middle class concert-goers of the early nineteenth century when popular and serious music had no place on the same programme, the middle class snobs believing that popular music was only for the 'unlearned' in music. Taking into account the price of the tickets for the festival it was obvious intended for the middle classes, gentry and nobility, the working man having no way of being able to afford the price of admission, in many cases more than a week's pay. The 'Account' author also found criticism in Braham's serious songs:

'We are astonished that a person of Mr Braham's acknowledged good sense and judgement should, time after time, commit such an outrage on the feelings of an audience, as to throw upon the pious ejaculation of the last line 'Prepare my God and meet Him', one of those

The 1827 Leicester Music Festival 71

W. Gardiner

AN ACCOUNT

OF

The Grand

MUSICAL FESTIVAL,

HELD

AT LEICESTER,

SEPTEMBER 4th, 5th, & 6th, 1827,

WITH

CRITICAL REMARKS

ON THE

Performers & Performances.

LEICESTER :
PRINTED BY A. COCKSHAW ;
AND SOLD BY
HURST, CHANCE, AND CO. ST. PAUL'S CHURCH
YARD, LONDON.

MDCCCXXVIII.

The title page of An Account of the Grand Music Festival held at Leicester, published in 1828. This must have been William Gardiner's copy for it is signed by him. (Leicestershire Record Office) vehement bursts of his voice, which in a theatre might pass for good taste, but which we consider a violation of it.'[32]

Another singer whose choice of songs came under criticism was Mrs Knyvett whose rendering of 'Midst Silent Shades' was too old fashioned for the writer who felt that 'the slow and equal vibrations of the last century are too inanimate and lifeless for the cravings of the modern ear.'[33]

Both of the above quotes, from the 'Account', seem to be contradictory. On the one hand Braham is being criticized for being too popular, whereas on the other hand Knyvett is not catering to the 'cravings of the modern ear!' It may be that the 'Account' was in fact the work of two critics, one attending the Tuesday concert in which Braham sung 'Blue Bonnets' and another was at the Wednesday event when Knyvett sang Bach's 'Midst Silent Shades'.

It would seem, however, as if the Leicester audiences were not as serious minded as Braham's critic would have us believe, for *The Journal* reported that another of the singers, De Begnis, sung two comic songs 'which excited much laughter'. Even the writer of the 'Account' had to concede that De Begnis brought 'a sort of sunshine and animation into the evening amusements' and that 'the drollery of De Begnis could not be surpassed'. One musician who, it seems, could do no wrong was the horn player Puzzi who 'subdued his audience into a soothing and pleasing melancholy'. Born in Parma in 1792, he was one of the most influential horn players of his day and as such one of the main attractions at the Festival.[34]

The more secular music was performed in the two Assembly Room evening concerts, both of which being packed out with two elevated rows at the end of the hall reserved for the patrons and their families. In order to accommodate the extra traffic there were similar rules in operation as there were for the morning concerts held at the church, carriages being instructed to come up Horsefair with their heads towards the Market Place and to let off their passengers at the Assembly Room's side door.[35]

Included amongst the orchestral works performed at the festival were some which are still well known and loved today, as well as others which have not stood the test of time and are now almost forgotten. The programme included exerts of works by Rossini (*Barber of Seville, Tancredi, The Thieving Magpie*), Mozart (selections from

Figaro and *Magic Flute*), Haydn's *Symphony No.12*, Weber's *Freischutz Overture* and Beethoven's *Symphony No.1*, which was chosen as being more intelligible than any of his others.[36]

The final morning of the festival saw a performance of the *Messiah* in which 'with music so fine, and a band so excellent' the *Hallelujah Chorus* was never done better, 'the simultaneous shocks from the orchestra [being] overpowering with the performers outvying each other in force and precision'. Indeed so well was it received that it had to be encored.' The *Leicester Journal* tells us that the church, while not full, was well attended, whereas the 'Account' paints a slightly better picture, telling us that 'as soon as the doors were opened the church overflowed.' Whether the church was full or only nearly full all sources are unanimous that it was one of the best performances ever heard in Leicester.[37]

Included among the music performed at the festival was Gardiner's *Judah*, the score of which he is seen holding in the portrait displayed in Newark Houses Museum. It was, however, felt that another fifty years would have to elapse before an orchestra would be able to do proper justice to the work, as there were no instruments at that time capable of producing the lower line of the scale. Only a man like Gardiner would write music incapable of being played! One should also not forget that little of Gardiner's work was original; it being, in the main, arrangements of tunes by Haydn, Mozart and Handel. In all fairness, however, he never claimed otherwise. To the late twentieth century ear most of his work is rather banal, and even some of his contemporaries were not entirely happy with the 'operation of Mr Gardiner's pruning knife.' On the other hand his arrangements of 'What Passion Cannot Music Rise and Quell', in which he had scored the cello solo for the horn, played by Puzzi, was very well received. In another example Gardiner was accused of *not* pruning! Concerning 'If God be for us who can be against us?' it was observed, 'why did not Mr Gardiner, who is avowedly of the new school, adopt the song as it stands abbreviated in the German copy?'[38]

In spite of these criticisms Gardiner must have been very pleased with the reception given to his arrangement of Haydn's 'The King shall Rejoice'

'We saw the joyous and buoyant effect of it depicted on the countenances of the performers, who were elated with the vivacity of the piece, that it was with difficulty the conductor could restrain the energies of his band from running away into an ungovernable velocity.'[39]

Even though the festival owed a lot to Gardiner for his tireless efforts on behalf of the committee, he did not get it all his way. Some of his choices of music requiring a 'little sober qualification from the experienced and sedate Mr Greatorex.'[40] The local press certainly realised that Gardiner had been the driving force behind the festival:

'No moderate share of eulogium is due on this occasion to Mr Gardiner. Exhaustless application and assiduity - exquisite taste in the selection - judgement in that contrasted arrangement by which attention was re-animated - unrivalled skill in their several adaptations - with a prompt fertility of resources for the many caprices and contingencies incident to a combination of such a magnitude, are very rarely united in one person. The event has proved his full possession of these attributes in an unusual degree, and most eminently have they contributed to the success and gratification.'[41]

The final event of the festival was a fancy dress ball held in the Assembly Rooms. Commencing at eight o'clock on the Thursday evening, such was the continuous music that there was 'scarcely time for the interchange of the usual courtesies of society', until the ball's conclusion at four the following morning. Fancy dress was not mandatory and most of the guests preferred either evening dress or military uniform. Amongst those who did enter into the spirit of the event were the Viscountess Tamworth, dressed as a Swiss peasant; Sir Frederick Fowke, as Sir Walter Raleigh, Lorraine Smith as a Tyrolean minstrel, and John Mansfield's wife Sarah who appeared dressed as a Spanish lady. Led by the music of Litoff's Full Quadrille Band, tickets for the evening were fifteen shillings each.[42]

Not only was the festival financially successful, after all expenses had been paid the Infirmary profited by £1,150 17s 7d, but it had also been a social success. In spite of the vast numbers of people which had thronged into the town there had been very little trouble and 'not a single accident had occurred which needed the services of the surgeon, coach maker or the police, the greatest decorum prevailed and not a single pickpocket succeeded in obtaining any booty'. This happy state of affairs was mainly due to the presence of thirty selected constables from the 'posse commitalis' of the Borough, who as well as Ellis and Ruthren, two principal officers from Bow Street, were deployed to detect any 'light fingered gentry from London.'[43]

Payment for the performers, which was made from Thomas Combe's Gallowtree Gate book shop, was on Thursday afternoon for those residing outside Leicester and Friday morning for the local musicians. As well as the principal performers there were also the members of the orchestra and chorus who were paid ten shillings each, plus an extra shilling for each rehearsal attended.[44]

With the dual success of the festival it was hoped that the town would repeat the venture in a few years time. However it was not to be, for the era of the grand music festivals ended with the coming of the Victorian Age. Most of the larger provincial towns formed their own choral and orchestral groups which catered mainly for the local population. In Leicester William Gardiner carried on with the choral group he had formed for the festival and, with the building of the 'New Hall', many musicians were invited to perform in concerts at Leicester. One of the first of these celebrated musicians to play in the town was Paganini in 1833. He was one of many, including Franz Liszt, brought to the town by Henry Nicholson, a musician who was to be at the fore of all the town's musical events for the next thirty years. Indeed, as we will see, throughout the nineteenth century Leicester was a mecca for musical entertainment, most concerts being given in the New Hall and, after its erection in 1853, the Temperance Hall. Leicester had indeed become a town of musical people.

Chapter 6

𝄞 ALLEGRO MA NON TROPPO 𝄞

The New Hall

By 1830 Leicester had become a town where music had been brought to a comparatively high state of perfection. Music teachers and music shops abounded, many middle-class homes had pianos, and as well as a fine choral society of one hundred members there were also many smaller choirs. However, in spite of all this, the town still did not boast a purpose-built concert hall. Some events, such as the well-attended 1831 New Year's Grand Concert, promoted by George Barker with tickets costing five shillings each, took place in the Guildhall. Other events, such as that of April 1831, which brought to the Leicester public the pianist George Aspull, took place in the Exchange.

Eight years earlier, Aspull, who had been playing since he was six, had been introduced to Rossini who, on hearing him play, proclaimed that he was the greatest instance of musical precocity and genius with which he had ever met.[1]

Towards the end of 1830 the town Radicals, by dint of the town Tories banning them from using the Guildhall for their gatherings, announced that they proposed to erect a new building which could be used for both public meetings and entertainments. The cost of fifteen thousand pounds was raised by selling shares at twenty pounds each.

In May 1831 local architect William Flint was selected to draw up plans for the building, and an invitation extended to builders to submit tenders.[2] Built in Greek revival style, with giant Doric pilasters, the hall, on the corner of Wellington and Belvoir Streets, opened in May 1832. At first commonly referred to as the Green Rooms, the party colour of the Radicals, it was not long before the building became generally known in the town simply as the 'New Hall'. It is still standing, now being used by the Leicester Library Services as the City Lending Library.

Leicester's 'New Hall', Wellington Street.

In November 1832 it was announced that as soon as enough subscriptions had been obtained, one guinea for gentlemen and half a guinea for ladies, a committee would be formed to arrange a series of subscription concerts. The first of this new series was under the stewardship of Dr John Hill, Thomas Bass Oliver, Charles Merridith and Thomas Paget. The main attraction of the first concert, which took place the following December, was Nicholas Bochsa who, as well as being skilful on almost every known instrument, was best known for his expertise on the harp, an instrument on which he was constantly discovering new musical effects. Harpist to Louis XVIII, in 1817 he had had to hurriedly leave his native France due to his part-time business in forged documents![3]

The highlight of the evening was Bochsa's *Fantastica for Harp and Violin* played by the composer and Nicholas Mori. Mori, who had made his public debut in 1804, aged eight, playing a concerto by his teacher François Barthelmon, was described as touching his violin as tenderly as a mother her child, but as playfully as the child its toy.[4]

A feature of these early concerts, which usually lasted about three hours, was that at the programme's conclusion the hall was cleared for dancing which lasted into the early hours. For those not so active card tables were set up in the side rooms. Catering solely for the middle classes, tickets for single concerts were seven shillings and sixpence each. The ladies used these musical events to vie with each other by showing off the richness of their gowns while the gentlemen, who stood at the back behind the sedentary ladies, were usually dressed in frock coats and tall hats which, incidently, they kept on during the performance.[5]

Among the musicians who appeared at these early concerts were the local singer Elizabeth Sharpe; Miss Sherriff from Covent Garden; Signor Begrez ('highly interesting as a singer in spite of being a foreigner'); Miss Atkinson, a pupil of Guynemer; Signor Giubilei, a pupil of De Begnis and singer at the Italian Opera; Maria Felicitia Malibran and Charles de Beriot.

Born in Belgium in 1802 De Beriot gave his first public performance when he was nine, making his London debut in 1826. Solo violinist to King Wilhem of the Netherlands, he was said to have adopted the technical brilliance of Paganini to the elegance and piquancy of the Parisian style. In March 1836 he married Maria Malibran, who unfortunately died some six months later.

Malibran had been born in Paris in 1808 and gone to New York City with her father, a tenor, in 1826 to promote Italian Opera. It was here she met and married local businessman François Malibran. A year later, on her husband's bankruptcy, she return to Paris alone, making her dèbut at that city's opera in 1828.[6]

The Musical Society

In April 1833, after almost thirty years, the Musical Society was resurrected. Incorporating the Choral Society, at first it was intended only to have a school for practice and improvement, 'to be useful and not ornamental', and to meet twice a month - once for rehearsal and once for a concert. However, the society became so popular that soon their New Hall rehearsals became public events with many subscribers paying half a guinea for an individual ticket or twenty-five shillings for one which would admit three. The first meeting, conducted by Edward Mammatt, included the singing of Mrs Weston, her sister Elizabeth Sharpe, Richard Toone and Isaac Handscomb, clerk of the

Handbill for the first subscription concert held in the New Hall, 6 December 1832. (Leicestershire Record Office) parish of St George. In September, in consequence of some unidentified misbehaviour amongst two of the band which had been engaged to accompany the singing, the Society had to announce that in future only a septet band would be used and the concerts only consist of songs, duets, glees and symphonies.[7]

By February 1834 the society's committee was getting short of money and, in spite of the success of the current season, they made an appeal for new subscribers. The response, however was not as good as expected and within the year the society had folded.[8]

Niccolò Paganini (1782–1840), (Grove's Dictionary)

Subscription Concerts

In 1833 the New Hall hosted two big special musical events. In June the town was visited by the Prussian Horn Band, a combination of twenty-three musicians who gave five concerts in the town, the last two being for the benefit of the Infirmary. The band was remarkable for each musician played an instrument which was only able to produce a single note. In this manner they played not only simple music but also symphonies by composers such as Haydn. Then, on 18 October, the great Niccolò Paganini played to an audience of only three hundred. His programme included 'Preludio e Rhondo Brilliante', 'Grand Variations on nel Cor Piu', 'Sonata Millitaire', which he played all on one string, and variations on the ever-popular 'Carnival of Venice'.[9]

Subscription tickets for the 1833–34 series of concerts were one guinea for gentlemen and fifteen shillings for ladies. Artists booked for the concerts included Maria Malibran, Giubilei and De Beriot, the band being led by local musician Henry Gill. This series of concerts was much better patronized than that of the previous season, with the attendance at the first concert far surpassing any event held in 1832.

The second concert, in November, included fifteen year old Clara Anastasia Novello who had begun singing lessons at the age of four and been admitted to the Paris Institution de Musique Religieuse when she was eleven. On her return to England in 1830 she had become a regular performer at the Philharmonic Ancient and Nobility Concerts in London singing in the first performance in England of Beethoven's *Mass in D*. A few months before her Leicester début she had sung in the Three Choirs Festival at Worcester.[10]

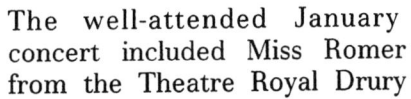

The well-attended January concert included Miss Romer from the Theatre Royal Drury

Sir Henry Bishop (1786–1855)
(Illustrated London News Dec 1851)

Lane, Giubilei and George Lindley, one of the country's foremost cellists. The orchestra, led by Guynemer, was without its wind section, most of whom being members of the Duke of Rutland's Militia Band which was on duty at Belvoir Castle, where the Duke was hosting guests at his birthday celebrations.[11]

With the dark winter evenings and the problems of artificial lighting in the first half of the century some of the concerts were held in the early afternoon, another indication of them being primarily for the middle classes. Indeed, the advertisement for the concert on the morning of Thursday 9 January 1834, actually stated that it was for the 'nobility and gentry'. Amongst those taking part in this event were Nicholas Bochsa, just back from a tour of Scotland and northern England where his new harp effects had created an unprecedented sensation; Nicholas Mori; and Henry Rowley Bishop.

Bishop, who in 1842 became the first musician to be honoured by a knighthood, was the director at Drury Lane, conductor of the Philharmonic Concerts and author of one of the best loved songs in the English language, 'Home Sweet Home'. Also on the programme was Bishop's wife, Anna, nee Riviere, who, three years previously, had made her professional debut as a soprano and was now lead singer of the Philharmonic Ancient and Nobility Concerts in London. Timed to begin at 1 pm the tickets for the concert were seven shillings each.[12]

1834 opened with a benefit concert to raise money to send Henry Hough, a promising young violinist, to London to further his musical education. Hough was a popular figure and the hall was full of his friends and supporters who had each paid three shillings for tickets. Hough certainly did not let his sponsors down for before long he joined his fellow Lestrians John Norton and John Ella in the orchestra of the Italian Opera.

In September there was a performance of local musicians including Samuel Wykes, Elizabeth Sharpe, Mr Rivett, Elizabeth Weston and Richard Toone. A bass singer with a full round voice, Toone was very well known in musical circles and took part in almost every music festival in the country. Locally he was a regular singer at the Rainbow and Dove, Northampton Square, where the landlord, Samuel Cleaver, held weekly glee parties.

Toone died in February 1857 and was buried in Welford Road Cemetery. He was interred in the same grave as Edmund Taylor, former choirmaster at Kidderminster, who had died five years earlier. The monument, now sadly disappeared, executed by Broadbent, was of plain white stone with, in the centre of an oval near the circular top, a sunken panel in which was carved a music book opened to 'I know that my Redeemer liveth'.[13]

In spite of the band being 'far superior to that of last year', the September concert was poorly supported. The people of Leicester, it seems, would flock to musicians from the capital but would not give support to the talented amateur musicians with which the town was blessed. The high price asked for tickets - ten shillings and sixpence - may also have contributed to the low turnout. The December concert which featured Isaac Handscomb, Elizabeth Weston and Samuel Wykes, was a little better supported, perhaps because the popular Guynemer was conducting.[14]

The first concert and ball of 1835, led by Guynemer and conducted by local music shopkeeper Charles Mavius, featured Franz Stockhausen, a German harpist, and his wife Margaret, a popular soprano singer.

Also taking part were John Parry the Welsh pianist, and Lucy Anderson, piano teacher to Princess Victoria, who had been the first woman pianist to play at the concerts of the London Philharmonic Society.

Other artists who appeared in the New Hall during the year included Mademoiselle Greisi; Luigi Lablache, one of the foremost bass singers of his day and singing teacher to Princess Victoria; and Buzzi and Piocianchettino, who were en route to the York Music Festival. The September ball featured Mr Brown, a dancing master from London, who exhibited his 'Improved Systems of Dancing Quadrilles'.[15]

The 1835-36 series of concerts, stewarded by Sir John Kaye, John Danvers, Edward Farnham, Dr George Shaw and Thomas Paget, proved to be the last for some time. The first of the promised concerts, took place in December when local musicians Henry Gill and Charles Mavius were joined by two of the leading names in contemporary English music, Anna Bishop, 'the most classical of all

Theatre Royal, Leicester. Opened in 1836, the theatre closed over a century later in 1947. (Spencer's Guide to Leicester)

English vocalists', and Robert Lindley, 'the finest violoncellist in the world', who delighted an audience of less than two hundred.[16]

The second concert, in February, was marred somewhat by the inconsiderate behaviour of some of the audience who wandered round the hall, chatting with their friends, while the performance was taking place. Among those trying to entertain those who wanted to listen were Sarah Jarvis, Elizabeth Sharpe, Samuel Wykes and Charles Wakely, a piano teacher who lived in High Street who had to cut his recital short because of the poorly-tuned piano. Also taking part was George Barker, who gave piano and singing lessons from a house, opposite the Stag and Pheasant, in Humberstone Gate. His performance, however, was not to the liking of the reporter from the *Journal* who, never one to mince words, wrote, 'we trust he will not be again invited to solicit his powers as a solo vocalist!' Interestingly enough a few weeks later Barker made his début at Covent Garden![17]

The season of concerts came to a premature end after the third of the series, which had ended with a ball led by the Leamington Quadrille Band, when the committee realised that they had overestimated the number of subscriptions and overspent. This, not surprisingly, caused some anger in the town, the general view being that the committee had failed to keep its contract for the four concerts because they had spent the money on importing talent when there had been good local musicians available. Some people tried to find out the names of the members of the committee - but in vain.[18]

Musical events also took place in the theatre which was demolished in 1834. In the September of its final year of existence, as well as putting on show the newly invented 'pianoforte flageolet', it produced the operatic farce 'No Song No Supper' and Auber's opera *Guy Mannering*. Starring the renowned tenor John Braham, tickets were relatively reasonably priced at one, two and three shillings each.[19]

On 12 September 1836 the new theatre, built between Horsefair and Market Streets at the cost of ten thousand pounds was opened under the management of James Monro. Designed by the County Architect William Parsons the building work was carried out by the local firm of W. & C. Herbert. At a time when seating in theatres usually consisted of plain benches it was with some pride that the management were able to announce that 'every second one has a rail at the back'.

In January 1837 those not affected by the epidemics, which were causing havoc in the town, could attend the concerts of operatic airs which were being put on at the theatre. In a time before streets were artificially illuminated and people had to depend on the light of the moon for nocturnal travel, the management, in an attempt to encourage patrons from the surrounding towns, announced that 'the moon will be of sufficient date to afford accommodation to country visitors'. Maybe one of the concert-goers was the Prince Esterhazy who was staying at the Bell Hotel, Humberstone Gate. This well-known building was demolished in the 1960s to make way for the Haymarket Shopping Centre.

In April 1840 the Amphitheatre, situated between the Bell Hotel and the Plough Inn, Humberstone Gate, opened under the management of James Monro, who had resigned his post at the Theatre in September 1838. Lasting only eight years, in 1848 it was sold to a Mr Adams for two thousand six hundred and ten pounds, during its brief period of existence it was host to many events including circuses and, in September 1846, a show featuring 'thirty-three Infant Dancers'.[20]

Braham returned to the town in 1846 when, with his two sons Charles and Hamilton, he gave a concert in the Amphitheatre, Humberstone Gate. With tickets at one shilling, children half price, it was an opportunity for those on small incomes to hear arguably, the greatest tenor of his day.

Bands

In the 1830s, as well as individual musicians, complete bands began to tour the country. This was mainly achieved by the advent of the railways which were able to transport large numbers of people much faster than the horse-drawn coaches. Although Strauss himself never came to Leicester, in September 1838 the town was visited by Herr Schallen, one of the original members of Strauss's band in Vienna, who, with his band, was touring England playing the music of the Waltz King. Tickets were three shillings and sixpence for which the audiences were treated to such musical gems as the 'Kadivoda Overture', the 'Philometer Waltz' and the 'Somnambula Waltz'. So successful was the concert, held in the New Hall, that Schallen had to return two months later.[21]

One of the most popular bands which came to Leicester was the illustrious Jullien Band, which visited the town annually from 1844 to

*Louis Antoine Jullien (1812–1860) brought his band to Leicester many times between 1844 and 1858. (*Illustrated London News *23 November 1850)*

1858, with the exception of 1854 when they were touring the United States. Like Gardiner, Louis Antoine Jullien was a devotee of Beethoven, and whenever he conducted works by that composer he would have a new pair of white gloves presented to him which he would wear while he conducted.

One of the highlights of his concerts was the playing of the 'Post Horn Galop' by the composer, Koenig. So popular was the band that in 1846 two hundred extra seats had to be erected in the Amphitheatre to accommodate the three thousand who wished to attend the concert.[22]

Born in 1812, Jullien, under the influence of his father who was a military bandsman, soon learnt to play the piccolo. After three years at the Paris Conservatoire he began promoting concerts of dance music at the Jardin Ture, where he became known as the Napoleon of Music. In 1840 debts drove him to England where he made his Drury Lane dèbut in June of that year. For a long time he was the object of unsparing ridicule, mainly due to his amplitude of spotless white waistcoat, ambrosial curls, superb moustache and the magnificent air with which he wielded his baton.

Allegro ma non Troppo

Each year he tried to bring some novelty into his concerts. In 1851 a French Drum Corps appeared in full uniform by permission of Prince Louis Napoleon. The drummers, however, in spite of being French, 'a strong recommendation to the public', did not live up to expectations and were considered no better than 'the boys of our own Guards'.

In 1849 Jullien introduced, for the first time in Leicester, the Monstre Ophicleide, the largest wind instrument ever made, which was played by Mr Prospère. Prospère, a Frenchman, was the foremost player of the ophicleide, an instrument which had been patented, as a replacement for the serpent, by Prosère's compatriot Jean Halary in 1821. The instrument, often unkindly called the 'chromatic bullock', lost its popularity with the introduction of the bass saxhorn tuba in the 1850s.[23]

Even in 1851 Jullien knew of the discomforts, if not the dangers, of passive smoking and requested that his concerts be non-smoking, It was not only cigars and cigarettes but also pipes that were smoked by some of the selfish and thoughtless attenders of concerts in the nineteenth century. Punch, who always referred to Jullien as the 'Great Mons', wryly noted that his farewell 'Mons-ter' concert, before leaving for a tour of the United States, ended with the song 'Farewell to the Mountain'.[24]

Jullien's last visit to Leicester, in April 1858, was accompanied by Louisa Vinning, (who had sprang instantly to fame two years earlier when she had stood in for an indisposed singer at a performance of the *Messiah*) Miss Ranoe and Mr Remenigi, who was solo violinist to the Queen. Led by Leray, the concert, which proved to be one of the best, included Haydn's *Symphony No. 94* 'The Surprise', Beethoven's overture to *Leonora* and arrangements of popular airs such as 'The Campbells are Coming' and 'Old Dog Tray'. Two years later, in March 1860, Jullien died bankrupt in Paris, leaving his widow and family destitute.[25]

Concerts for the People

In 1844 the ever-popular promenade concerts at the New Hall continued with the Weston and Nicholson Band who, a few weeks earlier, had provided the music for the annual Tradesman's Ball.[26] With tickets costing one shilling each they were a lot cheaper than those for the first concerts held in the New Hall. Nevertheless this was still almost a day's pay for the working man. At the May concert,

Henry Nicholson introduced his new flute solo 'Jenny Jones', the performance of which so delighted the audience that it had to be encored.

In July 1846 the local musicians held a benefit concert on behalf of Samuel Wykes, a professional musician who lived in Pocklington's Walk and who having been ill for some time was unable to make a living. For the concert Henry Nicholson, John Smith and Mary Deacon engaged the services of the American singer, Henry Russell, composer of 'Woodman spare that tree', who delighted the audience with his singing and anecdotes of 'our sable brethren'. The concert was such a success that, after expenses had been paid, thirty-five pounds was left to be presented to Wykes.[27]

An Englishman, Russell, who had first appeared on the stage when he was three, had studied with Rossini in Italy. He returned to England for a few months in 1833, before trying his fortune in North America where he settled at Rochester, New York. He wrote over two hundred and fifty songs, many of which were statements for social reform such

The Patent Dolce Campana Pedal Pianoforte,
This was the model which introduced the 'soft' pedal to the instrument.
(Illiustrated London News *27 July 1850)*

as 'The Maniac', which was concerned with conditions in mental institutions, and 'The Indian Hunter', whose sentiments condemned racial intolerance. Many of his songs are now forgotten, although two of them have survived - 'Cheer Boys Cheer' and 'Life on the Ocean Wave'.

The first concert held in the New Hall in 1848 was by the Collins family. Mr Collins, who was refered to as 'The English Paganini', played flute and violin. His five children, three and two sons accompanied him on instruments which included violins, piano and cello. The latter was played by fourteen year old Victoria, who delighted the small audience with her rendition of 'Tom Bowling'. The following May 'The Infant Harpists', Adolphe, Ernest and Fanny Lockwood from London, visited the town.[28]

In August 1848 François Femy returned to the town, to play such pieces as 'Robin Adaire' and 'Adeste Fidelis'. Supporting local musicians included Mr Adcock (who played a clarinet solo), Messrs Weston, Waldrom, Graham, Oldershaw, Foister, Henry Nicholson senior and junior and Mary Ann Deacon on harmonium and piano. The vocalists included William and Elizabeth Rowlett, Elizabeth Sharpe, Messrs Royce, Oldershaw, and Branston. Femy, supported by the same musicians, returned the following year, but the price of admission at two shillings and sixpence, was a big increase on the previous year's sixpence.

In August 1849 George Lake played a concertina solo at a poorly-attended concert in the New Hall, at which the tickets were a reasonable one shilling each. This was the first time that the instrument, invented some twenty years earlier by Charles Whetstone, had been publicly played in Leicester. Never a popular instrument, there was, however, one teacher in the Leicester who taught the instrument - Mrs Scaife of 12 Crescent Buildings.

An exotic treat that Christmas was the appearance in the New Hall of a band of Hungarian vocalists in national dress.[29]

With the end of the long depression of the 'Hungry Forties', during which fifty of the town musicians had given benefit concerts in the Theatre Royal to help relieve the suffering, the town put on a performance of the *Messiah*, the first time that the work had been performed in Leicester since the 1827 Festival. One of the audience, an unnamed 'celebrated singer', was so impressed with the concert that he commented that 'no other town in England could have got it up in such a magnificent time.' With tickets at three and five shillings each, the hall was so crowded that many people had to be turned away. The orchestra, led by Henry Gill, was conducted on this occasion by Mr Gutteridge, a man who used to practice in a room in a stone mason's yard at six in the morning.[30]

By the 1850s the railway had enabled the London musicians to travel to the provinces with greater ease and speed. It was now possible for them to give an evening concert in Leicester and return to sleep in their own beds within three hours of the performance. One of the country's leading singers who regularly visited Leicester during the rest of the century was Sims Reeves. He made his Leicester début in the New Hall in the first concert of the 1850-51 season which, arranged by Henry Nicholson with subscriptions at fifteen or twenty-one shillings, also included Helen Taylor (soprano), Charles Mavius and Henry Gill.[31]

Sims Reeves was born at Woolwich in 1821. By the age of fourteen he was proficient on several instruments and, after taking piano lessons from John Cramer, was appointed organist of the parish church of North Cray, Kent. He made his concert début in 1839 at Newcastle, making his London début with the Jullien Band at Drury Lane in 1847.

The second concert of the series was in December when the Choral Society performed Haydn's *Creation* complete for the first time in Leicester since 1827. Augmented by members of the Philharmonic and Royal Italian Opera orchestras of London, the Society, which had been rehearsing for the past two months in the Red Cross Street

Sims Reeves (1818–1900). A close friend of Henry Nicholson, Reeves was a regular performer at Leicester.
(Illustrated London News 11 Dec 1847)

school room, was led by the Nottingham musician Henry Farmer. Although the concert was well-supported, not all the audience were impressed by the novel inclusion in the orchestra of a big bass drum![32]

The next New Hall concert, in January 1851, was a performance of the *Messiah* with Mrs Sunderland, Miss M. Williams, Charles Lockey and Mr Machin, who was suffering from a heavy cold. The well-attended last concert of the season, in February, was 'unparalleled in the musical history of the town'. There being 'such an army of musical talent brought together such had never before been congregated in the town.' Those taking part included Sims Reeves, his wife, nee Lucombe, Frank Budda, Mr Wiley (violin), Mr Hausman (cello), Henry Nicholson (flute), Henry Gill (violin), John Smith (cornet), Thomas Weston (viola), Charles Mavius and Mary Deacon (piano).[33]

In January 1852, the Nicholson brothers, who had just returned from a tour of Scotland, put on a grand concert in the New Hall. Taking part were Sims Reeves, who sung the popular Victorian ballads 'Death of Nelson' and 'Down where the Bluebells Lie', Mrs Reeves, who sang Thomas Arne's 'Where the Bee Sucks', and Miss Wells, from the Exeter Hall, who delighted the audience with her rendering of 'The Swiss Girl'. Other musicians taking part included Mr Lawler; William George Cusins (piano); Henry Nicholson (flute); Henry Gill (violin); W. F. Reed (cello from the Royal Italian Opera); Alfred Nicholson (who was now principal oboe with the London Philharmonic); Mr Graham (viola); Mr Foister (horn) and Thomas Weston (bass). There was a large audience, paying from one to five shillings each. However, damp and the heat of the hall caused the piano keys to stick forcing Cusins to cut short his solos. Cusins was to become Master of the Queen's Musick in 1870. The last time, incidently, that the title included the archaic final 'k'.[34]

The Mechanics' Institute

In November 1838 the Leicester Mechanics' Institute, founded in 1833 'for the enlightenment of the lower orders', promoted a series of annual winter concerts, held from December to March, in the New Hall. In the summer of 1840 the Institute, in conjunction with their grand exhibition in the New Hall, arranged a series of special concerts. The final one, in September, which raised £75, had the attraction of the famous pianist and composer Franz Liszt. The concert was a sell out with the audience of 500 sitting between the exhibits. Liszt lived up to his reputation by thrilling the audience with

GRAND CONCERT
IN THE NEW HALL,
On *Wednesday Evening, the 9th of September*
M. LISZT,
The extraordinary Pianist,
Whose performances have been the wonder of the Royal Concerts and the Philharmonic, during the past season.

MLLE. DE' VARNY,
Prima Donna of the Operas at Milan, Paris, London, &c.
MISS LOUISA BASSANO,
Of the Nobility's Concerts.
MR. JOHN PARRY,
The admired English Vocalist,
MR. MORI.
MR. LAVENU,
Who will preside at the Pianoforte.
MR. RICHARDSON,
The celebrated Flautist.

The Committee beg to announce, that it is intended to restrict the Tickets of admission to the number that can be properly accommodated and seated, and as the arrangements in the Hall, with which they cannot interfere, render this number necessarily limited, they would advise that tickets be secured before the evening of performance, by which confusion and disappointment will be prevented.

Tickets, 6s. each, to be had at the door of the Hall, Messrs. Combe & Crossley's, and Miss Ella's.

To commence at a quarter-past eight.

Programmes of the Performance will be shortly published.
☞ It is not understood that Ladies will be expected to appear in full dress.

Left: *Franz von Liszt (1811–1886). (Grove's Dictionary)*
Right: *Advertisement in the* Leicester Chronicle *for Liszt's New Hall concert in September 1840.*

his amazing strength of finger which enabled him to execute the most rapid passages with amazing force, followed by a delicate shading down to the finest pianissimo.[35]

In September 1840 Henry Nicholson led a fourteen-piece wind band in a poorly-attended concert for the benefit of the Institute. The members, however, seemed to prefer the more popular songs and ballads such as those sung by a Mr Wilson, who gave three popular 'Scottish Evenings' in the January, February and March of 1843. Wilson, who was very popular with the town and often booked to return, also related anecdotes connected with the music.

With Alfred Nicholson on the Institute's committee few would be surprised that several concerts were arranged during the year. In May 1844 Nicholson formed a band of local musicians which, if the *Leicester Chronicle* is anything to go by, was the best ever heard in Leicester. Indeed, so impressed was the reporter that he contended that the music was almost too good for a general audience! At this concert Henry Gill, who led the band at this and other concerts, was made an honorary life member of the Institute.

In July 1850 the Institute promoted the *Messiah*, an event that was unique in that all the performers were from Leicester 'without foreign aid'. Those taking part included Mrs Parks (Leicester-born but living by then in Sheffield), Isaac Handscomb, George Löhr (organist of St Margaret's), Mr McEwen who led the orchestra, Elizabeth Rowlett, Miss Sharpe, Mrs Royce, Christopher Oldershaw and William Branston.[36]

In December 1850 the Institute held a Christmas concert which included the singing of Miss Cobb, Mr Royce, Christopher Oldershaw and William Branston to the accompaniment of George Löhr on the piano and harmonium. One of the pieces sung was a catch by Purcell which included the words 'God bless our Queen, What need we fear the Pope, The Jesuits Jews and Turks! for we defy the devil and all his works'. This was rapturously encored by the audience, coming as it did a few weeks after Pope Pius IX had attacked the Church of England by expressing the desire that England should become a Roman Catholic hierarchy. This speech had instigated many meetings all over the country condemning the 'papal aggression', as well as inspiring songs such as 'The Pope he is coming: O crikey; oh dear!' which was sung to the tune of 'The Campbells are coming'.[37]

William Gardiner

One of the regular attenders at the Mechanics' Institute's meetings was William Gardiner. At the close of every lecture, no matter what the subject, he used to get to his feet and begin to speak, but hardly before he had opened his mouth the audience would begin laughing, for they knew what he was going to say, for no matter the subject of the talk Gardiner would always ask a question relating to music. Once he had got the lecturer's eye Gardiner would try the patience of the audience with the lengthy and desultory conversation that always followed. He would try to bring music into everything and the story goes that one day while walking across some fields with some friends, one pointed to a man tossing up hay with a pitchfork and asked Gardiner what he could make of that in music. Gardiner laconically replied 'Oh he is simply sounding his A!'[38]

Thomas Gardiner, William's father had been leader of the Great Meeting choir, and sung at the coronation of George III. 'Billy', who

William Gardiner (1770–1853).
This painting, c.1821, which is attributed to William Artaud, shows Gardiner with his right elbow resting on the score of his Judah. (By kind permission of Leicester City Museums.)

subsequently drilled the Great Meeting choir, carried on the family tradition by singing at the coronation of Victoria.

In 1808 Gardiner published *Sacred Melodies*. This was in the main a selection of passages from the works of German composers such as Beethoven, Haydn and Mozart to which Gardiner had put the words of psalms for use by chapel choirs. As at this time many of the tunes used by the choirs were 'puritan tunes of the most mawkish and heartsickening kinds' the new arrangements soon became very popular all over the country.[39] In 1832 he wrote *Music of Nature* and a few years later, in 1836, published the first part of his autobiographical *Music and Friends*.

Always ready to help young musicians, one of those who owed his first musical instruction to Gardiner was William Keighley, who, as Trumpet Mayor of the Royal Horse Guards, was State Trumpeter at the coronations of George IV, William IV and Victoria. On the other hand, on one occasion in a stern voice of displeasure, Gardiner addressed a young man whom he had recommended as a piano accompanist and had failed to justify his expectations. He also helped John Hewitt and his two daughters of Southgate Street by setting harmonization exercises for their pupils', who, when between seven and fourteen years old, sat an annual examination.[40]

In August 1843 Gardiner was elected a Member of the Institute Historique de Paris. This was a far cry from his first visit to France in 1802, when he had been deported for expressing liberal views. A few weeks before receiving the honour he had lectured to the Mechanics' Institute on the theme of 'The Influence of Music on the Temper and the Passions'. A talk he had given to the Literary and Philosophical Society the previous year. Gardiner's theory was that while musicians were able to calm the savage breast they were unable to rouse angry passions. Composers, in Gardiner's view, were mostly humble, cheerful and good-natured while performers were, in general, petulant and selfish. Gardiner had enlisted five singers to help him illustrate his talk and one wonders what they thought about being described as petulant and selfish! Another of his theories was that music was particularly a feminine accomplishment, women invariably displaying more talent than men. Gardiner kept his audience entertained for two hours, ending the evening with the first performance of his arrangement of Rossini's *Viva Victoria*.[41]

Gardiner was next invited to speak to the Literary and Philosophical Society in 1851 when he took as his topic the 'Music of the Egyptians, Hebrews, and Greeks'. Having no primary examples he used musical illustrations by Handel, Haydn, Mozart and Beethoven performed by Mary Ann Deacon, William and Elizabeth Rowlett, Master Rowley of Lichfield, and Messrs Royce, Griffiths, Branston, Gill, Weston, Meerby, Graham, Brown and Oldershaw.[42]

Christopher Oldershaw, born in Newcastle, was editor of the *Leicester Mercury* and a fine amateur musician. As well as playing cello he was organist of Trinity Church and, in 1857, had the distinction of being invited to sing in St Martin's Hall, London. Secretary of the Mechanics' Institute in 1865, the members showed their appreciation of his services by presenting him with a cheque for £45.[43]

Gardiner was also well known for his ideas on acoustics, and often travelled great distances to advise the builders of new concert halls. In 1850 he was called upon to go to Brighton to advise on the best place for the organ in the Pavillion and, so it was said, the builders of a new concert hall in Boston Massachusetts referred to his *Music of Nature*, when they were constructing the building.[44]

Just before his death, in November 1853, Gardiner had his bust executed in clay by the Belgium artist Phyffer but this is now unfortunately lost.[45] The following year the last few copies of *Music and Friends*, cover price twenty-two shillings, were being offered at the reduced price of five shillings; in 1989 there was a set offered for sale in a Leicester bookshop for £240!

Chapter 7

♪ VIVACE ♪

The Opening of the Temperance Hall

Although the proposal to erect a Temperance Hall for public meetings, lectures, oratorios, concerts and other large meetings, was first mooted in February 1842, it was not for another seven years before a company was formed for the purpose, with an initial five hundred and fifty £10 shares. With this money the land was purchased and plans from architects sought. Out of the twenty-nine designs received the one chosen was that from J. Medland of Gloucester, who, two years earlier had built the chapels at the town's Welford Road Cemetery.

The site chosen, Hickling Square, was an area typical of the town, which consisted of houses and shops such as a butcher's, with the floor covered in sawdust, and a barber's, whose window display included toys and puddings in circular dishes. The twenty-four tenements and 370 square yards of land were purchased for £452 10s and the task of construction given to the local firms of Holland Smith and Lindley & Firn.[1]

On Whit Wednesday 1852, the foundation stone was laid and, after listening to the music of three bands, in spite of the rain, the crowd of about ten thousand moved on to the Wharf Street Cricket Ground to partake of a celebratory tea. By mid-August 1853 the finishing touches were completed as Frederick Winks, the younger brother of Joseph, local publisher and pastor of Carley Street Baptist Church, finished decorating the ceiling. In 1878 Frederick Winks and his son redecorated the hall and replaced the chandeliers with starlights. Three years later Frederick fell to his death while decorating Christ Church, Mountsorrel.[2]

The Temperance Hall which towered some fifty-seven feet over the surounding buildings was one of the tallest buildings in the neighbourhood and could be seen as people approached the town from the southeast. Officially opened by the Mayor, John Manning, at

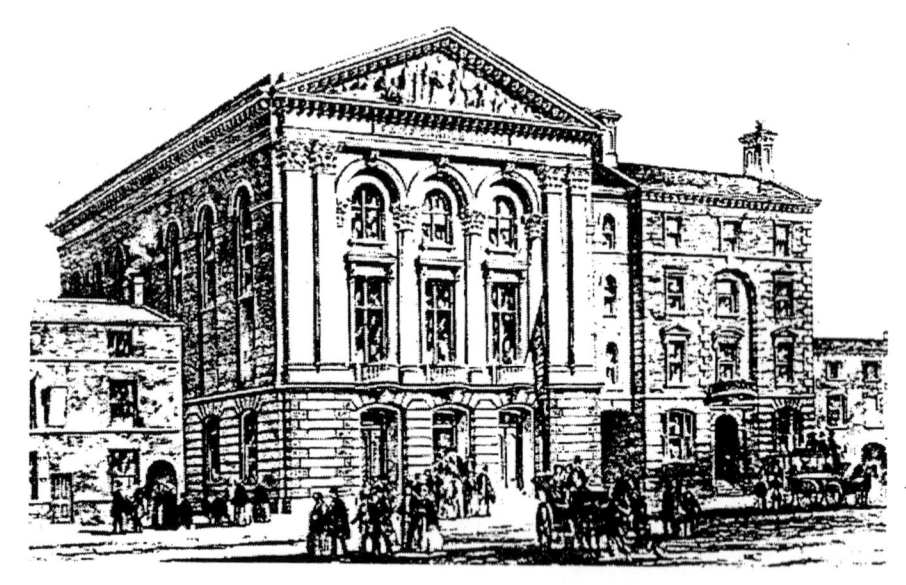

The Temperance Hall, Granby Street. Built in 1853 the Temperance Hall was the main concert hall in Leicester until the building of the De Montfort Hall in 1913. Although the hall is now demolished the Temperance Hotel, which adjoined the Hall, is still standing.(Leicestershire Record Office)

noon on Monday 19 September 1853, the ceremony was followed by an afternoon public tea meeting, tickets two shillings and sixpence, and an oration by John B. Gough, the celebrated temperance advocate. The next day there was a public breakfast, but with tickets costing two shillings each there would not have been many working people present.[3]

On Saturday 10 September the town's musicians met for their first rehearsal in the Hall. Rather incongruously, the first song sung on this occasion was a glee which commenced with the words 'Fill the shining goblet, and pass it freely round'. Indeed during the rehearsal, a barrel of beer was surreptitiously smuggled into the Hall and one nameless person threw a jug of beer at the wall, christening it the 'New Music Hall', a name that stuck for several years, much to the displeasure of Thomas Cook.[4]

On the morning of 19 October 1853, the grand opening concert, arranged by Henry Nicholson, took place with a performance of the *Messiah*. With over two hundred in the chorus, conducted by Charles

Lucas, Principal of the Royal Academy of Music, the singers, led by Mrs Weiss, included her husband Willoughby, Mary Ann Deacon, Elizabeth Wykes and William Branston. With tickets costing from three shillings to eight shillings and sixpence each this opening concert had an orchestra which, as well as local musicians, included some of the country's foremost instrumentalists:[5]

Violins: Henry Blagrove (leader), Henry Gill, Joseph Dando (Covent Garden), Clementi (Philharmonic Society), Ridgeway (Her Majesty's Theatre), William Blagrove, Henry Farmer (Nottingham), Smith (Rugby), Redgate (Nottingham), C. Weston, Kirkby (Nottingham), Winrow (Nottingham), Valentine Nicholson, Wale and Sansome. Violas: Robert Blagrove (Covent Garden), Graham, Rowlett and Smart. Cellos: Hausmann (Covent Garden), Selby (Nottingham), Waring (Derby) and Stanyon. Basses: Severn (Covent Garden), Thomas Weston, Samuel Deacon and Vernon. Flutes: Henry Nicholson, F. Collins (Her Majesty's Theatre). Oboes: John Norton (Her Majesty's Theatre), Smith. Clarinets: Henry Lazarus (Covent Garden) and Adcock Horns: Mann (Her Majesty's Theatre) and Foister. Bassoons: Waetzig (Her Majesty's Theatre) and Sale Trumpets: Elwood (Manchester) and John Smith. Trombones: W. Wesley, J. Wesley and Lawrence. Drums: Barnard.

Successful as it was, the opening concert did not get by without some last-minute hitches. Although the pouring rain did not deter the audience, two of the leading singers, Charles Lockey and his wife, mistook the date and did not arrive in the town until the afternoon. The performance of the *Messiah* had already started when it was realised that the Lockeys would not be present and at the shortest possible notice Mrs Weiss and Christopher Oldershaw took over the leading rôles. The chorus was also depleted by an unexpected 'strike' of a number of the altos who wanted more pay for their services. However, as they were the least efficient members of the choir, their absence was hardly noticed.[6]

Popular Music at the Hall

One of the problems encountered at the Hall was that too many musical events were booked for the same evening. Large concerts were held in the main concert room on the first floor, while other smaller musical parties took place at the same time in one or more of the other rooms on the ground floor. Soundproofing was not of the best kind as was experienced at the December 1853, 'Concert for the

Thomas Cook (1808–1892). As well as being the founder of the world-wide travel firm, Thomas Cook was also a temperance advocate and builder of the Temperance Hall. (Wyvern Vol. 1 Issue 14)

People' which had as the main attraction Sir Henry Bishop, who was described as the 'greatest living English composer'. The evening, however, was spoilt by the continuous thump thump of the music of two dancing parties in the lower rooms and the sound of Mr Smith's piano in the Lecture Theatre. Eleven years later the situation still had not improved for, in December 1864, it was reported that a concert had been marred by 'the vile scraping of some violins in another part of the building'.[7]

In 1869 Cook strongly opposed the Hall's application for a musical drama and opera licence saying that if he had known that this was how things were to turn out not a brick would have been laid. 'If I had my way,' he said at a meeting of the shareholders in 1869, 'people such as Vance etc would not have been allowed to perform in the Hall. What a burlesque the Temperance Theatre!' Cook, who went on to encourage the teetotallers of the town to buy up all the shares and make the Hall their own, must have been pleased when, in December 1853, it was the town's first recipient of piped water from Thornton Reservoir.[8]

Cook was not alone in his reservations concerning the use to which the building was being put, believing, as he did, that the Hall should only be used for morally uplifting events and not for popular 'working class' entertainment. In 1857 a shareholder complained about the way the management allowed the Hall to be used for large meetings of some of the 'most dissolute and profligate of the rising generation.' While he had no objection to gatherings of young people, 'who required so much instruction for their moral and spiritual development' he did, however, object to the Temperance Hall holding sixpenny balls and *soirées dansantes*. The reputation of the building, so he contended, was in jeopardy and if steps were not taken it would 'prove a great curse, and the means of leading many from the path of virtue to the broad path of iniquity.' Not only that but the worthy citizen was also convinced that this kind of entertainment would lead many to the 'haunts of vice', as well as 'seducing many from their homes to the public house and thus creating a love for everything that tends towards the downfall of morality'.[9]

This intolerant and bigoted middle class point of view was attacked by 'One who sings at the Loom' who pointed out that dancing had always been one of the joyous recreations of poor people and that it was nonsense to suggest that any building could be morally desecrated by gatherings of young people who wished 'to chase the golden hours with flying feet'. The framework knitter concluded by questioning the Shareholder's motives for wishing to prohibit 'these harmless meetings of the children of labour'. To the Loom Singer they appeared to emanate from one whose motto was 'Down with every liberty that is not our liberty'.[10]

The Shareholder's views were also attacked by 'A Looker-On' who, a few days earlier, had been to a *promenade dansante* which had been attended by about two hundred well-behaved young people. He had stayed for about four hours and during that time had not heard a word that 'the most virtuous and retiring female might not have listened to.[11]

In December 1862 Cook himself complained about the 'promiscuous dancing meetings' held on Monday nights, saying that at 11.30 pm, after the end of the dances, the young people went straight to the Black Horse, a nearby public house. This charge was denied by the publican who said that the few who did come in for a drink before going home were very well-behaved and caused no bother.[12]

Furnishings in the Temperance Hall

The Hall was obviously not the last word in luxury for, in the winter of 1866-67, curtains had to be erected in an attempt to keep away the draughts which were causing discomfort to those who sat near the door. This did not solve all the problems for the Hall was still bitterly cold, the gas lighting unreliable, and the seating uncomfortable, the narrow benches with hard rails being 'sufficient to cut ones back in two'.[13]

The Temperance Hall Organ

It was long thought that the Hall needed an organ and in 1865 Henry Ginn of New Street proposed that a public subscription be set up for such a purpose. The idea, which did not come to fruition, was that the organ would become the property of the Infirmary, that institution receiving the proceeds should the instrument be sold. After another fifteen years had elapsed, in 1880, with £90 in the bank (including £50 which had been put aside from the proceeds of the first two concerts held in the Hall), an organ, price £767, was purchased from the Leicester organ builder Joshua Porritt. Part of the cost was defrayed by Henry Nicholson who donated the income of all four of that season's Music Society concerts to the fund.[14]

The second concert of this series was notable as it introduced to the town Herbert Reeves, the son of the renowned tenor Sims Reeves. The third concert featured a band of twelve harps under the direction of French Davis. The fourth event was a Choral Society performance of *Israel in Egypt*, was honoured by Dr Keeton of Peterborough Cathedral, who presided at the new organ which had been officially opened on 19 May by Edmund Turpin. Nottingham-born Turpin, who was said to be the finest organist in the country, had first played in public, age sixteen, at the 1851 Great Exhibition.[15]

Jenny Lind

In February 1856, Jenny Lind, 'The Swedish Nightingale', appeared in concert at the Theatre Royal. With tickets costing up to a guinea each, the Hall was crowded and those who could not get in thronged the streets just to catch sight of the singer as she arrived and left. Indeed in some quarters it was felt that a royal visit could not have generated more stir. By the time the doors opened there was a long queue of carriages stretching down Granby Street and into London Road, the concert-goers wearing 'every luxury of dress which taste could suggest or wealth provide'.

As Lind came onto the stage some of the audience expressed a little disappointment as they felt she looked older than her thirty-six years. Accompanied on the piano by her husband, Otto Goldschmidt, the feeling of disappointment continued as she sung her first song, 'On Mighty Pens' from Haydn's *Creation*. As soon as she ceased singing the audience became restless as they vehemently discussed the singer, silence only being achieved by the entrance of Sainton with his violin.

Lind's next song 'Care Compagne', from *La Sonnambula*, went down a lot better, considered a magnificent performance it was rapturously encored.

Other songs in the programme included 'The Stars and the Maiden' (Mendelssohn), 'Quando Lasciai la Normandia', 'John Anderson my Jo' and 'The Swedish Echo Song'. The audience soon forgot the disappointment of the opening song and, hardly believing that such powers existed in the human voice, gave her an overwhelming reception as she retired amid immense applause. Financially one of the best concerts held at the Theatre, receipts were over £1000. After the concert, as was her custom, Miss Lind donated ten pounds of her fee to the Infirmary.[16]

Lind returned to Leicester six years later, in March 1862, when she was supported by Sims Reeves, Belletti, Henry Blagrove (viola), Alfredo Piatti (cello), and her husband, who conducted from the piano. The audience, who had paid from five shillings to one guinea each for tickets, arrived on special trains and began filling the Temperance Hall by six-thirty, an hour and a half before the time of the concert. Miss Lind did not let her Leicester audience down, giving a performance which was talked about long after the event.[17]

Jenny Lind (1820-1887). Jenny Lind, who made two visits to Leicester in 1856 and 1862, was born in Sweden, becoming a naturalised British subject in 1859. (Illustrated London News 1 Oct 1845)

Picco

One of the more unusual musicians who visited the town in the 1850s was Picco, a blind Sardinian minstrel who played a three-inch long three-holed pipe which he called his Pastoral Tibia. Picco, who evoked 'strains that would charm Apollo', gave his first concert in Leicester in

Above: *The Picco pipe. Only three inches long with three holes, Picco called it his Pastoral Tibia.*

Left: *Picco. Known as the Sardinian Minstrel, Picco made two visits to Leicester in 1856 and 1858.*

August 1856. A few weeks later he returned to the town with Alfred Mellor's Orchestral Union. The concert was an unparalleled success and Picco brought the house down with his variations on the 'Carnival of Venice'. In order to satisfy his Leicester admirers Picco made a third visit the following November when he shared the bill with Louisa Vinning who, as a child, had performed under the name of the Infant Sappho.[18]

Picco's next concert in Leicester, in November 1858, was held in the upper room of the three year old Corn Exchange. This event was used as an experiment to see if the building would be suitable as a concert venue. However, the acoustics proved to be dreadful and it was many years before the Exchange was used as a concert room again.[19] A few weeks later, in February 1859, Professor Kransky Baschik, an Hungarian, visited the town with an instrument manufactured by himself. Even smaller than Picco's pipe, it could be played in octaves and thirds.[20]

Family Combinations and Minstrel Troupes

In the mid-nineteenth century there were many musical families who used their talents by touring England giving concerts. In 1850 Henry

Nicholson brought to Leicester the Distin Family. The first saxhorn band in the country, the members consisted of John Distin, who had served at Waterloo as a member of the band of the Grenadier Guards and been principal trumpet in the private band of King George IV, and his three surviving sons. In 1844, while on a visit to Paris to try the new instruments being made by Adolphe Sax, the family had been heard by the Emperor Louis Phillip who was so impressed with their musicianship that he presented them with a silver horn. In 1846 Distin established a music shop in London, becoming Sax's British agents before, four years later, they begun manufacturing their own instruments as well as publishing *Distin's Brass Band Journal*.[21]

The Distins were to make frequent visits to Leicester playing such pieces as 'The Cuckoo Galop', 'Glory Galop', and 'The Soldier Tired'. The proceeds of their March 1852 concert (tickets one, two or three shillings each), went towards the Temperance Hall building fund.[22] Their fourth visit to the town, in January 1853, brought forth some

The Distin Family.
John Distin and his sons visited Leicester in 1850.
(Illustrated London News *December 1844)*

The Brousil Family.
The family made three visits to Leicester, in 1857, 1858 and 1859.
(Illustrated London News 12 March 1859)

adverse criticism, from a Thomas Ager who commented in the *Leicester Journal*:

'The programme is made up of a little concert music of the inferior stamp, a couple of solos remarkable only for their rapid and difficult exertion, a ballad nobody knows and 'The Singing Lesson' which is as old as the hills and withal Mr Distin's song 'Non Pia Andrai'. Now I have always considered that for an Englishman to sing in a foreign language to an English audience, is a worse anomaly than the mania for foreign valets, it is, to say the least of it, un-English, a perfect farce, and a libel on the glorious Apollo ... it is too bad to give us at a popular concert in 1853 a bill of fare no better than those provided in the reign of George III of blessed memory.'[23]

The sisters Sophie and Annie first visited Leicester in November 1853, and returned for a second visit in January 1855. The two impersonators portrayed such characters as Margery Muddles, Willie Wilful, Bobby Ploughshare (farmer's boy) and Harry Clifton (sailor). On their next visit, in January 1856, when they donated the proceeds of the concert to the Early Closing Association, the performance, was considered too risque in some quarters, some of the town clergy going as far as to condemn the act from the pulpit. This did not deter the sisters for they continued making regular visits to the town throughout the 1850s and 60s, making their farewell visit in 1875.[24]

The Brousil Family first appeared in Leicester with a series of three concerts in the Temperance Hall during June 1857. The family, consisting of three boys and three girls, aged between five and eighteen including twelve year old cellist Albin and thirteen year old violinist Bertha, returned in 1858 and 1859. Other family groups who visited the town include the five members of the Collins Family; and the Shapcotts, who, supported by the Blake sisters from Edinburgh, gave two concerts in Leicester in May 1850. In October 1869 the Temperance Hall was the venue for a concert by the Cremona Musical Union which consisted of the eight members of the Greenhead family: Charles (viola), Everard (viola), Henri (cornet), Lizzi (piano), Marie (cello), Miranda (flageolet and violin), Sophie (flute) and Zara (singer).[25]

Minstrel Troupes

The second half of the nineteenth century was the era of the minstrel troupes, either coloured bands from the United States or caucasian bands which 'blacked up'. In spite of owing much of their popularity to the strong anti-slavery sentiment which was strong in England, the image they evoked was false - the audience bringing away from their concerts an impression which was at variance with actual life. Very few of the songs were indiginous to the Afro-Americans, being composed by men like Stephen Foster and Dan Emmett. Indeed Emmett's *Dixieland* was appropriated, and used as an unofficial national anthem, by the Southern States during the unpleasantness of the early 1860s.

One visitor to Leicester was Henry Russell who, in 1847, delighted his Leicester audience with his 'admirable Nigger anecdotes and imitations.' Another concert in the same vein was given by Pell's nine-strong American Opera Troupe which appeared in the Temperance Hall in March 1858. The company portrayed 'through the medium of glees, songs, overtures, dances, lectures, refrains, sayings, and doings the oddities, peculiarities, comicalities, eccentricities and whimsicalities of the slaves and free blacks of America.' A few months later the Christy Minstrels, 'a talented troupe of ten American sable vocalists and instrumentalists' gave a series of three concerts in the Temperance Hall.[26]

The visits of these 'sable vocalists' were very popular and even influenced the music of the waits who abandoned their repertoire of English music for a selection of minstrel songs, such as 'Willie we have

A coloured opera troupe of the mid–nineteenth century.
*(*Illustrated London News *November 1858)*

missed you', played to the accompaniment of bones and banjos. One 'Staunch Conservative' of the town, who described himself as 'Anti-Nigger in the Night', complained that while he had no objection to listening to 'Nigger Melodies' before he went to bed, as he believed a hearty laugh was good for the digestion, he did, however, have a decided objection to being awakened by a wretched band under his bedroom window at three o'clock in the morning![27]

Other minstrel troupes which played to full houses in the town included, in 1860, the Charlestown Opera Troupe; in 1862 The African Opera Troupe; in 1864 Christy's Minstrels returned, now described as 'these laughter provoking nigger parodizers'. In the same year came Harry Templeton's Minstrels and Original African Opera Troupe; in 1866 the Amateur Kentucky Minstrels, a group of local men who gave a concert for the benefit of the blind; Butterworth's celebrated Christy Minstrels; in 1867 the Kentucky Minstrels, the Charles Christy Minstrels.

In July 1869, a company of sixteen 'real ex-American slaves' with their 'brass band' and 'Japanese Tommy' appeared in the Hall. 'Japanese Tommy' was described as 'the most wonderful specimen of Black humanity in existence, being 36 years of age and only 34 inches high'. In Christmas week 1869 the Royal Christy and the Queen's Minstrel

Band performed in the Leicester, ending each show with a 'clearly sung and highly amusing' burlesque on *Il Trovatore*.[28]

In October 1862 the recently-opened Alhambra Music Hall in Belgrave Gate, under the proprietorship of Dan Cook, presented to the Leicester public Edwards and Townshend 'the only true delineators of Negro life.[29] In October 1864, William Paul, known as 'The Apostle' and who had a teetotal coffee bar in his Belgrave Gate theatre, which was patrolled by uniformed guards, gave the town the Alabama Minstrels.[30] A month later the Brothers Traves 'nigger delineators' appeared in the Oxford Music Hall, Gladstone Street.[31]

Although some of these bands called themselves 'Christy' they were not the original band under Edward Christy who had arrived in England in 1857. Such was the concern of the original band, who were based in London, that throughout 1869 and the early seventies the newspapers carried notices which stated that 'provincial towns have been visited by hosts of unscrupulous persons who have gone about with exhibitions of the most wretched and degrading character calling themselves the Christy Minstrels'.

Accepting that the term 'Christy' had become a generic term used by almost all minstrel troupes, in the Spring of 1872 the original company changed their name to Moore and Burgess Minstrels. Although the original company had broken up, in 1865 Messrs Moore and Burgess reorganised the surviving members into what they claimed was the largest and most magnificent company of its kind in the world. By 1873 it was conceded that the title of 'Christy Minstrels' had fallen into irretrievable disgrace and in 1874 Moore and Burgess finally announced that the title of 'Christy Minstrels' was now totally extinct. The troupe, however, did not disband for, with no falling off in the popularity of good minstrelsy, they were still visiting the town in 1898.[32]

There were also troupes of female minstrels who visited Leicester such as Amy Washington's thirty-one strong 'Great Washington Lady Troupe' and Andrew Merrylee's Virginia Female Christy Minstrels. The latter's performance being described as depicting 'the essence of Negro life in wild and grotesque plantation extravaganzas', brought forth the observation that one or two of the young ladies looked much like young gentlemen! In spite of the suspect gender the Virginia Female Christy Minstrels returned in 1874 and again in 1881.

The practice of female impersonation in bands was not confined to Merrylee's company for in January 1894 the Anglo-Viennese Ladies' Orchestra played at the Floral Hall. A misnomer if ever there was one, the band had only one lady in it - a trombonist. In 1883 Professor Andres's Alpin Young Ladies Choir introduced to the town 'the marvellous Electric Pianista, the most marvellous triumph in music that electric science has yet achieved'.[33]

In 1880, the twenty-strong Livermore Minstrels, dressed in the costume of George II, announced their arrival in the town by parading the streets led by their own brass band. Regular visitors to Leicester, two years later the company included American and Australian artists. In 1896 the band changed its line up from mainly brass to harp, two violins, viola, cello, flute, clarinet, cornet, trombone and drums. The following year they attracted large audiences when they featured the 23-27 inch high 'Colibris Liliputanians', described as 'nine of the smallest people which exist'.[34]

Other regular visitors to the town were William and Harry Matthews' Christy Minstrels. Established in 1864 and led by Sam Haynes, the forty strong company was reputed to be one of the best troupes travelling under the cognomen Christy. They usually included a novelty act in their programme, such as in 1874 when they featured a baby elephant; two years later a party of American Skaters; and, in 1897, scenes from the Turko-Greek War, the Queen passing St Paul's, and a Venetian Bath.[35]

Local Bands of Minstrels

In 1873 W. B. Maxfield and his team of minstrels appeared at the Conservative Club, St Nicholas Street. A few weeks later the Tennessee Minstrels gave a concert in the Temperance Hall which raised just over £8 for the benefit of the Infirmary and Blind Institute. In November 1876 the Albion Amateur Minstrels performed in St John's church hall. Their line-up was F. Morrall; Frederick Samwell; William Lucas; J. Gaskill, who sung for the first time in Leicester 'Silver Threads among the Gold'; J. Adcock; W. J. Wills; and John Gamble, piano.[36] The Nottingham Christy Minstrels, sixteen 'coloured gentlemen' under the direction of the Esmonde Brothers, came to Leicester in March 1876 to give a concert in aid of the Nottingham Amateur Christy Minstrel Life Boat Fund. In 1894 the Domino Minstrels gave a concert in the Temperance Hall for the benefit of the Railway Benevolent Institution Orphanage.[37]

The Tyrolean Minstrels who were invited to Leicester by Charles Mavius in 1852. (Illustrated London News 6 Decemebr 1851)

British Music

It was not only the music of America which was in demand. Enthusiasm for music of the British Isles, especially Ireland and Scotland led, in 1843, to Mr Wilson visiting Leicester to give 'A Nicht wi' Burns', returning the following February with 'Anither Nicht wi' Burns', and a month later 'Mary Queen of Scots'. In January 1855 Irish music was under the spotlight as Mrs F. E. Grosvenor gave a Temperance Hall concert entitled 'Melodies of Scotland and Ireland'.[38] Then, in November 1856, as part of Henry Nicholson's 'Concerts for the People', the Brothers Fraser, violinists, with Miss Poyzer and Miss Aldridge presented 'National Songs of Scotland'. A few weeks later Lizzy Stuart gave her Temperance Hall audience 'A Peep at Scotland through Songs', a concert which was repeated to a crowded house in January 1858.[39]

European Music

More exotic were the two concerts promoted by Charles Mavius in the Theatre Royal in 1852. The first, in March, featured the Tyrolean Minstrels from the Zillerthal. Led by Simon Holaus the members - Veit Ram, Ludwig Reiner, Klier and Margreitler wore national dress as they sung and played melodies from their homeland. Twenty-two years later, in 1874, the singers returned to give four more concerts in the Temperance Hall.[40]

Mavius's second promotion in 1852 was in May when he brought to Leicester the Hungarian Music Company. Led by Kaloedy, the musicians, wore national dress with scarlet coats, and played all their music from memory, as many German bands still do today. Originally booked for two concerts such was the demand that they stayed for four. The fourteen 'stout little fellows', who positioned themselves in a body 'as closely packed together as sticks in a faggot', consisted of five violins, bass, two clarinets, saxhorn, tenor cornet and a cello which was played by a left-handed man who held the instrument in his right hand.[41]

In March 1853 the Theatre was visited by the unique Hoffmann's Organophonic Band or 'human voice orchestra'. Wearing military uniform the twelve members, who imitated by voice alone a complete orchestra of instruments, caused such a sensation that they returned to the town in 1856.[42] In April 1862 The Swiss Female Singers, Fredericke Keller, Schenk and Johanna Clausen, who had been in London for the past three months and were now on the way, via a somewhat circuitous route, to St Petersburg, appeared dressed in national costume in the Temperance Hall. The Alleghanians - Carrie Hiffert, George Weeks, Walter Field and J. M. Bowlard, regarded in some circles as the best vocal quartet in the world, visited the town in 1874 and 1875.[43]

Among the other exotic bands which visited Leicester in the last quarter of the nineteenth century were Arthur Brogden's Swiss choir who, in 1883, played in the newly opened Cook Memorial Hall which had been built in Archdeacon Lane by Thomas Cook in memory of his daughter Annie (who had tragically died from an escape of gas from a bathroom heater). In 1891 and 1893 the twelve members of the Blue Hungarian Band played to almost empty seats in the Floral Hall.[44]

The Floral Hall

Built in 1876 in Belgrave Gate, the Floral Hall was on two floors, the first being a music hall while the ground floor was used as a roller skating rink. Built to plans drawn up by James Bird & Son, the building was two hunded feet long by eighty feet wide and covered by a circular glass roof. The cost of £5,660 was met by a flotation of shares at five pounds each with a special offer for those purchasing fifty shares who received life membership of the hall with free admission to all events. Opened by the Mayor, William Winterton, in December 1876, the first concert, under the direction of Henry Nicholson, was by the massed bands of the Coldstream Guards, the Yeomanry Cavalry, the Leicestershire Militia and the Pipers of the Royal Scots Fusiliers.[45]

Chapter 8

🎼 THE NICHOLSON FAMILY 🎼

Henry Nicholson

1816 was a good year for music in Leicester. It was the year that Londoner Henry Nicholson (1784–1862) moved to Leicester, on the invitation of the Duke of Rutland, whom he had met at Waterloo. The duke had been impressed with Nicholson's musical knowledge, and asked him to come to Leicester to form a band for his private use. The musicians had many and varied duties including giving concerts in aid of the Framework Knitters' Relief Fund and forming part of the procession which went through the town proclaiming the death of George III in 1822. They also performed at the annual firework displays on the Wharf Street Cricket Ground; during the annual Race Week; and, each January, at Belvoir Castle during the Duke's birthday celebrations.[1]

Nicholson, who soon integrated himself into the town's musical circles, became friendly with local bassoonist John Waldrom, with whom he formed a quadrille band and established a music shop in Market Street.[2] In 1831 poll books show him to have been a Tory. In anger Nicholson fined several members of the band a week's pay when they had joined the post-election celebrations by helping chair through the town the two new Liberal MPs, William Evans and Wynn Ellis.[3] In 1841 some of the band refused, at the last minute, to take part in a concert with a group of musicians from London, objecting to their small fees compared with those being offered to the musicians from the capital.

Known throughout the musical world as a fine flute player, Nicholson played in many provincial music festivals including Derby in 1825, Birmingham in 1826 and Dublin in 1831. It was at the latter that he became acquainted with Paganini, whom he invited to Leicester. Nicholson, a no mean player of the ophicleide also gave lessons on

Ward's Patent Flute.

flute, cornet and saxhorn. He tested every new type of flute which was put on the market including, in 1846, Ward's Patent Flute and, in 1849, Siccama's New Patent Diatonic Flute.

Cornelius Ward was London's first manufacturer of Boehm's conical flute which had been introduced in 1832. The first English flute to use needle springs, Ward adapted the instrument by building it on an open hand system with silver ring keys controlled by wires and cranks. Abel Siccama's instrument was similar to the Boehm flute but with open high E, F, G and A.

A provider of 'the most efficient brass, military and quadrille bands', by 1859 Nicholson was advertising his band, formed in 1839, as the 'Royal Quadrille Band' under the patronage of the Duchess and Princess Mary of Cambridge. Contactable either at 14 Halford or 79 Nicholas Street, the line up included the finest musicians of the area including Nicholson's sons Alfred (oboe), Henry (flute) and Valentine (violin).

Other members of the band were Mr Richardson (flute); Henry Farmer (piano); W. F. Reed (cello); Mr Chapman; Mr Lole; Mr Kilby; Mr Chyma (flagolette); J. Wesley; Mr Adcock; Mr Foister (viola); John Smith (cornet); W. Stracher (harp); Thomas Selby (bass); C. Weston (violin); H. Weston (Manchester); James Pole (harp); Roxbee (clarinet); Messrs Tilley, Harrison, Redgate, Kirk, and Thomas Weston (violins).[4]

C. Weston, born in 1812, was a violin teacher and music copier who lived in High Street. A member of the town council, he had three musical sons: Thomas who played bass in the Opera House orchestra and two others who, on their father's death in 1894, were living in Manchester and London.[5]

The 1850s was a busy decade for Nicholson for, as well as playing at the annual Licensed Victuallers Association's ball in 1853, where he introduced *La Gorlitza*, 'an extremely pretty dance', he spent the summer season playing at the Cheltenham Pump Room in Harrogate. In June 1854 the Yeomanry Band, under his direction, played at the Derby Arboretum Fête Day and, a week later, at the Lincoln Royal Agricultural Show. As well as being an instrumentalist Nicholson also copied and arranged music, such as his piano arrangement of the 'Travatore Waltzes' (Verdi) which was published in 1857.[6]

In October 1859, five hundred people attended a testimonial concert to mark Nicholson's thirty-sixth anniversary with the band of the Prince Albert's Own Leicestershire Yeomanry Cavalry. During the evening he was presented with a silver cup inscribed 'As a token of affection from the band of the PAOLYC and as a grateful acknowledgement of undeviating kindness received from him during a period of thirty-six years this cup is presented to the bandmaster Henry Nicholson'.

When Henry Nicholson died in November 1862, his memory was perpetuated by a fine Gothick monument, which was placed over his

The Nicholson family grave in Welford Road Cemetery, Leicester.

grave in Welford Road Cemetery. Paid for by the officers and men of the Cavalry, it was made by local mason John Firn from a sketch by Henry Goddard.[7]

Henry Nicholson had three musical sons:

Henry Nicholson junior

Born in 1825, Henry Nicholson junior made his first public appearance in 1836. Under the gaze of his proud father, young Henry took his place with his father's Duke of Rutland's Band for a concert held on the Wharf Street Cricket Ground, on the corner of Wharf Street and Humberstone Road. Henry officially joined the band four years later.

From an early age Henry showed his musical talent both as a player and a composer, writing, in celebration of the Queen's visit to the town in 1843, a march which was later to be adapted as the Regimental March of the Leicestershire Yeomanry Cavalry.[8]

In 1844, the year that Henry joined Jullien's famous orchestra in London, he promoted the first of what were to become annual concerts, a tradition which was to last in Leicester for almost half a century. The start of the concert given in March 1845 was delayed for a few minutes and the audience began stamping their feet, whether from the cold or impatience is not clear.[9]

Two years later Henry played in the first English performance of Mendelssohn's *Elijah* at Birmingham Town Hall. Conducted by the composer, Nicholson used the opportunity to get the maestro to sign his flute case. He continued this custom, collecting many famous musician's autographs over the next half century, including, on his visit to Leicester in 1903, that of the American 'March King', John Philip Sousa, who signed just below the name of Kubelik. Sadly the case is now lost.[10]

During the 1846 Leicester May Fair Henry and his brother, Alfred, used the Amphitheatre for a series of six promenade concerts. Utilizing mainly local musicians, with tickets at one shilling each, the venture was not too well supported, the first two concerts only attracting an audience of about thirty each! The Wednesday performance, however, which included the 'Little Musical Giant Camillo Sivori', said to be the best violinist since Paganini, was a sell out, Sivori's rendition of *The Carnival of Venice* being rapturously encored.[11]

The concept of the promenade concert had originated from France, and the first in England was held in London in December 1838. Unlike such concerts today, where the audience is static, those attending these early events literally did promenade. However, it would seem that music was a secondary concern to the dress and elegance of the middle classes who used the opportunity to show off their fashions.

In November 1852 Nicholson, who had spent the summer performing in Brighton, announced his intention of promoting a series of concerts with admission as low as sixpence so that all sections of society could enjoy them. As we have seen tickets for most concerts were way beyond the means of the working man, but now all would be able to attend performances of classical music. One such concert was in

A scene from a London concert. Although this is a concert held in London, the same scene would have been seen at concerts in the provinces, albeit on a lesser scale. A point to note is that, even in the concert hall, the gentlemen are still wearing their top hats.
(Illustrated London News, 26 October 1850)

February 1854 when the working people of the town got their first chance to hear the *Messiah* at a price they could afford. So popular was the venture that the same work, at the same price, was repeated the following year.[12]

The last concert of the 1853–54 season saw the Leicester premiere of *Judas Maccabeus*. At one of the rehearsals George Smallfield, who had been the proprietor of the *Leicestershire Mercury* for the past thirteen years and was now leaving the town, was presented with a bound copy of Mendelssohn's *Elijah*. Those taking part in the performance included Mrs Parkes, Mary Deacon, Oldershaw, Royce, William Branston, William Briggs, Lawler, Thomas Weston (leader) and Henry Gill (conductor) who played the violin which Döbler had played at the first performance of Beethoven's music in Leicester in 1794, and which Gill had purchased at the sale of the German's effects in 1836. In spite of losing money on the series Nicholson was not deterred for he continued to promote his concerts even though he often had to subsidise them out of his own pocket.[13]

The Nicholson brothers' 1855 annual concert, described as the 'musical event of the season', featured the singing of Sims Reeves and his wife accompanied by Mr Farquharson on the piano. A few days before the concert, which also featured the Duke of Rutland's Militia Band which played Rossini's Overture to *William Tell* and Auber's *Zanetta*, Henry Nicholson had played in Bath where he was praised as being the finest of living flautists.[14]

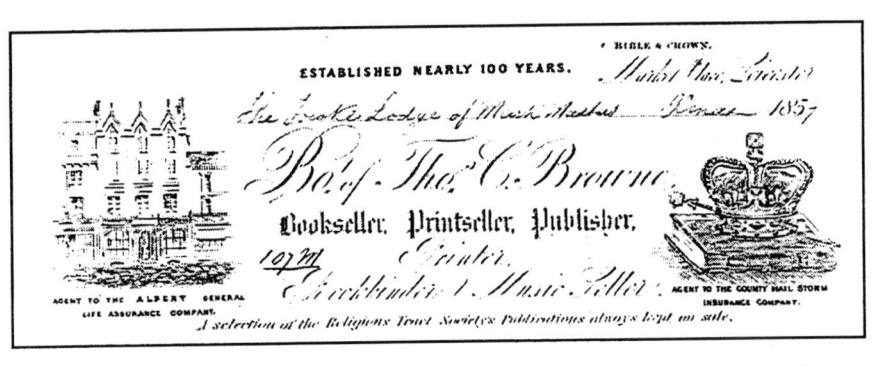

Bill head of Thomas Chapman Browne, a bookseller of the Bible and Crown in the Market Place who, in conjunction with Henry Nicholson junior, produced musical works in Leicester in the mid-1800s.
(Leicestershire Record Office)

On New Year's Eve 1855 Henry Nicholson, in conjunction with Thomas Chapman Browne, a bookseller of the Bible and Crown in the Market Place, produced Mendelssohn's *Elijah* for the first time in Leicester. The production, which cost Nicholson over £100, was conducted by his brother Alfred and included among the one hundred and twenty performers Mr and Miss Weiss, Julia Breadon, Fanny Huddart and Willsie Cooper. Unfortunately the pleasure of the fifteen hundred people present, who had paid from one to six shillings each for tickets, was marred somewhat by those who got up to leave as soon as the first note of the final chorus was struck, making it impossible for those who stayed to hear the music above the 'perfect babel of confusion and noise'. This practice, which seems to have been a regular occurrence in the nineteenth century, did not deter

The seven feet diameter drum, made by John Distin for the 1857 Crystal Palace Handel Festival. (Illustrated London News, 27 June 1857)

Nicholson from putting on another performance of the same work the following December.[15]

In 1857 Nicholson commenced his 'Concerts for the People' which were held in the New Hall with tickets from threepence each making them available to all incomes. The artists appearing in the fourth series, which commenced in October 1860, subscriptions five and ten shillings, included Richard Blagrove the concertinist. Never a popular instrument at the best of times, Blagrove's performance was described as suggesting the idea of a first-rate workman on a miserable tool. Another artist who came to Leicester in 1860 was John Ogden, 'the Irish Ambassador', who appeared with Charles Woodman, billed as 'The English Picco'.[16]

In 1857, Henry Nicholson, playing double-bass, made the first of his many appearances at the triennial Crystal Palace Handel Festival. This was the year that the Festival featured the seven foot diameter monster bass drum which had been manufactured, from the largest buffalo hide ever imported into England, by John Distin.[17] Other experienced Leicester musicians invited to be part of the three hundred strong band and one thousand members of the chorus included Mary Ann Deacon, William and Elizabeth Rowlett, Elizabeth Bailey, Alfred Paget, Mr Royce, George Löhr, Mr Buttery, William Briggs, Cleaver, John Wood (choirmaster of Holy Trinity), Harry Wye, William Branston, Joseph Muston who played in Nicholson's place in 1894, T. L. Selby who would become organist at St Peter's, Gedling, and Henry Gill's daughter Frances Anne, a piano and singing teacher of 13 New Street, who had been a pupil of William Sterndale Bennett and Maria Garcia.

Frances Gill also promoted concerts such as those in October 1859 and the autumn of 1866, when she gave a series of formal classical chamber concerts and piano recitals in the Masonic Hall at which morning dress had to be worn. As well as conducting the Belgrave Musical Society, Frances also turned her hand to composing; in 1880 her cantata *The Lord of Burleigh* was given its Leicester debut in St Margaret's Church.[18]

In September 1857 Nicholson promoted a performance of Haydn's *Creation*. Conducted by his brother, Alfred, the two hundred singers were led by Clara Novello, Mary Ann Deacon, Charles Oldershaw and L. W. Thomas. Novello, who had last visited the town in 1855, had to perform in her travelling clothes as her luggage had been lost on the journey.[19]

Local Talent Unfairly Neglected

The December 1857 concert included in its line up Miss Poyzer, Mary Deacon, Mr Sansome, 'a rising young vocalist of considerable promise', Valentine Nicholson and John Farmer, organist and violinist of Nottingham. The large audience which attended gave lie to the common feeling that the people of Leicester only supported concerts of musicians from London and the Continent. Indeed, three years earlier, after a poorly-attended concert which had been promoted by Mary Ann Deacon and which had featured some of the best singers in the country, it was observed that the apathy of the people of Leicester to support amusements generally was a 'reputation that had long been held, and one which they seemed determined to enjoy'.[20]

Throughout the nineteenth century continual complaints were made that, while concerts by 'foreign' talent were as a rule well supported, those by local musicians usually played to half-empty halls. In 1846 one of the local newspapers felt moved to comment that it was a stigma that Leicester never supported local talent; and again, three years later, 'Perhaps there is no town in England in which there is more musical talent than Leicester yet in no town is music less supported.' This apathy continued all through the century, for in 1893, it was still being observed that one of the mysteries of musical life in Leicester was that concerts given by local artists were never met with the success they deserved.[21]

The March 1858 'Concert for the People' included the singing of William Thorpe Briggs who the following month, above a large number of other applicants, was appointed to a vacancy in the Worcester Cathedral Choir. At his farewell concert, which included the best instrumentalists and singers in Leicester, Briggs was presented with a silver cup which was inscribed 'a memorial of public services and private worth from his musical associates and fellow townsmen of Leicester to their friend Mr W. T. Briggs on his leaving them for a distant residence. Presented 7th June 1858'.[22]

Baptised at St Margaret's in March 1827, Briggs often returned home to take part in concerts such as in October 1860 when he assisted Mr Pearsall and the Lichfield Cathedral Choir in one of their 'popular historical musical entertainments'. In August 1880 Briggs, who had become a Gentleman of the Chapel Royal Windsor some fourteen years previously, left his home in the Horseshoe Cloisters, Windsor Castle, only to be found two days later floating in the Thames.[23]

In May 1858 the *Leicester Journal* published a long article concerning music making in Leicester. Although the town was one of the most musically-aware in England, Leicester's reputation of being the town where first-rate music could be heard for a minimum of expense was mainly a result of the efforts of Henry Nicholson junior whose concerts were well-known throughout the country as being better than those in any other comparable towns, it was contended that Leicester was still some twenty years behind most German towns. The *Journal* went on to suggest that the town should have a college organization which would admit amateurs of all ages to membership, after they had submitted themselves to an audition 'by a board of examiners, composed of the acknowledged heads of the profession resident in Leicester'. Once the applicant had successfully passed this examination they would become Junior Associates, giving them the right to appear in the orchestra at public concerts, after which there could be another more difficult examination which would entitle the member to become a 'Senior Associate'.[24]

In March 1859 Nicholson's band and the Philharmonic Society once again presented the *Messiah*, the lead parts being taken by Mrs Sunderland, Miss Palmer, Julia Bleaden, L. W. Thomas and Sims Reeves. With memories of the 1855 production of *Elijah*, there was a five minute interval after the 'Hallelujah Chorus' in order to allow those who wanted to leave early. However, in spite of this arrangement, there were still some people who got up to leave during the final chorus. The same thing happened the next month at the annual concert of the Amateur Harmonic Society when, much to the disgust of George Löhr, the Society's conductor, many of the audience left before the playing of the national anthem, a discourtesy which, along with the constant opening and shutting of the doors, was to be often repeated in following years.[25]

Henry Nicholson Attains National Recognition

Nicholson, who was known as the 'Prince of English Flautists', was one of only two nineteenth century Leicester citizens (the other was Elliot Galer) mentioned in the magazine *Punch* which once described him as 'tootling on his flootle like a mocking bird'. Vice-president of the Birmingham Flute Society, in 1864 he had the honour of playing

Left: Henry Nicholson (1825–1907). Known as the 'Prince of English Flautists', Henry Nicholson was the foremost musician in nineteenth century Leicester. (Wyvern, 27 November 1891)

Right: Charles Santley (1834–1922), who had studied in Milan under Nava, made his English professional debut in 1857. He joined the newly-formed Carl Rosa Opera Company in 1875 and was knighted by King Edward VII in 1907. (Illustrated London News, 19 November 1859)

before the Queen at Buckingham Palace, while the following year he was appointed first flute of the Edinburgh Philharmonic Society.[26]

In 1867 Mary Deacon, on behalf of the Philharmonic Society, presented Nicholson, who had founded the Society some eleven years earlier, with a gold Albert watch chain and an ivory baton mounted with gold and stones, supplied by Distin's of London. Four years later the Society gave Nicholson, who was ill from rheumatic fever, a grand benefit concert which included Sims Reeves, Charles Santley, Catherine Stephens (who was now 73), Helen Alton, Henry Lazarus, William Shakespeare and Nicholson's son William, the family's third generation flute player. The full house showed how highly Nicholson was regarded in the town.[27]

In 1870 Henry Nicholson began promoting weekly 'popular' concerts. The first of these, in October, featured the members of the Anemonic Union - M. Barnett (oboe); Henry Lazarus (clarinet); T. E. Mann (horn); Hutchins (bassoon); William Shakespeare (piano); Miss Thaddeus Wells (singer); and Nicholson himself. As the winter set in attendances at the concerts improved; that featuring French Davis, a harpist, drawing a full house. In 1882 Davis and his band of seven harps returned to the town with Kathleen Wills, a pianist who played a composition by Nicholson's second son Arthur, entitled *Reverie*. Arthur published a number of minor pieces including *Piccadilly Polka, Coach Club Galop, Banjo Polka* and *Love Fetters Waltz*.[28]

At this period the harp was a popular instrument and most concerts included solo harpists such as Theresa Carreno; Elsie Jansen, Harpist to the Emperor of Germany; and Aptommas who, described variously as 'the Paganini of the Harp' or 'the Thalberg of the Harp', had first visited Leicester in 1869, making his farewell visit to the town in 1884. In spite of being musically successful many of these weekly concerts attracted audiences 'scarcely worthy of Leicester'.[29]

It was not only the music that was at issue but also the names of the artists. The mid-nineteenth century was a time when many musicians practiced the ridiculous custom of Germanizing and Italicising their plain English names. Two examples of this were Michael O'Kelly, who called himself 'Ochelly', and Basil Cameron who, for reasons best known to himself, chose the appellation 'Hindenburg'. Charles Dickens satirised this curious preference for foreign names in 'The Dancing Academy' in which the dancing master is a certain Signor Billsmethi![30]

Henry Nicholson, a genial and generous man who lent many a struggling professional a helping hand, was responsible for both promoting local talent and bringing many 'names' to Leicester. Two of these were Adelina Patti (the Marchioness de Caux) and Charles Hallé, whose piano playing on his first visit to the town in 1868 caused a sensation.

Charles Hallé, was born Carl Halle in 1819 at Hagen, Westphalia. His father was organist at the local church and was a great influence on his son who gave his first public performance while only four years old. When Carl was sixteen he went to Darnstadt where he studied under Riack and Weber. The following year, 1836, he moved to Paris where he francocised his name and mixed with the foremost musicians of the day including Wagner and Liszt. In 1843 he made his first visit to England when he gave two concerts in the Hanover Square Rooms.

Hallé returned to Paris where he remained until the 1848 French Revolution which drove him back to England where he eventually settled in Manchester, a town known for its influencial German community. He threw himself heartily into the musical life of his adopted town and, in 1850, gave the first of what were to become annual series of piano recitals. In 1857 he formed what was to become the celebrated Hallé Orchestra. In 1880 the University of Edinbugh awarded him an honorary doctorate and, in 1888 he was knighted by Queen Victoria. Charles Hallé, whose second wife was the celebrated violinist Wilma Norman Neruda, died in 1895.

As we have seen, a regular performer at Nicholson's annual concerts was Sims Reeves. In 1876 he toured Australia and was paid the then almost unheard of sum of £300 a concert. Such was his love of Leicester, or may be more correctly his deep friendship with Nicholson, that in November 1878 he turned down a 150 guinea engagement at Covent Garden so that he could perform in Leicester.[31]

Another notable visitor to these concerts was Mrs Howard Paul who, in 1861, as a mark of solidarity with the Union in this first year of the American Civil War, introduced, in costume, her 'far famed notorious song The Star Spangled Banner'. Amongst her impersonations she included Sims Reeves singing Dibdin's 'Tom Bowling', which was so like the original in voice, manner, style and appearance that the audience was quite startled.

Henry's sons William (flute), and Alfred (piano), made their first public appearance the following month at a concert which also featured Henry Nicholson's Bradgate House Brass Band. The Christmas concert of 1861, a performance of the *Messiah*, commenced with the *Dead March in Saul* as a mark of respect to the recently deceased Prince Albert.[32]

Known all over the Kingdom, Nicholson made regular tours of England, Scotland and Ireland, usually in the company of his friends Sims Reeves, Charles Santley and Thomas Burnett Laxton, one of the town's foremost bass singers. On one such tour, organised by William

> ## In Memoriam - Henry Nicholson:
> ### by Arthur B. Talbot
>
> Lay it aside the flute he held so dear,
> Nor o'er its keys let stumbling fingers stray.
> His love for it was life long, deep, sincere,
> And 'tis a "melancholy flute" today.
>
> Still'd is the breath that erstwhile made it play
> In notes like angels, voices sweet and clear,
> Or zephyrs whispering in a fairy ear
> Or Philomel, triumphant loud and gay.
>
> He loved the sad and sorrowful to cheer
> And strewed with pleasant memories his way.
> And we, who come Love's tribute here to pay
> With bated breath stand listening to hear -
>
> In answer to the prayer we oft shall pray
> The ghostly music o'er the silent bier
> The voice of nature, that from far or near
> Will sing earth's melodies when man is clay
> Eternal echoes flung from sphere to sphere.

Pyatt of Nottingham, for which Nicholson was correspondence secretary, the performers presented him with a leather case.[33]

In November 1898 there was a large audience for Nicholson's farewell concert held in the Temperance Hall. His old friend Sims Reeves, in spite of having stated in 1881 that that year's concert was 'positively the last time that he will sing in Leicester', sung as a special favour to his old colleague. The town had just cause to be grateful to 'Harry', many of whose promotions had not even covered costs. His 1860 production of Mendlessohn's *Elijah*, for example, resulted in him being out of pocket by over £150.[34]

A large man who needed help to get onto his horse,[35] Henry Nicholson died, age 82, in his Hinckley Road home in September 1907. After the funeral service, held at the church of St Mary de Castro, he was buried in the family plot in Welford Road Cemetery.

Alfred Nicholson (1828–1909). Brother of Henry, Alfred made his name as an oboeist. In his later years he took over as bandmaster of the Leicester Yeomanry Band. (Leicester Commemoration Exhibition of 1897 Catalogue.)

Alfred Nicholson

Alfred, Henry Nicholson senior's second son, born in 1828, began his professional career in 1845 when he was appointed first oboe in the orchestra of the Royal Italian Opera. The following year, in September 1846, while playing in a concert at Birmingham, he was offered a post in the orchestra of the Prince's Theatre, London. He made his last appearance in Leicester before leaving for the capital during the Race Week concert where he delighted the audience with the oboe solo, *La Sonnambula*, which he had made his own. Three years later he was appointed first oboe of the London Philharmonic.[36]

In 1868 Alfred Nicholson was too ill to work and, in an age before 'Income Support', a testimonial concert was arranged for his benefit. It spite of tickets costing between five and seven shillings and sixpence each, the concert, which was graced by the presence of the Duke of Rutland, was a sell out. The highlight of the evening was the first performance in Leicester of John Francis Barnett's *Ancient Mariner*. The two hundred-strong chorus, which had been rehearsing for the past eight months, and a band of fifty, made up from the best players of the orchestras of the Royal Italian Opera, Her Majesty's Theatre and the Crystal Palace, were conducted by the composer himself. The London critics pronounced the performance the best yet, while Barnett himself admitted that he had never heard the choruses sung with more precision and effect.

Among those who helped the evening be the success it was, were Fanny Holland, Bessie Palmer, Fanny Reeves, Vernon Rigby and Mr Renwich, while the solo instrumentalists were Colin Chip Reed (cello); Barrett (oboe); Henry Nicholson (flute); John Harper (trumpet); Henry Lazarus (clarinet); and a violin quartet consisting of Weist Hill, Viotti Collins, Mr Amor and Valentine Nicholson.[37]

Able to transpose music from sight, Alfred was in great demand all over the country. One day in 1879, during a tour of Scotland, he was delayed in leaving his hotel and missed his train - a most fortunate event for the train he had been due to use was that which was involved in the Tay Bridge disaster.

A more pleasant event occured on his 1883 tour when his second daughter was born. He named her Adelina, after Adelina Patti, with whom he was touring.[38]

In spite of these heavy commitments Nicholson still found time to be the musical director of the town's Yeomanry and Militia Bands as well as to collect musical instruments. One of these, an ophicleide, he presented to what is now part of the Charles Moore Collection, held in the Library at the University of Leicester. Alfred Nicholson died at his home, 48 Church Gate, on the site of the present Swiss Cottage restaurant, on 2 November 1909.

Valentine Nicholson

Valentine Nicholson, born in 1837, was Henry senior's youngest son. Valentine taught violin, clarinet and piano from the family home at 14 Halford Street. Although not achieving the eminence of his older brothers, such was his mastery over his instrument that in 1856, during the interval of a concert by the London Grand Opera, his playing of a 'very difficult solo on the violin with such exquisite taste and feeling' was awarded by a hearty burst of applause.[39]

Chapter 9

♪ CANTABILE ♪

In some quarters of Victorian England there was a general antipathy towards drama as a whole, of which opera was an example. This wide-spread distrust of opera derived from a certain amount of anti-Roman Catholic feeling coupled with an ingrained xenophobia, the vast majority of librettos being in Italian. The fact that grand opera so frequently dealt with violence and erotic passions was also a factor which inhibited the pious from tolerating it. Opera was, as it still is today, very

Left: *Elliot Galer was the first manager of the Leicester Royal Opera House.*
(Wyvern *2 February 1894)*
Right: *Fanny Reeves, the singer wife of Elliot Galer.*
(Wyvern *15 October 1897.)*

expensive to produce and the preserve of the rich. Indeed it was not until the 1860s that the art became wide-spread in the provinces.

A regular attraction at the Theatre Royal in the 1850s was Elliot Galer's Drury Lane Opera Company. Productions such as Donizetti's *Lucrezia Borgia*, performed in Leicester for the first time in September 1856; Verdi's *Il Trovatore*; Bellini's *La Sonnambula*; and Gay's *The Beggar's Opera* kept the Leicester music lovers abreast with all the latest works, and re-acquainted them with old favourites. October 1858 saw the Leicester premier of *La Traviata*, conducted by Meyer Lutz. With tickets priced from sixpence to three shillings each, Verdi's music was available to every pocket.[1]

Born in Cambridge, Elliot Galer, an amateur actor, had trained as an architect in Norwich before going to Milan for voice training under Lampert. On his return to England he joined the Drury Lane Company and, in early 1854, made his professional debut in the rôle of Harry Bertram in Bishop's *Guy Mannering*. Shortly after his marriage to Fanny Reeves his career was tragically cut short by a serious carriage accident which led to his premature retirement from the stage.

In February 1864, Galer and his wife produced 'The Haunted Mill' and 'Cousin Kate' in the Temperance Hall. The performance so excited the jealousy of Henry Powell, the manager of the Theatre, that he summonsed Galer for a violation of the Act of Parliament which prohibited unlicenced dramatic performances. As the Temperance Hall did not have a permit for such performances the Bench found that the duologue was an infringement of the Act and fined Galer five pounds. Galer's next engagement was at Shrewsbury where he was again summonsed. However, the mayor of that town stopped the case observing that it was more like persecution than prosecution.[2]

Galer also wrote plays such as *Spiders and Flies*, *With the Colours, A True Story* and *Found in Exile*. In 1873 he returned to Leicester as the lessee of the Theatre Royal before, in 1877, taking over the newly-built Opera House. On the death of his wife in 1897, Galer, who had a number of race horses, settled in Surrey where he died in 1901.[3]

The Royal Opera House

Although proposals for an Opera House and Music Hall were first put forward in 1869, with an offer of one thousand £10 shares, it was not

Left: *Thomas Tertius Paget (1807–1892). Thomas Paget was the main backer of the Royal Opera House. (Wyvern 21 October 1892)*

Below: *The Leicester Royal Opera House, Silver Street, opened in 1877 and closed in 1953. (Robert Read's Modern Leicester)*

until October 1876 that excavations for the building commenced in Silver Street. Designed by Charles Phipps of London, construction took nearly a year at a total cost of £35,000. Most of this sum was supplied by Thomas Tertius Paget, High Sheriff of the County, who used his influence to install his friend Galer as the Opera's sole proprietor.

The House opened in September 1877 with a grand concert arranged by Henry Nicholson. One of the guest singers was Sims Reeves who, suffering from a heavy cold, had to return to his hotel as soon as he had completed his part of the programme. this was unbeknown to the audience who were still calling for encores.[4]

With a growing taste for operatic music in Leicester, and the country in general, in 1870 the town was visited by two opera companies. In March, Cooper's British Operatic Association produced Offenbach's *Orpheus in the Underworld* (first produced in London in 1865) and Donizetti's *Poliuto* (first produced in London in 1852). Then, in May, Loveday's English Opera Company, 'the most complete and best organised company in Europe' made their fifth visit to the town. Six years later, while Her Majesty's Opera Company were playing at the Temperance Hall, there was a minor problem when Jules de Swert's cello was accidentally broken by an hotel porter. Fortunately, a replacement instrument was soon procured and the tour was able to continue.[5]

In May 1879 Leicester had the honour of being the first provincial town to hear Bizet's *Carmen* sung in English. Emily Soldene, who had purchased the sole rights for producing the English version of that opera in the provinces, presented the work to a crowded Theatre Royal. Already playing to packed houses at Her Majesty's Opera House and Covent Garden in London, the interest taken by Leicester music lovers was immense, with many people queuing in the streets for hours before the doors opened. Some of the arias were already known in the town, for at a Musical Society concert a few weeks previously, Valleria had sung 'Parlami de mia Madre'.

Although Soldene considered that the Theatre was too small - the stage dimensions were only forty-eight by twenty-five feet and the auditorium had a capacity of only about thirteen hundred - she was back in Leicester with Carmen in 1880, the same year in which Hughnotti's Comic Opera Company brought Strauss's *Die Fledermaus* to the Theatre Royal.[6]

In 1879 Leicester's music lovers were able to see their first full production of a Gilbert and Sullivan operetta when *HMS Pinafore*, which had been written a year previously, was performed in the Theatre Royal by the d'Oyly Carte Opera Company.[7] The Company became regular visitors to the town and brought many of the Savoy Operas, such as *The Pirates of Penzance* in 1881, 1882 and 1883; *The Mikado* in 1893 and 1895; *Trial by Jury* and *The Gondoliers* in 1894.

Other visiting opera companies were the National Grand Opera who, in 1881, produced *Il Trovatore* (Verdi), *Lucrezia Borgia* (Donizetti), *La Traviata* (Verdi) and William Wallace's *Maritana*. Wallace believed that opera should be in the vernacular and was one of a group of composers who challenged the old hegemony of Italian opera. *Maritana* received its premiere at Drury Lane in 1845 and was an instant success.

In 1882 the Royal English Opera produced *Il Trovatore*, *La Sonnambula* and Nissler's *The Piper of Hamelin*.

In 1885 and 1896 the Carl Rosa Opera Company visited Leicester with productions of *Carmen*, *Esmeralda* (Arthur Goring Thomas), *Mignon* (Ambroise Thomas), *Mephistopheles*, *The Bohemian Girl* (Balfe), *Il Trovatore* and *Falka*. Written by Henry Farnie, this now-forgotten work was pronounced 'the wittiest, prettiest, liveliest, sprightliest opera on tour'.[8]

Carl Rosa, a violinist, was born in Hamburg in 1842. When he was twelve he had toured England, Germany and Denmark before studying at the conservatories at Leipzig and Paris. His first post after graduating, in 1863, was as Konzertmeister at Hamburg. Three years later he moved to London where he joined a concert tour of the USA. In September 1775 his newly formed opera company opened its first season in London with *The Marriage of Figaro*. Rosa was responsible for the first performances in English of such operas as *The Flying Dutchman* (1876), *Lohengrin* (1880) and *Aida* (1880).

In September 1892 the Leicester audiences got their first chance to hear the music of Wagner when Herbert Marshall included in his winter concerts excerpts from *Tannhäuser*, a work written some fifty years earlier. Four years later the Opera House produced the complete work as well as *The Flying Dutchman*. The English music-lovers were very conservative and it was a long time before they accepted the new style of music written by Wagner. Although Wagner had visited London in 1855 it was only to conduct music by other composers and not to introduce his own work. Another reason which accounted for the delay in producing Wagner's operas was the difficulty in staging them, indeed, even in Germany, he had to build his own theatre in Bayreuth before he was able to get all the effects he wanted. The Leicester performance was well received apart from the criticism that the orchestra was too small.[9]

Charity Concerts

In the 1850s there were both local and national charities which benefited from musical events in Leicester. The two main local issues were that of the Newark Orphanage, for whose benefit Henry Nicholson conducted a concert at the Theatre Royal in May 1851, and that of the Leicester branch of the Early Closing Association. Founded in 1842, the aim of the association was, at a time when some stores were staying open until ten or even later, to have them closed by seven in the evening so that the shop workers could have more free time.

One of the musicians who gave his support to the association was Ellis Roberts, Harpist to the Prince of Wales, whose concert in January 1853 was presided over by William Gardiner. As we have already seen, in 1856 the slightly risque Sophia and Annie appeared on behalf of the Association. In 1858 Agnus Fairbairn and the Bennett Sisters gave two popular concerts at the Theatre Royal for the same cause.[10]

In 1854 there were two events for the benefit of the families of the soldiers and sailors who were fighting in the Crimea. In May a band concert on the cricket ground raised five pounds, while the following October there was a gala evening in the Theatre Royal which, illuminated by gas for the occasion, was decorated with the flags of England, France and Turkey. The highlight of the evening was Alfred Nicholson's *Battle Symphony*, a musical description of the Battle of the Alma, which was played by the massed bands of the Yeomanry, Militia, and Duke of Rutland. Conducted by John Farmer the bands were in a specially-erected bandstand in the centre of the stage, the orchestra pit being boarded over to accommodate the large number of musicians taking part.[11]

In May of the same year the Hungarian pianist Zerdahalji played in a Temperance Hall concert for the benefit of the Hungarian exiles who had been arriving from the USA in the mistaken belief that they could join the British army and fight against Russia in the Crimea. Finding themselves destitute, and not having the money to return home, they had to rely on charity to support themselves.[12]

In January 1860 the New Philharmonic Society put on a performance of Haydn's *Creation* for the benefit of William Branston, a local yarn agent and popular bass singer who was retiring. An unusual feature of the concert was that the orchestra consisted only of stringed instruments, there being no woodwind or brass. Although there were many good amateur string players in the town, there was not such a big pool of wind players upon which the local orchestras could call. It is possible that the wind players, who were mostly also members of either the Yeomanry or Militia bands, were on duty elsewhere. In September the New Hall was the venue for a concert by E. Land's London Glee and Madrigal Union who sung for the benefit of the new school at Belgrave.[13]

In January 1861 James Lee Summers, 'the celebrated blind pianist', played a recital at the Temperance Hall for the benefit of the local Blind Institute. In spite of this admirable cause only about fifty bothered to support the concert. The poor attendance, it was felt, was partly due to the bad weather. The same excuse was given a few days later when a lecture, illustrated by songs, entitled 'The Sphere of Social Life', by the popular Leicester-born ballad singer George Barker, was also marred by a poor attendance. Barker returned to the Temperance Hall in October 1866 when his programme included some of his own songs such as 'Mary Blane', 'White Squall' and the 'Irish Emigrant'. He lived at Aylestone, and, as well as setting words to music and giving lessons, was one of the lecturers at the West London Youth Institute.[14]

In 1862 the Yeomanry, Militia and Rifle bands played at the Blind Institute Bazaar. In November 1865 the Institute was the recipient of £42, the proceeds of the New Philharmonic Society's Leicester début of *St Paul*. Five years later they benefited from another £23 which was raised by a grand concert held in the Temperance Hall.[15]

In November 1861 Dr Mark brought his orchestra, consisting of young people, to Leicester to raise funds towards the building of the Doctor's national institute for poor boys and girls with musical talent. This great enterprise, to be called the Royal Albert College, was to have free admission and education for orphans and poor children gifted with musical genius. Dr Mark and 'his little men' returned to Leicester in 1864 and 1866.[16]

The first half of the 1860s was marred by the American Civil War. One of the effects of which was a cessation of shipments of cotton from the southern states to the manufacturing areas of Lancashire where there were over two thousand factories employing over 500,000 workers. Many towns gave help in one way or another, Leicester's contribution was a performance of the *Messiah* by the town's three music societies - Amateur Harmonic, Philharmonic and Amateur Instrumental. Under the baton of Henry Nicholson they raised over £120 for the Lancashire Relief Fund.[17]

The Infirmary, as well as continuing its annual balls and concerts, was also aided in its funds by Dr H. T. Leslie, organist at Bishop Street Chapel and owner of the music hall over Kinder's carriage showroom in Halford Street. In 1866 his newly-formed choir of over 300 children gave their first public appearance was at the Band of Hope Festival. The following March they gave three concerts, accompanied by the Band of the Working Men's Club, for the benefit of the Infirmary and Orphanage. In April of the same year the Infirmary also benefited by over £20 from a musical evening held in the Assembly Room, arranged by Mrs Arthur Sergeant of Charles Street, at which tickets were a costly three shillings and sixpence each.[18]

The winter of 1866 was a bad one with gales and storms. After one such storm, when a ship had been lost, the mayor's wife, Mrs Hodges, suggested that Leicester should raise a fund for the purchase of a lifeboat at an estimated cost of £4,000. A public meeting took place and various ideas were put forward including a 'grand musical entertainment' in the Temperance Hall, for which tickets were a modest threepence each. The money was soon raised and in May, accompanied by the music of the Rifle Band, the boat was launched on the River Soar before going into service at Gorleston, Norfolk.[19]

In 1871 Harry Morgan Dare, a double bass player and composer of songs, wrote *The Lifeboat*. Dedicated to Mrs Hodges, the song was put to music by Rosario Aspa. Dare's youngest son, Harry, who became a proficient violinist, was a perfectionist who, on one occasion when his playing was far below his usual standard, threw down his instrument and stamped on it. Dare's daughter Isabel had a fine contralto voice, while her younger sister Clara was an admirable pianist.[20]

The Leicester Lifeboat, launched in 1866. (Leicestershire Record Office.)

In 1867 and 1868 there were a number of concerts in the town to help pay for the 'Haymarket Memorial Structure', what we now know as the Clock Tower. The event in November 1867 raised £43.[21] Erected by public subscription at a cost of about £1000 the tower was designed by Henry Goddard and built by Samuel Barfield of Welford Road. Work, over the centre of the town's most important sewer system, commenced on Monday, 2 March 1868, the thirty-two masons involved completing the work, with the exception of the statues, by the beginning of June.

In November 1868 A. Landergan, the organist of St Mary's who gave lessons from 30 Lancaster Terrace, gave a piano recital to a small audience in the Temperance Hall. Assisted by the singers Gustave and Martonelli Garcia and violinist Henry Farmer, the concert was in aid of the building fund for St Mary's new parish school, which opened the following Easter Monday. St John's church was also supporting an infants' school and in October 1869 a grand concert in aid of that institution featured some of the foremost musicians of the day including Mrs Thaddeus Wells, Henry Nicholson, Mr Crozier (oboe),

Henry Lazarus (clarinet), Mr Harper (horn) and Mr Wootton (bassoon).[22]

In 1874, under the patronage of the Earl of Shaftesbury, the Jubilee Singers, a party of freed slaves from South Carolina visited Leicester. They were raising raise funds to continue their education at the recently founded Fisk University in Nashville, Tennessee. The popular singers returned many times to Leicester, their last visit being in 1897.[23]

Other funds which benefited from concerts in Leicester included the Bengal famine of 1874 and the Indian famines of 1877 and 1897. Leicester Football Club benefited from a concert in 1883, while two concerts in 1883 and 1884 raised just over eight pounds for the St John's Ambulance Brigade who were buying a new ambulance.[24]

Throughout the last decade of the nineteenth century there were annual concerts for the benefit of the People's Dispensary. For a small sum each week this local charity enabled the poor, when ill, to be visited by a doctor and obtain medicines from the town chemists. These concerts, which included the singing of James McRobie, a sports outfitter of 43 Granby Street and William Quinn, a solicitor, bass singer and choirmaster of St Saviours, were very popular and raised between £60 and £80 each year.[25]

Leicester Clock Tower, built in 1868. (Spencer's Guide to Leicester.)

Chapter 10

𝄞 A CAPELLA 𝄞

In 1547 the plainer forms of protestant worship were officially decreed for use in place of the elaborate ritual of the Church of Rome. In compliance with this edict churches were striped of all their 'symbols of popery', which, as well as the adornments and imagery around the altar, also included the organ. St Martin's sold their organ chamber for eight shillings and sixpence and the case for three shillings. The pipes were sold for sixteen shillings to local bell founder Thomas Newcombe, who no doubt melted them down and recycled the metal for his bells. St Margaret's, who must have had a larger instrument, received ten shillings for its organ case and one pound eight shillings for the pipes.[1]

With the accession of Queen Mary organs were reinstated both at St Margaret's, who paid their organist Richard Lilling five shillings a year, and St Martin's, who paid an unnamed organist three shillings and fourpence. However, on Elizabeth coming to the throne, the revival was over and music was again taken out of divine service. Once again St Margaret's lost its organ, no doubt being part of the 'popish monuments of superstition' which in 1568 the vicar John Lounde consigned to the town ditch which ran on the line of Church Gate.[2] In place of the hitherto fine music a psalter was provided for the clerk who led the congregation singing, it not being until after the Restoration that music once again began to play a major part in worship.

Nineteenth Century Organists and Choirmasters

In the summer of 1826 a meeting was called to discuss raising funds to buy an organ for the soon-to-be-opened church of St George - the first Anglican church to be founded in Leicester since the Reformation. However, it was not until December 1832 that the instrument, built by England, was installed and ready to be played by Miss Ella at the Christmas celebrations. In August 1846, just a few weeks after Samuel

Deacon, Henry Nicholson, Thomas Weston and Isaac Handscomb (the parish clerk) had performed in a concert of sacred music to celebrate the re-opening of the church after renovations, the church was struck by lightning.[3]

In 1848 Ella was followed by Mr Shelmerdine, a music teacher from Melton Mowbray, who in turn was succeeded, three years later, by nineteen year old Elizabeth Wykes, who, with her father Samuel, gave music lessons from their home in Pocklington's Walk. In 1856, with Elizabeth's sister, Sophia, as organist, it was felt necessary to enlarge and renovate the instrument, a task which eventually was executed by Samuel Groves of London who, four years earlier, had built a new organ, costing £305, for the Great Meeting.[4]

With the formation of the Society for the Propagation of Church Music in the 1840s the metrical psalter fell into disuse as a number of modern hymn books appeared culminating in 1861 with the first edition of *Hymns Ancient and Modern*. From now on choir members were expected to be able to read music and, with anthems and canticles being rapidly introduced into parish churches, there was much discussion among church musicians about the proper use of the organ. With the restoration of old fabric, and new churches being built, organs became more common and many town churches began employing professional organists and choirmasters. The social standing of church musicians was further enhanced in 1864 with the formation of the Royal College of Organists.

George Augustus Löhr

The first full-time professional church organist in Leicester was George Augustus Löhr. Born in Norwich in 1824, Löhr received his early music training, as a chorister, at Magdalen College, Oxford before attending the universities of Leipzig and Munich. Assistant to Dr Zachariah Buck of Norwich Cathedral, Löhr came to Leicester in 1845 to take up the appointment of organist at St Margaret's Church, a post he held for forty years. By the beginning of 1846, from his home at 34 Granby Street, he was teaching music, with fees ranging from one guinea a quarter. A few months later, with an ever-increasing number of pupils, Löhr was giving piano and singing lessons from a room in John Shouler's draper's shop in Hotel Street.[5]

One of Löhr's pupils was the daughter of Henry Martin Mills Hanford, the headmaster of the Alderman Newton School and choirmaster of

St Mark's. Miss Hanford, who married E. C. Elton, was organist of the church of St Nicholas, from 1868 to 1879, for which she received a salary of £20 a year.[6]

September 1861 saw the first of many annual music festivals organised by Löhr when over two hundred singers from the associated choirs of the district sung in a packed St John's Church. The largest of these festivals was in 1867 when nineteen choirs with over three hundred choristers took part. The following year there were not so many participants because the music had not been distributed until the last minute and some felt that they could not do justice to the music with so little rehearsal.[7]

Löhr was a very conservative musician. Not until 1876, and then only after much persuasion from his sons and other young musicians, did he consent to have the organ, which as we saw in the Prelude had been tuned so as not to interfere with the bells, tuned to concert pitch. A local examiner for the Royal Academy of Music, Löhr died in September 1897 and was buried in Welford Road Cemetery where there is a memorial to his memory. His wife Sophia died twelve years later in 1909.

One of Löhr's pupils was William Henry Barrow, who, in 1874, when he was sixteen, became deputy organist at St Martin's. A year later he took over at St George's, where a new organ was about to be built by the Bryceson Brothers. Barrow, who worked in his father's piano shop at 2 Argyle Terrace, Belgrave Road, also played cello and, in non-musical moments, enjoyed a game of whist or chess. A linguist, he spoke French, Spanish and Italian, as well as studying microscopy and entomology. He was awarded his doctorate from the University of Dublin in 1891.

George Augustus Löhr (1824–1897), organist at St Margaret's Church from 1845 to 1885. (Wyvern 3 September 1897)

One of Barrow's pupils, Walter Groocock, became organist at St Leonard's. During the Boer War, in which national pride in music echoed the poetry of Kipling, Groocock wrote a song patriotically entitled 'Sons of England'. During the war there were a number of musical events arranged in Leicester such as, in February 1900, when the Leicester Association of Dancing Masters arranged an all-night ball in the County Rooms. The tickets cost 3s 6d each, and, as the musicians gave their services free, all proceeds went to the fund.[8]

Löhr's three sons:

Charles became an ecclesiastical architect and was responsible for the choir stalls at St John's. George, who became organist of St Judas, Southsea, wrote a symphony which was performed in London in January 1875. In 1877 Löhr's third son, Richard Harvey, while organist at St Mark's, was awarded the Santley Prize of ten guineas for the best accompanist able to transpose music from sight. Although Richard eventually settled in London he regularly visited Leicester to give lessons and recitals. Held in the Museum Lecture Hall, with tickets costing five shillings each, these gatherings were obviously aimed at the middle classes. Indeed the reports of the concerts take pains to mention that they were attended by a 'fashionable audience'.[9]

Löhr's nephew Frederick, organist of the parish church in Helston, Cornwall, also made occasional visits to Leicester. On one of these visits, in March 1872, a packed concert in the Temperance Hall (which also featured Sims Reeves and Helen Dalton), his 'Ave Maria' for solo, band and chorus was performed to an 'appreciative audience'.[10]

Edwin John Crow

Born in 1843 at Sittingbourne, Kent, the son of a groom, Edwin Crow commenced his musical career, age nine, as a choirboy at Rochester Cathedral. In 1853, after studying piano under Philip Armes, he became articled to John Hopkins, organist of that Cathedral. Five years later Crow came to Leicester as assistant to George Löhr at St Margaret's. The following year he became organist at Holy Trinity Church, taking over from Reuben Stewart, a man who combined carving and gilding with teaching organ, piano and violin from his 36 Humberstone Gate home. By 1870 Crow was choirmaster of St Andrew's, Victoria Place and giving lessons, at one guinea a quarter, from 41 Friar Lane. From 1865-68 he was at the Royal

Academy of Music and in 1869 elected to a seat on the Council of the Royal College of Organists. In 1872 the University of Cambridge awarded Crow a Bachelor of Music and, ten years later a Doctor of Music.[11]

A local examiner for the College, in 1871 Crow was appointed organist and choirmaster of St John's where, in December of that year, he led a concert in aid of the Dover Street Infant School. In November 1871 his popular part singing class, which had been established in 1866, gave a benefit concert in aid of the victims of a fire that had engulfed the Wisconsin prairies. Now living at 73 London Road, in May 1872 the members of his music class presented him with a silver baton. Two months later the Company of Organists awarded him the first prize in a competition for the best setting of the Office of Holy Communion. In September 1873 Crow was appointed choirmaster and, the following year, organist at Ripon Cathedral, where he remained until his death, at his home in Harrogate, in December 1908. There is a memorial to Crow's memory in Ripon Cathedral.[12]

Joseph T. Stone

In 1870 Joseph Stone, teacher and sheet music seller of 1 Portland Street, took over from Frederick Cambridge as organist and choirmaster at St Mary de Castro. Cambridge, a music teacher of 10 Crescent Street, had been organist at Trinity Church, before, in 1855, becoming choirmaster and organist at St Mary's on an annual salary of £35. By 1874 Stone was also giving lessons in Melton Mowbray, Loughborough and Hinckley as well as having published *A Complete Course of Instruction for the Pianoforte*, *The First Six Months at the Piano* and *Theoretical and Practical Instruction for Singing*. Stone was succeeded at St Mary's by Henry Ellis.[13]

Henry Bramley Ellis

Without doubt the most influential organist of St Mary de Castro in the nineteenth century was Henry Bramley Ellis. Born in 1841, his father, Edward, was the senior verger at Newark church while his uncle, Matthew Bramley of Southwell, was the man who first cultivated the Bramley Apple. When he was sixteen Ellis, who had been a choirboy since he was eight, became articled to Dr Deale of Southwell Minster. Five years later he took his first step on the professional ladder when he became Deale's assistant.

In 1864, age twenty-three, he was appointed organist at St Andrew's Halstead, Essex, where he built up that town's Musical Society to one of the finest in the country. Indeed ten years later, when he left Halstead prior to coming to St John's Albion Street, Leicester, the Society presented him with fifty pounds as a token of their appreciation of his musical services. In August 1878 he moved from St John's to take over as organist and conductor of the forty-strong choir at the church of St Mary de Castro, a position he held until his death in 1910.[14]

Ellis threw himself into the musical life of the town joining the Anemonic Union as pianist (other members included Henry Nicholson, Mr Vaughan, Dr Orton, Thomas Wykes, William and Frank Rowlett) and the Leicester Musical Society as assistant conductor. On the disbanding of the Society in September 1876 some of the former members formed the Leicester Amateur Vocal Society with Ellis as conductor. In 1879 he succeeded William Wale (organist of the Humberstone Road Wesleyan Chapel, who had just been awarded his Bachelor of Music from the University of Oxford) as director of the Orchestral Union, before, in 1886, becoming conductor of the Philharmonic Society.[15]

In 1880 the organ, which in 1850 had been built against the south wall of St Mary de Castro by Foster and Allen of Hull, was re-erected and enlarged by Joshua Porritt on each side of the East Window.[16] In the nineteenth century the main cause of damage to church organs was the pall of smoke which filled the sacred edifice when the flues of the stoves failed to fulfil their function. This meant that the instrument had to be cleaned regularly and, in more extreme cases, replaced. Before electric power became freely available organs were

Henry Bramley Ellis (1841–1910) was organist at the church of St Mary de Castro from 1878 to 1910. (Wyvern 26 February 1892)

operated by human organ blowers - in the case of some of the largest instruments up to three men had to be employed in this task.

A born conductor, whose love of music was infectious, Ellis was always clear and lucid in expressing his ideas to the musicians under his control. Quick to detect blunders, it was said that if even his best friend played a wrong note he would be corrected even if it meant the loss of the friendship. A popular man, as well as being a writer of songs such as *Ah Sweet Thou Little Knowest*, he was often in demand for organ recitals, such as that in the Humberstone Road Wesleyan Chapel in August 1875. At a testimonial concert in 1890 the people of the town showed their high esteem of Ellis by presenting him with three hundred pounds, a watch and a portrait of himself.[17]

Ellis lived at Stanhope Lodge, 67 New Walk and had six children. His daughter Ethelwyn taught piano and singing at Wyggeston School until her retirement in 1937. In 1898 one of his sons, Leonard, organist of St Paul's, Southampton, married one of his father's prime pupils, Sybil Eva Windley. Sybil, who had gone on to study at the Royal Academy of Music, was the daughter of Thomas Windley, mayor of Leicester in 1899. Ellis's other sons were Harold, Gerald, Cecil, and Sydney.[18]

One of Henry Ellis's pupils was Richard Craven, who had been a choirboy under Mary Ann Deacon, from whom he had his first private lessons. In 1875 Craven was appointed organist at Wigston where a new organ

Henry Bramley Ellis. This caricature of the popular Leicester musician was published in the 1891 Christmas Day edition of the Wyvern.

had just been built by Thomas Ingram. Eleven years later, in 1886, he moved to Victoria Road Church, taking over from Thomas Handyman Scott (a piano and organ teacher who had come to Leicester in 1876). Accompanist to the Choral and Philharmonic Societies, Craven also conducted the Syston Choral Society as well as, in 1889, founding the YMCA Orchestra.[19]

Mary Scott

In 1857 Mary Scott who, with her sister Catherine Cook, had been giving piano lessons since 1830, moved from the organ bench at St Margaret's to that of St Martin's. She was a popular lady and after her first decade with the church the members of the choir presented her with a clock. The following year the two ladies, who had been joined by their recently widowed niece Mrs Wood, moved to the 350-year old 'Old Confratory' at 5 Highcross Street, a move necessitated by their Welford Place house being demolished to make way for road widening. Their sojourn in the new home was short for, in 1874, it too was demolished. Mary Scott retired in 1869, her position at St Martin's being taking over by John Morland.[20]

John Morland

John Morland became choirmaster and organist at St Martin's in 1870 at an annual salary of £30. At this time Joshua Porritt added two new couplers and pedals to the organ. In 1873 it became the largest in the county when it was rebuilt and enlarged by J. W. Walker & Son of London at a cost of sixteen hundred pounds. With seven hundred pounds still owing on the instrument, it was re-opened in March 1873 by Edward Hopkins, of the Temple Church, London and composer of the hymn tune 'Ellers'.[21]

This was not the first time that the organ had been repaired. As early as 1778 Snetzler had been paid ten guineas for work on the instrument and in 1845 new pipes were added by Holditch of London. Three years later the instrument was moved from the west gallery to the north transept, where it remained until 1861, when, because of restoration work on the tower, it was transferred to west end of the great south aisle. Formerly used as the vestry, this area of the church is now nominated St George's Regimental Chapel.

During Morland's brief stay at the church he formed the St Martin's Musical Society which gave regular concerts in either the Masonic Hall, Halford Street, or the Assembly Room, Hotel Street. In July

1875 when Morland, who lived at 6 West Street, left Leicester to take up the post of organist at Caernarfon, he was presented with a writing desk, a six-volume set of cathedral music and a purse containing fifty pounds.[22] Morland, whose brother James was organist at Holy Trinity, was succeeded by Charles Hancock.

Charles Hancock

A Londoner, born in Islington in 1852, Charles Hancock arrived in Leicester in 1875. A noted boy chorister at St Michael's Cornhill, he had been elected a member of the choir in St George's Chapel Windsor at the age of nine. The following year, on the death of his father, a subscription was raised to give him a start in the music profession - Queen Victoria herself is believed to have contributed. During Hancock's apprenticeship to the Windsor organist Sir George Elvey he took piano lessons from Dr Keeton, as well as finding time to be accompanist to the Windsor and Eton Choral Society and deputy conductor of the Amateur Madrigal Society. At the end of his training he was appointed Elvey's assistant and played for five royal weddings including those of the Dukes of Albany and Connaught. In 1875 he was appointed Organist and Choirmaster at St Martin's, a post he held for over half a century until his death in 1927. Such was Hancock's influence that as early as 1876 it was said that 'the name of Mr Hancock will appear in the musical history of the town when it is written'![23]

Charles Hancock (1852–1927). Organist of St Martin's church from 1875 to 1927. (Wyvern 9 December 1892)

At Easter 1876 St Martin's new organ still had not been paid for and a recital from Bach's *Passion* in aid of the organ fund was organised. This raised another thirty-five pounds. The *Passion* was to become a regular feature of Easter services at the church, and it must have been comforting for the 'lower orders' to know that 'all classes' were invited to the recital of 1882 when two hundred vocalists sung Haydn's rather than Bach's *Passion*. In 1877 a recital by Hancock raised another sixteen pounds for the organ fund, while in 1881 there was a series of three recitals at the church by Hancock, Henry Ellis and W. Parsons of St John's for the same fund.

In 1877, in an age before State Pensions, a benefit concert was organised on behalf of Abraham Martin, an elderly bass singer in St Martin's choir. Hancock played at the concert, held in the Assembly Room, and the full house raised nearly thirty-five pounds for the singer. In August 1884, on the occasion of Hancock's marriage with Mary Jane Johnson of Foss Road, at a social gathering in the Waterloo Hall, Waterloo Street, the Choral Society presented Hancock and his new bride, who were now living at 27 New Walk, with a clock. In his thanks the newly married man told the assembled guests that any present which continually beat time would always be a constant reminder of the Society.[24]

In 1880 the Church Congress was held in Leicester and a large temporary hall, which could hold over four thousand, was built near the railway station in Campbell Street. Before it was dismantled Hancock arranged a concert, by the Amateur Harmonic Society and St Martin's Choir, which featured Haydn's *Toy Symphony* and a new march

George Elvey, organist St. George's Chapel, Windsor. Charles Hancock's first professional appointment was that of Elvey's assistant.
(Illustrated London News
2 April 1871)

written by Hancock. The tickets were a modest one shilling each with all the proceeds donated to the Infirmary.[25]

Hancock was founder of the Leicester New Musical Society. During the February 1893 rehearsal Mary Ann Deacon, on behalf of the members, presented him with a standard floor lamp, a five volume calf-bound set of Grove's *Dictionary of Music* and a cheque. Henry Nicholson, who was unable to be present, wrote to the Society expressing his apologies for not being at the presentation, adding that no one could entertain a higher regard for or hold in more affectionate esteem Hancock's qualities both as a gentleman and as a musician.[26]

In 1899 Hancock, described as 'organist of our Cathedral Church', was honoured both by the New Musical Society and St Martin's choir. The former gave him a testimonial concert in the Temperance Hall, 'in appreciation of great services rendered to music in Leicester over twenty-five years'. In February Mr J. Jackson, the senior member of St Martin's choir, presented Hancock with an oak-framed photograph of himself signed by the members of the choir. Two years later, in October 1901, he was presented with an illuminated address and a cheque for two hundred and fifty-five pounds, the proceeds of a collection made amongst the foremost citizens and musicians in the town. The address was inscribed 'As a mark of high personal esteem in recognition of his great attainments and in grateful acknowledgement of eminent services rendered by him during twenty-five years residence in Leicester to the cause of musical education in the Borough'.[27]

This reference to the 'Cathedral Church' is anachronistic as Leicester was not re-established as a See until 1927. However, St Martin's had long established itself as the place of worship and burial of the town's elite. The willingness of a man of Hancock's status to serve as organist clearly reflected the quasi-cathedral status of St Martin's.

Hancock not only played a leading part in the musical life of his adopted town, but he was also the conductor of the Derby Choral Union. In 1897 he brought the Union to give a concert in Leicester for the benefit of the Infirmary. With tickets at a very reasonable one shilling each the concert raised one hundred and two pounds for that worthy institution.

At the final rehearsal for this concert the Society showed their appreciation of Hancock by presenting him with a baton and a bicycle. Five years later, in 1902, he was honoured to be chosen as one of the choristers at the Coronation of Edward VII. A founder member of the National Society of Professional Musicians, Hancock was also Secretary for the London Trinity College of Music. It was said that no matter however badly the band played or the choir sang he always displayed a remarkable calmness and serenity.[28]

Charles Hancock died at his home, 11 De Montfort Square, in February, 1927, and was buried in Welford Road Cemetery. As well as the memorial in the cemetery a tablet was erected to his memory in St Martin's which reads:

This tablet and panelling / Are erected on the site of / the old organ by the / Widow and daughter of / Charles Hancock / Mus Bac OXON FRCO / Faithful friend and / Organist of this church / From 1875–1927. This / Is a loving tribute / To his memory.

Hancock's Pupils

Hancock was also a teacher of music. One of his more notable pupils was Beatrice, the daughter of Joseph Foster, a hosier and amateur violinist of Guthlaxton Street who died in 1904. A member of the New Musical and Philharmonic Societies, in 1892 (aged 15) Beatrice won a piano scholarship to the Royal College of Music. There, in 1895, she was elected to a Pringle Scholarship worth £100. Her playing soon achieved national recognition, for the *Musical Times*, in a report of a concert where she had played Beethoven's *Sonata in C Minor, opus 111*, stated that she had very successfully surmounted the work's technical difficulties. Her first appearance in her home town after this was in January 1896 when, at a Philharmonic Society concert, in front of her adoring Leicester audience, she was presented with a bouquet.

At another London concert, in December 1897, where she played Tchaikovsky's *Concerto in B flat*, *The Times* prophesied that she should have a 'decided future'. However, Beatrice Foster soon after returned to Leicester to teach and promote minor concerts in the town, such as that in the Temperance Hall in November 1899.[29]

Another of Hancock's notable pupils was Walter Bunney, an architect by profession who lived at 19 Upper King Street. Bunney also studied the organ under Hayden Keeton of Peterborough Cathedral and took singing lessons from William Shakespeare and Monteith Randell of Birmingham. About 1884, Bunney became organist and choirmaster of Holy Trinity. In 1899 he founded the Trinity Church-based male voice Leicester Orpheus Society. After a twenty-year stay at Holy

Trinity, in 1904, Walter Bunney felt the need for a change and moved to St Peter's.[30]

Nonconformist Chapels

Leicester's large dissenting congregations had a fine tradition of music and many nonconformist chapels followed their Anglican counterparts by introducing fixed organs rather than the hitherto-usual harmonium. Bishop Street Wesleyan Chapel, built in 1815 had a band which consisted of violins, flutes and a cello which was played by Samuel Cartwright, a descendant of John Cartwright, who had been mayor of Leicester in 1772 (the year that John Wesley made his last visit to the town). In 1866 the chapel's organ was enlarged by the addition of 16 foot pedal pipes by Hadfield and Earee of London, but by 1878 the instrument had to be rebuilt. The cost of this was met partly by trust funds and partly by the proceeds of a sale of work.

Ranshall Rowe

The organist at this time was Ranshall Rowe who had been appointed to the post in 1872. Except for the years 1882-1888, when he played for Gallowtree Gate Chapel, he remained at Bishop Street chapel until about 1905. A printer and stationer in his father's business, which had been established in 1839, Rowe was an original member of the Orchestral Union. His grandfather, George Hambly Rowe, had been the Chapel Superintendent and lived in Chapel House, on the site of the present Sunday School building.[31]

The Rowlett Family

William Rowlett (1786–1866), a member of first reformed council in 1836, was a bass singer in the Great Meeting choir. This was at a time when Lutheran psalmody was a rallying point among seceders with psalm singing prevalent among the more pious families. The most musical of non-conformist chapels in the town, the Great Meeting was the first to soften from the lugubrious tunes of the seventeenth and eighteenth centuries to the more sprightly ones which were being composed towards the beginning of the nineteenth century. In the 1850s Henry Farmer, a violinist from the Nottingham High Pavement Chapel, along with Rowlett and Henry Nicholson used to accompany the singing from the organ loft.[32]

William's (1813–83) son, also called William, a hosiery manufacturer, was the chapel's choirmaster. His marriage to Elizabeth Sharpe in the

Great Meeting, on 26 July 1837, is believed to be have been the first such ceremony in a non-conformist place of worship in England. The year 1860 was an eventful year for Rowlett for not only did he become Secretary of the Leicester Chamber of Commerce, but he also established the precedent that it was he who had complete authority over the choir and not the organist, Henry Gill, (who was eventually dismissed).[33]

William Tertius Rowlett was apprenticed in his father's factory, Messrs Rowlett Son & Russell. In 1866, aged 28, he founded his own business as a yarn merchant and agent in Silver Street. William Tertius, who married Mary Elizabeth Homer from Earl Shilton in 1870, learnt to play the organ and in 1886 became the first organist of the newly-opened Victoria Road church. With his brother Frank (1842–1907) and Thomas Atkins Wykes he formed a highly-regarded reed trio. He taught himself French, German, Italian and, aged 70, Spanish. In 1884 he translated Professor Gustav *Willkomm's Technologie der Wirkerei* which became the country's leading textbook of framework knitting. In 1889, in recognition of this work, he was awarded a silver medal by the City and Guilds Institute of London.[34]

In November 1900 ill-health forced William Tertius Rowlett to resign from both the Orchestral Union and his civic duties. He was President of the Leicester Chamber of Commerce from 1897–1900 and councillor for Knighton Ward. Rowlett's health did not improve and in 1905 he had to relinquish his post as organist at Clarendon Park in order to go to Canada to recuperate. The holiday must have done him good for twelve years later, on his 79th birthday, 25 May 1917, he presented the prizes at the annual Deacon Prize Trust competition.[35] William Rowlett died in February 1924 and was buried in Welford Road Cemetery where there is a memorial to his memory.

The Wykes Family

Thomas Atkins Wykes (1841–1905) was organist for the Great Meeting for 26 years, relinquishing the position in 1890 to his 27 year old son Lewis, the fifth member of the family to hold the post. Thomas was considered the best amateur bassoon player in the country, and was in demand for many of provincial festivals including Peterborough and Lincoln. He was also the arranger for a very popular trio that also included the brothers Frank (clarinet) and William Rowlett (oboe), and, with the addition of Henry Ellis (piano), a quartet.[36]

In 1860, Wykes became Secretary of the Chamber of Commerce and, three years later of the Infirmary Board where he was also the secretary to the Trustees of the Sutton Charity. Founded by Benjamin Sutton this charity gives (it is still in operation) pecuniary help to poor people on leaving the Infirmary to enable them to get back on their feet during convalescence.[37] Thomas Wykes, who had received his first musical instruction from Mary Ann Deacon, was the senior member of Wykes Brothers & Mantle, chartered accountants and official corporation auditors, a firm which had been founded by his brother J. A. Wykes in 1859.

Thomas Atkins Wykes, organist at the Great Meeting (1854–1890). (Wyvern 12 April 1895)

A lover of cricket and member of almost every local music society Thomas Wykes died while at a Chamber of Commerce Convention at the Hotel du Nord, Brussels in 1905. His wife Clara, the daughter of William and Elizabeth Rowlett, had died two years previously.

Organ Builders

To meet the needs of the rapidly growing population, many new churches were built in the second half of the nineteenth century. These churches needed organs and one of the main organ builders in Leicester was Stephen Taylor of Clyde Street who had started up in business in 1866. Taylor prided himself as a thoroughly artistic and conscientious workman, his wide experience combined with a real love for his work, affording a sufficient guarantee that nothing of an inferior character was ever turned out of his workshops. Indeed, when F. Dunkerton, assistant organist of Lincoln Cathedral, heard Taylor's organ at Wellingore he was moved to comment that it was worth 'ten of our box of whistles.' Taylor would not lower the standard of his work to compete with any other local or provincial builder contending that lowness of price was not necessarily cheapness.[38]

The firm built many organs including: All Saints (1868); St George's Square, London (1871 played by Arthur Sullivan); Ripon Cathedral (1872); St Peter's (organist W J Bunney); St Saviour's (1878); Christ Church (1879): Thurmaston (1881) Ashfordby All Saints (1885); Loughborough Holy Trinity (1886); John Baptist (1886); All Saints (1887); St Leonard's (1887); St Michael and All Angels (1892); St Margaret's (1893); St Matthew's (1901); St Cuthberts Great Glen (1909); Stoneygate Baptist; Syston SS Peter and Paul; Cosby St Michael; Wigston St Thomas; Aylestone St Andrew; and Norwich Thorpe.[39]

Stephen Taylor's musical sons

John H. Taylor, who became the director of the Leicester Amateur Musical and Dramatic club, sung his first comic song in public in 1879. As a young man he was a member of the Apollo Glee Union, a variety company organised by local man William Noble. Taylor was a piano dealer who started his business with a shop at 62 Granby Street, from where he sold pianos from nine shillings a month and organs from five shillings a month. In 1905 he moved to larger premises, next to the Temperance Hall. Taught the organ by Dr Frederick Iliffe of Kibworth (who became organist of St Barnabas at Oxford), at the age of 15 he was appointed the organist of

John Taylor was the director of the Leicester Amateur Musical and Dramatic Club.
(Leicester Guardian *1905 issue 706)*

newly-opened St Leonard's before taking the same post at St Mary's Knighton, St Mark's, St Bartholomew's Quorn, and, in 1895, St John's.[40]

In 1888, at the age of 16, Cardinal Taylor, a pupil of William Barrow, became organist of Holy Cross. Said to be able to play all of Mendelssohn's organ works from memory, in 1889, he succeeded his brother as organist at St Bartholomew's, Quorn. In 1891 he took over the organ at St Peter's and, in 1894, the year after he had become a Fellow of the Royal College of Organists he moved on to St Mary's, Humberstone. He was often asked to preside at special services for many of the local chapels including the re-opening of Hill Street chapel in 1897. After a period of three years away from Leicester he returned in 1902 as organist of St Paul's.[41]

The choirmaster at Holy Cross, the town's Roman Catholic Church in Wellington Street, was Joseph Winterhalder junior, a jeweller and watchmaker of 21 Belvoir Street who had succeeded his father in the post in 1887. A talented amateur musician Winterhalder produced many works at the church including Rossini's *Stabat Mater*. This popular work was performed a number of times in the town during the last two decades of the century including in 1896 when the band was conducted by Johann Klee, the leader of the Opera House orchestra. A composer in his own right Klee wrote *St Dominica*, a mass which was regularly performed in the church, and a comic opera *Queen of Love*, which was produced in the town's opera house during the 1900 Christmas season.

Billhead of Joseph Winterhalder. Winterhalder, a jeweller by profession, was choirmaster at Holy Cross Roman Catholic church.
(Leicestershire Record Office.)

Joshua Porritt

Stephen Taylor's main local competitor was Joshua Porritt. An organ builder of Silver Street, Porritt believed his to be the largest such establishment in the country, claiming to be the only organ builder in Leicester who had served an apprenticeship in the trade.[42] Examples of his work include St Mary's; Holy Trinity, Coventry (1868); St Luke's (1869); the Unitarian Church, Friar Lane, Derby (1869); St Patrick's, Royal East Street (1873); St Peter's (1875); St Luke's; Oxford Street Chapel (1882); Melbourne Hall (1882), which he enlarged in 1897; Blaby Baptist Chapel (1897) and Clarendon Park (1901).

Porritt also built a new organ for the Great Meeting in 1882. The original organ, which had been built in 1800 at the cost of £35.6s, was replaced in 1856 when Löhr, who had been asked to inspect the instrument, found that the metal pipes were so rotten and the machinery so defective that any money spent on it would be wasted. This organ, built by Samuel Groves of New Road, London, at a cost of £245, did not last long, for Porritt was asked to build a new one 16 years later.[43]

Campanology

From the thirteenth century the shape of bells evolved from being long and thin to the fatter wider shape which we know today. Although it was not until about 1600 that bells regularly begin to bear an inscription there are rare examples of thirteenth century bells bearing the donator's name such as at Caversfield, Oxfordshire (c.1207) and Thorley Isle of Wight (c.1260). Littleborough, Nottinghamshire, has a bell of about 1170 which bears the inscription *Santa Maria*.

The first itinerant bell founders cast their bells inside the church where they were to hang. Not until the mid-fourteenth century do we find a bell founder recorded in Leicester. John Stafford, MP for the Borough in four parliaments, who was also mayor in 1367, 1370, 1371 and 1381, had his foundry and home near All Saints Church where he was a member of the Gild of the Assumption of the Blessed Virgin Mary. One of Stafford's bells was still being rung in St Cuthbert's Great Glen in 1890, when it had to be recast due it having a crack in it. Still living in 1392, Stafford was succeeded by William Miles, who died in 1506 and Thomas Newcombe who died in 1520. Newcombe's widow Margaret married Thomas Bett who took over the foundry in 1521 and became mayor in 1529.

For the next 150 years the business was carried on by: Robert Newcombe, died 1557; Robert's son Edward who was mayor in 1599 and who left Leicester in 1616 for Newport Pagnall Buckinghamshire; Francis Watts, died 1600 and Francis's son Hugh, in whose lifetime the Leicester foundry closed, who died in 1650.[44]

The first recorded peal in Leicester was in 1773 when, in spite of one of the ropes failing, a complete peal of 5040 Grandsire Triples was rung at St Margaret's by William Bull, Mark Graham, Joseph Kirk, John Martin, Thomas Miles, Thomas Mitchell, William Ryder, Thomas Scott and Joseph Smith in three hours and eighteen minutes.[45]

St Margaret's, whose bells had been replaced in 1714, had the finest bells in the area and was often in the news. In 1777 the Leicester Society of Change Ringers decided to go for a record peal of 10,080 Grandsire Caters. After four attempts, in one of which they had got as far as 9,000 when one man missed his sally, thereby losing the peal, they finally succeeded on 25 February when 5,000 changes were rung in the morning with the peal completed in the afternoon in the time of seven hours and twelve minutes. The next day the campanologists chaired three of the oldest members through the principal streets of the town, while a collection of just over £33 was made from the inhabitants. Those who rung on this momentous occasion were: Thomas Armstrong, William Bull, Mark Graham, John Martin, William Ryder, Thomas Scott, James Slack, Joseph Smith, William Thacker, Benjaman Warburton and Richard Wright.[46]

In 1787 a new peal of ten bells was cast for St Martin's by Mr Arnold, a clever craftsman but a poor musician, who, unable to tune the bells himself, asked a group of local musicians to help him in this task. It was decided that the treble bell was too sharp and a man was set to work with a pick-axe to chip away the inside of the bell's mouth to flatten it. After three days, during which the whole town was subjected to the noise of this work, the bell was found to be more out of tune than before and had to be recast. By September 1787 the bells were ready and a grand opening peal, lasting three hours and thirty-seven minutes was rung by Thomas Armstrong, John Blower, Thomas Dudley, Daniel Langley, John Martin, Thomas Sibson,

St Margaret's bell ringers of 1895. Back row: J.H. Potterton, J.A. Harding, W.H. Smith, E.E. Smith, T.W. Preston, A. Lord. Front row: A. Potterton, F. Cooke (captain), J. Morris (secretary) and F.E. Harding. (Leicestershire Record Office)

Thomas Scott, Joseph Smith, Bejamam Warburton and Richard Wright.[47]

In the nineteenth century Leicester had an excellent team of campanologists led by Edward Biggs of St Margaret's Church. In 1834 they rung in the new year with a peal of 1834 Grandsire Triples in one hour and twenty minutes. Two years earlier, at the church of St Mary de Castro, the team (consisting of Biggs, Robert Stringer, John Smart, John Russell, Thomas Langham and John Harper) had rung a 'true and complete peal' of 5040 Grandsire Triples.[48]

For many years the ringers came together each Easter at alternate churches, where they would ring a peal of Grandsire Triples, usually 5040 but on Easter Monday 1848, when the peal came from the tower of St Margaret's, the eleven bell ringers rung no less than 6012 in three hours and fifty-five minutes. In 1852, when the ringing came from St Mary's, the 5040 changes were executed in the much quicker time of three hours three minutes, and, two years later, at St Martin's in three hours and fifteen minutes. At St George's Church, in January 1857, the new bells, cast by Taylor and Son of Loughborough, were rung for the first time, the day ending with the twenty ringers of the town enjoying a dinner at the Anchor Inn.[49]

In 1871, a few weeks after the ringers of St Margaret's had rung in the year with 1871 Grandsire Triples in one hour sixteen minutes, there was a concert at the Temperance Hall for the benefit of Thomas Langham who was one of the oldest change ringers in Leicester. In April 1872, a few weeks after St Mary's had rung a peal of 5040 changes in three hours nine minutes, Langham, aged 67, who had taught all of Leicester's ringers, rang his last peal of 5040 changes in two hours fifty-nine minutes, the same as the peal he had rung at the opening of the bells in 1831.[50]

In May 1873 the bells of St Mark's, the tenor weighing 23 cwt, were inaugurated by Stephen Cooper, Thomas Armstrong, Arthur Brown, William Cooper, Edward Biggs, John Cooper, Thomas Wilson and William Walker. The peal of 5040 Grandsire Triples, composed by the recently deceased John Martin, was rung in three hours two minutes. In November, however, the peal was pronounced false and the bells had to be re-opened in November with 5040 changes rung in three hours by James Jarvis, Ralph Fox, John Crossley, John Cooper, Stephen Spencer, Alfred Millis, John Buttery and William Walker.[51] The following month the ringers of St Mark's and St Margaret's united to ring in the year with 1872 changes in one hour nineteen minutes.

Some times the activities of the bell ringers did not meet with the approval of those who heard them. In November 1879, for instance, Judge Barrow was presiding over the County Court sessions at the Castle on the same day as the Bishop was holding confirmations in the nearby church of St Mary de Castro. Disturbed by the ringing of the church bells, the judge sent over a court official to ask the bishop to stop the ringing. However, in spite of several requests by the judge the bishop refused to cease ringing the bells and the court had to be adjourned till the next day.[52]

In June 1880 St Margaret's bell ringers had a narrow escape when a large stone fell from the mullions of the west window, narrowly missing the men who were standing talking outside the entrance to the belfry. In 1883 there was a move to form a society of bell ringers in the town which would train young men in the art of campanology. Although several Leicester churches had peals, it was the same group of itinerant change ringers, mainly from St Margaret's, who went from church to church. On occasions the local press would announce the names of the ringers and from these lists we can see how often the same names keep turning up.[53]

1847: Thomas Allen, Edward Biggs, Samuel Green, James Johnson, Thomas Langham, Joseph Pickard, John Seddon and William Warden.
1848: Edward Biggs, Frederick Hubbard, John and Thomas Johnson, Thomas Langham, William Langley, Thomas Mills, Joseph Pickard, John Russell, John Seddon and John Smart.
1852: Edward Biggs, Arthur Brown, Charles Burrell, Jonathan Hitchcock, James Johnson, Thomas Langham, Samuel Neile and John Smart.
1858: Robert Allen, Edward Biggs, Arthur Brown, William Clark, William Davies, John Johnson, Joseph Pickard and John Smart.
1864: Charles and H Bail, Arthur Brown, H Cuthbert, Thomas Langham, Alfred Millis, John and Thomas Wilson.
1868: Charles Bail, Edward Biggs, Stephen and William Cooper, William Harding, John Jarvis, Thomas Langhorn, John Metcalf, Alfred Millis, John and Thomas Wilson.
1871: Thomas Armstrong, Edward Biggs, Arthur Brown, John Buttery, Stephen and William Cooper, Ralph Fox, Thomas Langham, Alfred Millis and William Walker.
1872: Thomas Armstrong, Arthur Brown, John Buttery, John Cooper, Ralph Fox, Alfred Millis and Charles de Quincey.
1877: George Burrows, John Buttery, Stephen and William Cooper, James Jarvis, William Walker, John and Thomas Wilson.
1878: George Burrows, John Buttery, John, Stephen and William Cooper, Charles Edward de Quincey (steeple keeper of St Mary's), William Walker, John and Thomas Wilson.
1879: William Bail, George Burrows, John Buttery, John, Stephen and William Cooper, William Walker and John Wilson.
1880: William Bail, George Burrows, John Buttery, John, Stephen and William Cooper, John and Thomas Wilson.
1881: Thomas Armstrong, Edwin Ashwell, Arthur Brown, Guido Dickinson, Alfred Millis, John Moore, George and Joseph Needham.

Chapter 11

𝄞 ALLA MARCIA 𝄞

Brass bands, a peculiarly English and Welsh development, came into existence as a result of the philanthropic efforts of factory owners to enrich the lives of their workforce. The first band of which we know is that of the Blaina Ironworks, Monmouthshire, which was formed in 1823, while one of the first brass bands in Leicester seems to have been that which was formed in 1847 by Henry Nicholson and John Smith from the 'most efficient members' of the Duke of Rutland's and the Leicestershire Yeomanry bands.[1]

There were, however, brass bands in the area as early as July 1843 when, at a Grand Gala on the Freeman's Piece, in celebration of the conversion of part of the land into allotments, the people were serenaded by two bands, one from the town and the other from Newtown Linford. As well as the music the event, which drew a crowd of almost 15,000 (a third of the then population of the town), included many stalls and activities such as races, bowling, dancing and ninepins.[2]

John Alfred Smith

The main force behind the brass band movement in nineteenth century Leicester was John Alfred Smith. Born in Sileby in 1825 he learnt to play the cornet,

John Alfred Smith, the founder of the brass band movement in Leicester. (Wyvern Vol. 2 No.50)

joining his father, who played clarinet, as a member of the Duke of Rutland's private band when he was thirteen. His father, a former member of the town waits, run an upholsterer's and piano shop in Market Street. In a moment of youthful high spirits young John is said to have carved his initials in the Belvoir Castle bandroom door.[3]

By 1847 Smith was teaching from his home at 11 Belgrave Gate, opening his first piano shop at 13 King Street ten years later. Recognized as 'the cornet player of the district' Smith founded no less than sixteen local brass bands including the Midland Railway (in existence by 1860), the Loughborough Volunteers and the Leicester Temperance Band. He was, however, specially connected with the Police Band and that of Rawson's factory in Church Gate. The latter was the first amateur band in the town, which, in 1860, became the band of the newly-formed Leicester Volunteer Rifle Corps. In 1860 Rawson's band played a series of summer concerts on Victoria Park, a tradition of open air music which was to last for the next seventeen years.[4]

During 1861 and 1862 the Rifle Band held a concerted fund raising effort. In April £60 was raised at an amateur dramatic evening held in the Theatre Royal, while a few weeks earlier the band had taken part in a concert of popular music which had included the singing of Miss Stuart and Christopher Oldershaw as well as the piano playing of Mary Deacon. The February 1863 concert, which had been planned for the previous December but postponed because of the death of Prince Albert, included the singing of a

Robert Read's shop in Southgate Street. Read supplied uniforms to most of the bands in Leicester.
(Modern Leicester)

The only known person on this late nineteenth century photograph of Yeomanry Band members is John Lawrence (seated on the right).

Mr Burge, an impersonator who, we are told, 'lacked good taste if not good sense', so much so that at the end of the concert Francis Ptacek, the evening's guest conductor, announced that in future he would stick to 'genuine music' and not introduce into his performances 'characteristic representations'.[5]

Throughout the thirty years of its existence the band played at many and varied events such as concerts on the Race Course (the present Victoria Park), the Market Place, Town Hall Square and in the Temperance Hall. The band was also in demand for fêtes such as that held on the Peacock Grounds, Belgrave Road on Whit Monday 1876. In 1872 the bandsmen were supplied with new uniforms made by Robert Read of Southgate Street, while five years later, the same year that the Volunteers moved their headquarters from 22 Cank Street to the School of Art building in Pocklington's Walk, they changed the colour of their uniforms to scarlet.[6]

In October 1889, the adjutant of the Regiment asked Smith to resign. Upon appealing to Sir Henry Halford, the colonel of the regiment, as to why he had been asked to relinquish his post Halford replied that owing to Smith's numerous engagements he believed that Smith was not able to give the time to the band that he felt necessary. The implication was that the band had so deteriorated that, in the interests of the Regiment, it was necessary to reorganize it.[7]

The situation came to a head in January 1891 when the members of the band, so incensed at the shabby treatment meted out to Smith, signed a letter in support of their bandmaster which they sent to Halford. A few days later the band committee visited Smith at his house, The Limes, 76 London Road, both to express their condolences on the death of his wife Mary and to express their support for him as their leader. Thomas Taylor, tuba player and an original member of the band, in praise of his erstwhile bandmaster said 'Nothing can take away from Mr Smith the merit of all the good work he has done in Leicester for the cultivation of instrumental music. The offices of the Regiment may deprive him of his old position but they cannot take away from him the public appreciation of his efforts or the esteem we all feel for him.' Smith bravely replied that the main thing was to cherish happy memories and not dwell on disappointed hopes.[8]

On his retirement in 1900 Smith, who never accepted any money for his services, presented to the town the silver cornet which had been given him by Henry Halford in 1863, and a silver tankard which had belonged to the Corporation since 1601, but which had been acquired by his father at the sale of the Corporation property in 1836. A genial gentleman, after a short illness he died at his home, age 75, in January 1901. Having no surviving family he left most of his money to local hospitals and institutions.[9]

Open Air Band Concerts

The town's first open air brass band concert took place on the Wharf Street Cricket Ground in May 1853. In spite of the bad weather six hundred people paid sixpence each to share this novel experience which Londoners had been able to enjoy since at least 1851. The following week over 1,500 attended the Militia Review Day, also on the Cricket Ground, when the united bands of the Duke of Rutland, Prince Albert's Own Yeomanry Cavalry and Henry Nicholson's Military Band filled the air with martial music. The Yeomanry Band had been formed in 1803 as the Leicestershire Regiment of Gentlemen and Yeomanry Cavalry and had changed its name in 1844 to Prince Albert's Own Leicestershire Regiment of Yeomanry Cavalry. On parades the band was usually preceded by pickaxe-carrying Pioneers.[10]

A few weeks later Nicholson planned to hold a concert in the ruins of Bradgate Park but because of heavy rain, the concert was moved to a large room in the New Inn, Newtown Linford, where 150 people gathered to hear Nicholson's twenty-strong band. The following weekend was fine and the band was able to give a grand open air concert on the Wharf Street cricket ground while Mr Green made one of his popular balloon ascents. Special trains were laid on from the

Victoria Park Pavilion. Built in 1865, the pavilion was destroyed by a bomb in World War II. (Leicestershire Record Office)

neighbouring towns to enable as many as possible to attend this holiday event.[11]

In 1854 a temporary bandstand, illuminated by gas, was built complete with a platform for dancing and a boarded promenade, designed to enable 'the most nervous invalid feel perfectly secure against damp grass,' while, with true English optimism, a marquee was also erected 'as shelter from the sun.' The next year the bands, conducted by Henry Nicholson and Francis Ptacek, played from the pavilion balcony, a situation which was far from satisfactory diminishing, as it did, the effect of the music'.[12]

As ever, the paternal Victorian middle classes were concerned about the welfare of the working people. It was considered that the concerts, which often terminated by firework displays organised by Mr Wilkes 'the celebrated pyrotechnic artist', should end before ten so that the audience could get a good night's rest before starting work at six the next morning. The starting time of these concerts was also of concern, for when it was announced that the arrangements had been finalized for two band performances each week of the summer, it was complained that the proposed time of commencement, 6.30pm, was too early for working people, many of whom did not finished work until 6 o'clock.[13]

*Victoria Park Bandstand, erected in 1857.
(Leicestershire Record Office)*

Whit Monday 1857 saw over 6,000 attending the first open air concert of the year. Stationed in the newly-built bandstand, the band had to compete with the flocks of sheep that roamed the grass of the Race Course. At first there were three concerts a week but by the beginning of July, due to the committee not getting the backing they had expected, the frequency had gone down to two and by the middle of the month one a week, the series terminating at the end of July. All was not lost, however, for in August the Band of the Leicester Militia offered their services free of charge for the final four concerts of the season.[14]

Examples of music played at these park concerts include: the march 'Seventh Hussars'; the waltz 'Ever of Thee'; Donizetti's 'Daughter of the Regiment'; Bishop's 'Home Sweet Home'; the 'Tyrolean Alpen Sanger March'; Henry Nicholson's 'Parade March'; Tinney's 'Victory Galop'; a selection from Vinzenzo Bellini's *La Sonnambula*; the 'Chorus of Druids' from the same composer's *Norma*; Hauser's 'Defiler March'; d'Albert's waltz 'Nymph of the Waves'; Linley's song 'Bonney Jean'; Mendelssohn's 'Lieder ohne Wörte' and Laurent's waltz 'Maud'.

1859 was a busy year for the Nicholson Band for, as well as their park commitments, they played at a bazaar and fête in aid of Melbourne parish church, Derbyshire. Billed as the 'celebrated band of the Leicestershire Militia' a few days later they played at the Derby Arboretum Anniversary Fête where Henry Nicholson played a solo on the recently invented baritone tuba. Many who learnt to play in the band went on to have musical careers, such as cornet player John Buchanhan who, taught by Nicholson and Ptacek, was to join the Band of the Guards.[15]

The 1861 season of concerts commenced in July and consisted mainly of the playing of the Rifle Band. However, by August the funds had run out and the two subscription collectors, William Weston, a butcher of Humberstone Gate, and Benjamin Nedwell of Welford Place, announced that the series had to be abandoned. The 1862 season of concerts on the Race Course was given by the Temperance and Albion (the works band of Samuel Odames of Watling Street) bands, both conducted by John Smith who was at the time selling brass instruments made by Distin. Since 1857, when £140 was collected, the amount raised in subscriptions had decreased every year falling to an all-time low in 1862 with only twelve shillings being donated! The two bands offered their services free of charge so that the concerts could continue giving pleasure to the mainly working class audiences who put on their best clothes to enjoy the free concerts of popular music.[16]

Apart from the occasional cricket match at which military bands were in attendance, the lack of financial support meant there was a period of about ten years without these summer park concerts, until the Rifle Band recommenced them in 1874. Also in that year there was a fête on the Belgrave Road Ground to celebrate the wedding of the Duke of Edinburgh, where, as well as over 1000 horses, the largest-ever balloon and Mr Paine, 'the great Pyrotechnist' whose display featured 'The Siege of Paris', there were six military bands on hand to play for the dancing. The admission for the seven hour programme was one shilling.[17]

By 1900 band concerts in the town's parks - Abbey, Victoria, Fosse Road and Spinney Hills - as well as Town Hall Square, were a regular part of town life. Most of the best bands of the town took part, including the Rifle Corps, Military, Gas Works, Highfields and Police.

Sunday Band Concerts

Although occasional band concerts on the Sabbath had taken place as early as 1834, it was not until 1856 that an effort was made to hold these on a regular basis. In July of that year 15,000 mainly working class people thronged to the Race Course to hear the 'People's Band', which was comprised of thirteen of the town's musicians, who believed that the town inhabitants had as much right to hear music on Sundays as on any other day of the week. With the ever-present threat of prosecution, boxes were provided for contributions towards the expenses of defending such action if taken by the tenants of the Race Course.[18]

The nineteenth century was a time of devout fundamental religious activity, especially among the middle classes. To them allowing Sunday amusements would bring the country 'down to the level of France'. Sir Benjamin Hall contended that by providing band concerts the authorities were inciting civil disturbance. The strains of martial music, he went on to say, were wholly out of accordance with the sacred repose of the Sabbath.[19]

In 1855 the National Sunday League was formed, and, in December 1856, the children of Leicester were invited to take part in an essay competition on the subject 'Sunday amusements are inconsistent with the Word of God and are opposed to the wellbeing of Society'. It is not surprising therefore that this 'fearful Sabbath desecration' of public band concerts caused no little concern amongst churchmen, not only in Leicester but also in other towns such as Manchester where in August 1856 sixty-two ministers and 170 Sunday school teachers marched to protest against 'these unhallowed proceedings'.[20]

In July 1857 there was another attempt to revive the Sunday concerts, during the course of which the lessees of the Race Course presented every member of the band with a letter to the effect that not only were they opposed to such performances, but also were the magistrates and town council, the notice ending with the warning that anyone playing music on a Sunday would be 'prosecuted as the law directs'. The concerts continued and in August all the members of the band were issued with a summons to attend the county court.

The following Tuesday Thomas Keighley, supported by Charles Billson, appeared before the court charged not for playing in the park, but with trespass. In spite of the defence hingeing on the fact that as

*'The Unholy Alliance.' A cartoon of 1897 showing the devil, a preacher and a bandsman arm in arm. Some people thought that Sunday band concerts were wrong and as such should not be allowed.
(Wyvern 11 June 1897)*

the general public were allowed on the grounds, Keighley could not be guilty of a trespass, he was, nevertheless, fined a nominal one pound for 'damage' caused to the park. Not being able to play on the Race Course, the following week the band defiantly moved to a patch of land on Upper Brunswick Street, Humberstone Road, where, to a large audience, they played their last concert.[21]

It was not until the 1890s that the subject of Sunday band concerts returned to the fore in Leicester's musical life. Although by 1891 such concerts were still banned in Leicester, they were allowed in other places such as Windsor. While the town's good bands, such as the Police, Gas Works and Highfields were not allowed to play in any public place on Sundays, the town's Salvation Army band, whose first open air concert in May 1881 had attracted a crowd of over a thousand, had the reputation of playing 'most discordant music' on Sundays with nothing done to stop them. Indeed their music was so bad that on more than one occasion it was said that instead of doing good the noise of the band was such as to only cause bad language![22]

Alla Marcia

The town's military bands were also permitted to play on Sundays when they were on duty. However, this music was not always of the highest class, an example being in June 1893 when the Rifle Band, returning from Church Parade, marched down London Road incongruously playing 'The Man who Broke the Bank at Monte Carlo'.[23]

It was not until 1895 that bands were officially granted permission to give Sunday afternoon park concerts of sacred music. This move was partly welcomed by the Sunday School Union, who wrote to the Council requesting that the times of the concerts be put back from 3.00 to 3.30 so that they did not clash with Sunday Schools which ended at 3.00. The move was, however, condemned by the more conservative Carley Street Baptist Church. In much the same way as hunts today which, although legal, attract a large group of protesters, so did these early concerts which were accompanied by a large police presence which kept a large ring around the band.[24]

Francis Ptacek

In August 1855, with the Crimea War into its second year, a Grand Military Fête, with three military bands in full uniform, took place on the Cricket Ground. The highlight of the evening was a grand

Leicester Market Place in 1877.

172   *Musical Leicester*

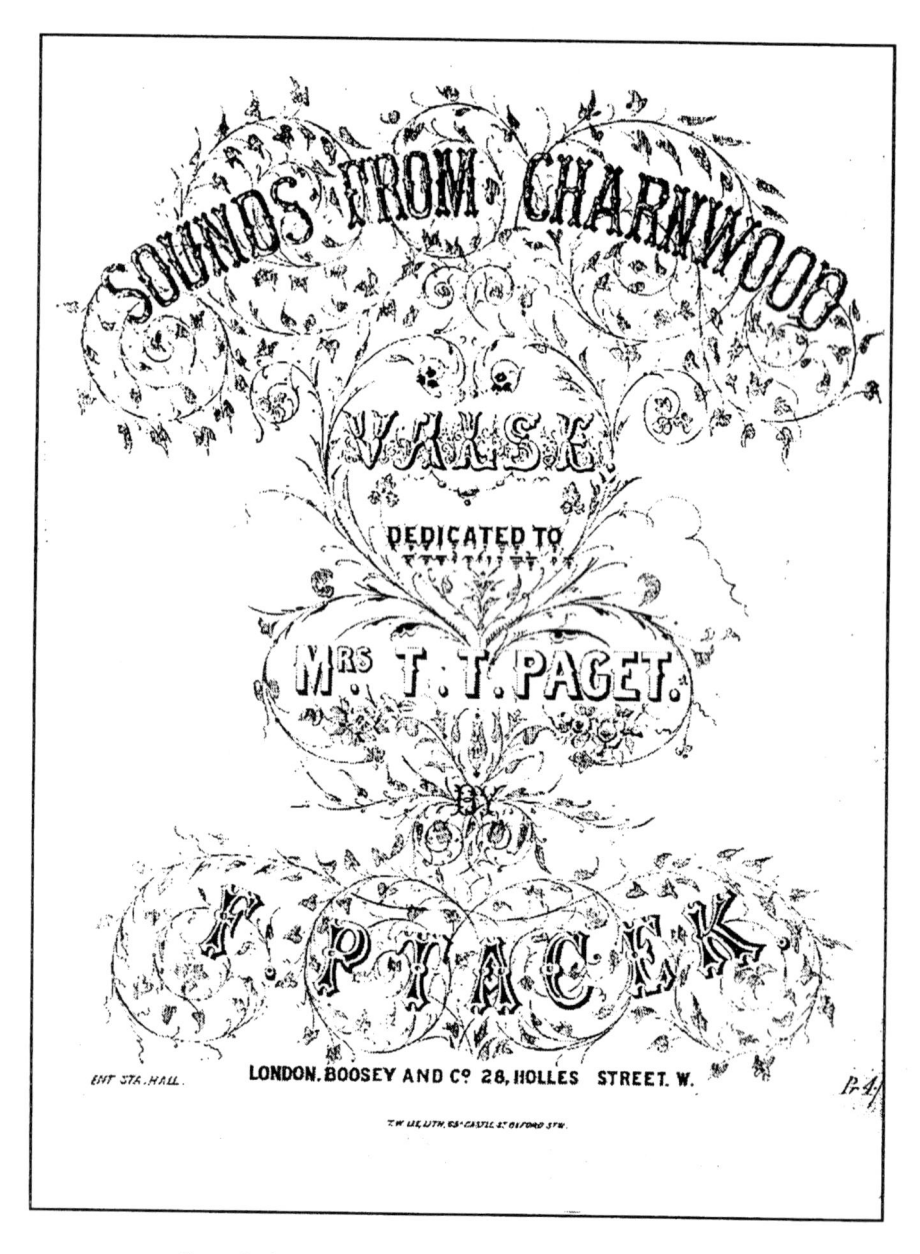

Sounds from Charnwood, *which included the song*
'Old John of Bradgate Park' composed by Francis Ptacek, published in 1865.
(Leicestershire Record Office)

'pyrotechnic representation' of the siege and bombardment of Sebastopol. The following November the reformed Militia Band, under Francis Ptacek, gave a concert in the Market Place before travelling to Aldershot for the winter. After returning from Aldershot, where the band had played before the Queen, the Militia was posted to Cork. The sea crossing was so rough that it took them six days to get there.[25]

Ptacek was a member of the Prague Conservatoire who the previous year had been invited by Major Neal, whose wife was Czech, to take over the militia band. As well as his band and teaching commitments Ptacek also promoted concerts of popular music in the New Hall which featured George Cave, the country's foremost concertina player and Mr Ramsden, who sang 'Sally in Our Alley' and, to some consternation, 'The Vicar of Bray', with its 'profane first verse'. The first verse of the song ends with the words 'And damned are those who dare resist, Or touch the Lord's Anointed'. It was, no doubt this line to which Victorian taste objected.

Other performers at the concert were Rosa Hersee, Fanny Reeve's niece, who sung some of the popular ballads of the day such as 'Sing Birdie Sing', and the flautist Sidney Pratten. The fourth concert of 1864, which featured Fanny Reeves, Elliot Galer, Henry Lazarus and cornet player John Clarke, was crowded with the season ticket holders having to endure a 'crushing and scrambling' as they made their way to their seats in the gallery. This problem resulted from the practice of not opening the doors until half an hour before the commencement of the concert, causing the *Journal* to advise the hall keeper to let the audience in as they arrived without them having to queue up outside.[26]

In May 1864 Ptacek, who was by now Professor of Instrumental Music at Southfields College for Young Ladies, had his photograph taken with the forty-strong Militia Band by the local photographer John Burton. He obviously thought that this was an official photograph for the band records, as he was very surprised the following month when during an open air concert in the Market Place it was presented to him. In 1865 Ptacek published 'Sounds from Charnwood', a waltz which included the song 'Old John of Bradgate Park', which he dedicated to Mrs Thomas T. Paget.[27]

In May 1867 Ptacek, as a 'matter of honour', resigned as Bandmaster of the Militia Band. The position was taken over by Henry Nicholson, who stayed in the post for the next thirty-two years. Ptacek soon formed another band from many former members of the Militia who, in August of that year, playing instruments made by Courtois of Paris, gave their first public concert on the Race Course to a crowd of over 8,000.[28]

The following December the people of Leicester showed their esteem of Ptacek by giving him a benefit concert in the Temperance Hall. During the evening he was presented with a purse, made by Mrs Neal, containing 150 guineas 'as an acknowledgement of twelve years' work in cultivating the musical taste of the town'. The 200 performers included his band and the New Orpheus Society, of which he was conductor. Twelve years later, in the Spring of 1879, on Ptacek's retirement as bandmaster, the former members of the Militia who had been present when he had taken over the band at Aldershot some twenty-four years previously, and were now members of his private band, presented him with an oil painting of himself executed by the Haymarket studio of Burton & Son.[29]

Music critic of *The Bee*, a local weekly sports and entertainment magazine, in 1882 Ptacek stated that he thought Leicester should be able to support a band of about thirty to play every day in the newly opened Abbey Park. The expenses of such a band, he contended, could be met by the sale of programmes and a subscription list. The band, Ptacek believed, could be run on the same lines as the Militia band with the mayor being considered the colonel and the aldermen and councillors the majors and captains. An idea which, needless to say, never caught on.[30]

Organist of St George's Church Ptacek also taught music from his home in Welford Road, where he composed his overture 'Glengarrif'. The news of his death was received with great sadness in Leicester, especially as it was so unexpected. He had gone to Kent to spend Christmas with his friend Herr Sawerthal, bandmaster of the Royal Engineers and, as he was preparing to come home, he suffered a fatal heart attack on 7 January 1886 aged 55.

On hearing of the news of his death Nicholson said 'I cannot forbear placing on record my high esteem of his character, both as an artist and a gentleman.' Thomas Paget saying: 'It only required to know my friend Herr Ptacek to esteem, to respect and to love him.' In his will Ptacek left just over £1781 with instructions that his funeral be as plain and unostentatious as possible. The remaining inscription on his weatherworn tomb in Welford Road Cemetery states:[31]

An accomplished musician, he was endeared to his many pupils and to all who knew him, not more by his varied attainments than by his honesty and frankness and by the warmth of his attachments. Those who sorrow, over his grave may well say he came among us as a stranger and he departs leaving many warm and devoted friends.

Local Bands

Villages such as Newtown Linford, Belgrave, and Great Glen formed bands, as did the Temperance Society and some of the local factories, the owners of which seeing the bands as a suitable social adjunct to the work place. Examples of such factory bands in Leicester include the Bowbridge factory of Archibald Turner; Hodges & Sons; the Midland Railway; Evans & Stafford; and N. Corah & Sons. One of the members of Corah's St Margaret's Works Band was cornet player David Geary who had been a member of the Town Waits and Leicester Military, Yeomanry and Saxe-Coburg Street bands, as well as playing horn in the Opera House Orchestra. His two brothers, Tom and James, were also local musicians, the former being leader of the Police Band and the latter flautist in the Theatre Royal Orchestra.[32]

The first civilian drum and fife corps in the town was founded by the Leicester Band of Hope in 1854 under the instruction of Arthur Moulds. St Martin's Drum and Fife Band (Secretary John Tolton, a draper of 246A Belgrave Street, and bandmaster John Freestone of New Park Street) was formed about 1870 and were regular performers on Victoria Park as well as playing on Bradgate Park during the Easter weekend. They gave annual concerts in the Working Men's Institute, Union Street, which often included unusual combinations of instruments such as the trio of two violins and an euphonium, played by J. Jelley. Five years earlier he had played in the 1870 production of the *Messiah*. Well-known outside Leicester, at the Manchester Belle Vue contest of 1875 the band came fourth.[33]

The Police Band

The town Police Band was formed in 1874. The eighteen musicians, who under the direction of John Smith, were a regular sight in the parks, also gave annual concerts in aid of local charities such as the Discharged Prisoners' Aid Association. In 1877 Joseph Simpkin, a grocer of Market Street, arranged a collection for the members of the

Leicester Borough Police Band 1900. The top hatted figure to the left of the drum is the bandmaster John Smith. (Leicestershire Constabulary)

band in appreciation of their efforts in giving free concerts in Town Hall Square.[34]

In October 1881 several thousand attended a concert given by the Band in the Floral Hall for the benefit of its own funds. The guest singer on this occasion was Alice Askew of 51 Filbert Street, who had been a pupil of Madam Gilbert and had made her London début some six years earlier. On her return home she set up as a teacher, arranging occasional concerts on behalf of local good causes such as the Borough Asylum.[35]

A year later the band, which rehearsed in the Guildhall, gave a concert in the Floral Hall for the benefit of the proposed Royal College of Music. The music chosen for this concert was not to the general liking for it was described as being badly arranged by 'persons who lacked the very rudiments of harmony' who made the sound noisy but never full. The evening also included songs by Miss Blackwall, Miss Birch and Charles Birch, a piano, violin and singing teacher. The singers were accompanied by Dr Johnston, the police surgeon, who played a piano that could hardly be heard.[36]

Two of the more notable members of the band were Inspector McCormack, who became bandmaster of the Birmingham City Police

Band, and Tom Geary, an accomplished cornet player, who joined the band as deputy bandmaster in 1883. On the death of Smith he took over as director until the band folded in 1906.

Other Brass Bands

Caleb Palmer, born in Sileby, used to copy out the music for the Sileby and Quorn band before moving to Leicester in 1879. He joined the Rifle Band, taking lessons from John Smith and Andrew Humberstone, before, in 1888, founding the Gas Works Band. The thirty musicians, mostly all taught by Palmer, made their first appearance at a garden-party at the home of John Stafford, Elmsleigh Hall, Stoughton Road.[37]

Caleb Palmer, bandmaster of the Municipal Gas Works Band. (Wyvern 16 June 1899)

With the reorganisation of the Rifle Band and the break-up in 1894 of Major John Richardson's reed band, one of the few bands left showing promise was that of the Municipal Gas Works which was under Palmer's leadership. Known for the kindly, gentlemanly way in which he managed his bands, he also ran the Gas Works string band and the Caillard Boys Home band. Palmer, who had a collection of over 100 photographs of the most famous musicians of the world, died in November 1899.[38]

Andrew Humberstone, born in 1857, joined the Rifle Volunteer Band in 1871, and, on resigning when Smith was dismissed, joined the Yeomanry band. On his death, at the relatively young age of 36, Alfred Brant wrote the following in his memory:[39]

The Bandsman's Burial

We bear our comrade to his tomb,
With music brightening sorrow's gloom
A bandsman good was he, we say,
Who could right well the cornet play.
Strike up! In crowds the mourners come,
As on we march with muffled drum.
Euphoniums with their tenderest breath
Proclaim the pity of his death;
The trombones blare in tones profound,
Like dirges pealing underground,
Bombardoms mightily outroll
And, with this requiem, thrill the soul.

The trumpets with their vibrant swell,
Recall the sounds he loved so well;
As sweet and sad as Love's goodbye,
The clarinets make low reply
But ah! the bandsmen wait in vain
To hear their comrade's crowning strain.

Strike up once more for Music's voice
Can make the mourner's heart rejoice.
Let grief depart, the 'Dead March' cease,
Our brother bandsman rests in peace;
And who would cheer the World but he
Who links his life with melody.

In the 1890s the number of brass and reed bands in the town increased at a vast rate. Many of them took part in a massed band concert in May 1898 for the benefit for John Clarke of the Floral Hall. As well as the attraction of the band and pipes of the Gordon Highlanders, the concert included such local bands as the Rifle Volunteer Band (now under the direction of Stephan Plant), Leicester Military Band (Alfred Nicholson), Gas Works Band (Caleb Palmer), the Highfields Band (John Chapman), Albion Band (Frank Gilbert), Theatre Royal Band (Carl Hamlyn), New Tivoli Band (John Lowe) and the New Empire Band (Thomas Richardson).[40]

One of the town's top combinations was the Highfields Brass Band who won first prize at the 1900 Easter Monday Contest at Rugby. The following year, under the baton of T. Seddon the musicians walked

The Leicester Imperial Prize Band 1903.
(Leicester Guardian 5 December 1903)

off with the top prize at the Crystal Palace Contest. One of the members of the band, which in 1902 changed its name to the Leicester Imperial Prize Band, was John Robert Markham, a wringing machine maker of Upper Conduit Street, who founded the Leicester Brass Band Festival. A Conservative, Markham also played tenor horn and trombone in the Wesley Temperance and Borough Workhouse Bands as well as being organist of the Leicester Symphony Orchestra..[41]

Band Contests

Brass bands' popularity grew for two main reasons, the main one being the advent of the railways, which made travel easier for the working man. The other was the improvements in the manufacture of brass instruments, which made both fingering and blowing easier. With this wide-spread popularity it is not surprising that it was not long before bands began to compete with other in friendly rivalry.

The first known brass band contest was held near Hull in 1845. In these early days the participating bands were restricted to twelve players (as against twenty-five today) and played arrangements of works by composers such as Weber, Rossini and Mozart. The most distinguished of these early bandsmen was Enderby Jackson, a conductor and arranger, who, in 1854, established the principle of all participating bands in a contest playing the same test piece.

In 1858 Sheffield held a contest at which only six of the twenty-six bands which entered were allowed to take part. Not to be outdone, the following year, on 15 August 1859, Leicester hosted its first Brass Band Contest. Managed by Nicholson and Smith the event, attended by between six and seven thousand spectators, took place on the Wharf Street Cricket Ground. Judged by F. Farmer of Nottingham; Mr Newham, of the South Nottingham Yeomanry Cavalry; Thomas Weston of Leicester; and Enderby Jackson, who composed the test piece 'The Prize Waltz', the top three bands were Northampton, Chesterfield and Newtown Linford.[42]

The following year, what had become known as the Annual Midlands Brass Band Contest took place at the Cricket Ground, on Monday 20 August. The top three of the thirteen bands which took part were Chesterfield, Newtown Linford and Sutton in Ashfield with Leicester's Midland Railway Band fourth. The novelty of brass band contests in Leicester soon wore off. The 1864 event only attracted five bands - Chesterfield Rifle Corps, Matlock Rifle Corps, Wednesday Rifle Corps, Nottingham Temperance, and Rothwell Saxhorn Band. National annual contests soon became established both at Manchester Belle Vue (from 1853) and the Crystal Palace (from 1860) although some local towns still held the occasional contest such as Nottingham in 1875 and Matlock in 1878.[43]

In October 1899 Leicester was once again the centre for a national contest. Arranged by John Clarke, manager of the Floral Hall, there were over sixty entries out of which only the first twenty-eight received could take part. On the day of the contest the people of the town were given a grand display as all the bands marched from London Road station to the Floral Hall. One of the bands which drew special attention was the Arael Griffin Band from Wales which had to travel overnight on the Friday and did not get home again until the next Monday. Judged by J. Ord Hume of Fleet, Hants; J. O. Shepherd from Liverpool and William Barrow of Leicester, the contest was won by the Kenneling Rifle Band.[44]

Visiting Bands

Leicester was often the venue for concerts by visiting brass and military bands. The first such concert was at the Theatre Royal in 1848 when the twenty-four members of the Nottingham-based Royal Irish Dragoon Guards band played under Herrn Tieke. In 1858 the band of the Grenadiers gave a concert in the Temperance Hall. In

August 1872 the band of the Grenadier Guards, under Dan Godfrey, returned to the town to play in a well-attended concert on G. Harrison's grounds on the Belgrave Road. This concert was to help raise funds to improve the Rutland statue and erect that to John Biggs.[45]

In August 1877 the Floral Hall, now under the management of Edward Watson, was the venue for a grand military promenade concert by the Grenadier Guards, the Pipes of the Scots Fusiliers, the Leicester Military and the Yeomanry bands. In an age before air conditioning the building was cooled by huge blocks of Wenham Lake Ice, supplied by Alfred Panter, a fishmonger of 26 Granby Street, which were piled in front of the platform. This very popular concert, tickets sixpence to three shillings each, drew an audience of 5481.[46]

The Leicester Commemoration Exhibition

Although brass bands had been in existence for over forty years it was in the 1890s that they gained the popularity that they still have today. Two bands, still in existence, which became regular visitors to the town were Black Dyke Mills, founded in 1855, and Besses O' th' Barn, founded in 1853. In 1903, just outside the period covered by this book John Philip Sousa, the 'March King', brought his band to Leicester.[47]

The Leicester Commemoration Exhibition, to celebrate Victoria's sixty years on the Throne, was held in the Floral Hall from 13 March to 24 April 1897. On the first day the Band of the Grenadier Guards gave two concerts, while the town bell ringers rung simultaneously from the church belfries all afternoon from two till seven. Other bands which gave concerts on every day of the exhibition were: the First Life Guards, the Royal Marines, the Royal Engineers, the 3rd Battalion Leicestershire Regiment (conducted by Henry Nicholson), the Gordon Highlanders, the Leicestershire Military Band (conducted by Alfred Nicholson), the First Battalion Rifle Volunteer Band, the Corporation Gas Department (Caleb Palmer), the Lea Mills Brass Band, the Rushden Temperance Silver Prize Band, the Black Dyke Mills Band, the Besses o' th' Barn Brass Band and the Royal Treorchy Male Voice Choir.[48]

Chapter 12

𝄞 TUTTI 𝄞

The Harmonic Society

In 1841 the Harmonic Society commenced their meetings at the Bell Inn, on the site of the present Haymarket Shopping Complex, Humberstone Gate. With the lack of public rooms in the town almost the only accommodation available for social meetings were the large rooms offered by the local inns, such as the White Lion which was holding weekly music meetings in 1866.[1] The Harmonic Society, which was devoted to harmony 'both music and social', was instituted on strictly non-party lines, an innovation for the town which was divided both politically (Liberal and Tory) and religiously (Established Church and Dissenters). Many people from all sections of society enjoyed these convivial meetings which included songs from a group of glee singers who enjoyed the meetings so much that they did not charge for their services.

The sixty-strong Leicester Amateur Harmonic Society, founded by George Löhr in 1856, gave very popular annual concerts in the Temperance Hall. That of 1860 was marred for the pedants of the town by the poor Latin pronunciations: the word *coeli* being pronounced 'chee-li', *descendit* 'deshendit' and *pacem* 'pah-chem'. In 1866, at the Society's eleventh annual concert, presentations were made to both George Löhr, who received a long-handled silver baton, and Mary Deacon, the Society's accompanist, who was given a gold pendant brooch. The 1870 concert, which featured Rossini's *Messe Solonelle*, included Löhr's son Harvey who played harmonium at this his first public performance. In 1876, with Henry Ellis as conductor and Mary Deacon as accompanist, the Amateur Harmonic Society merged with the vocal portion of the New Musical Society to become the Amateur Vocal Society.[2]

During its twenty-seven years of existence the Society, which folded in 1903 because of the difficulty of getting tenors and basses, produced such works as Barnett's *The Building of the Ship*, Haydn's *The Creation*, Farmer's *Christ and His Soldiers* and, in 1884, Handel's *Saul*. Conducted by D. T. Jackson with William Bunney on organ, tickets for this event, which lasted until nearly midnight, were from a reasonable sixpence to one shilling and sixpence each. Owing to the lack of experienced singers for this ambitious work some of the lead singers had to take several parts. James McRobie, for example, who took the parts of both Saul and Samuel, had to answer his own questions! After the concert the Midland Railway laid on a special train to return concert-goers home to Loughborough. In 1899 the Society produced *Light of Life*, the first time any of Edward Elgar's works had been heard in Leicester.[3]

The Madrigal Society

In September 1851 Alfred and Henry Nicholson promoted a concert by the London-based English Glee and Madrigal Union which consisted of Mrs Endersohn, Miss W. Williams, Mr Lockey, Mr Francis, Mr Land and Mr Phillips. The all-English composers concert was well-attended, the Union being asked to return to Leicester the following November and December, and again in September 1852. Such was the impact on the town by the Union that, in February 1852, the Literary Society considered putting on a Madrigal performance, believing that a musical section of the Society could be formed. This was, however, considered inexpedient so, under Alfred Paget, a separate society was formed with Henry May, an employee of the Bank of England, as conductor. Using the New Walk museum as a rehearsal room, the thirty-seven members, all amateur with the exception of twelve of the choristers from St Margaret's and the Alderman Newton Green Coat School, used their first concert, in 1854, to obtain funds to pay off the debt incurred by the museum's purchase of the 200 million year old saurian fossils which had been found at Barrow-on-Soar in 1851. At this first concert, in a packed New Hall, some of the madrigalians even brought along their liveried servants to conduct the visitors to their places.[4]

The New Choral Society

The New Choral Society was founded in December 1875 when, at a rehearsal for a musical service in the Curzon Street chapel, the possibility was mooted of organising a choral society for the benefit of the working classes. Many of those who joined had been members of the defunct Choral Society (which had been under the direction of

William Goodrich), the Orpheus or the New Philharmonic Societies. Conducted by Charles Hancock, one of the New Choral Society's members was Joseph Wood, born in 1808 and a printer by trade, who had been drummer for the old Choral Society and had built an organ at Harvey Lane Chapel, where he was organist. Wood was also known for his musical evenings which he held at his home with his friends Thomas Weston (violin); Mr Fozzard (viola); and J. Sladen (cello).[5]

The singer Helene Lemmens-Sherrington was one of the many musical visitors to Leicester in the second half of the 19th century.
(Illustrated London News 20 August 1859)

The new Society's first public performance of *Samson* in April 1876, saw the largest choir that had ever appeared in the Temperance Hall. The 200 members were augmented by singers from London including Helene Lemmens-Sherrington who, born in Preston, Lancashire in 1834, had studied at the Brussels Conservatoire before making her London début in 1856. Such was the esteem felt by the members for their conductor that a few weeks later they presented Hancock with a bound score of *Elijah* and a purse containing six pounds and twelve shillings.[6]

The following January the Society produced, for the first time in Leicester, Mendelssohn's *Hymn of Praise*, and, two years after the composer's death, William Sterndale Bennett's *May Queen*. Conducted by Henry Nicholson, the principal singers at this well-attended concert were Sophie Ferrari, Miss Ibbotson, Miss C. Blackwell, Henry Guy and Lewis Thomas. First produced at the 1858 Leeds Festival the *May Queen* is one of the best known of Bennett's works. Born at Sheffield in 1816, Bennett's musical genius showed as a boy, indeed he was admitted into the Royal Academy of Music before he was ten years old.[7]

In December 1876 the 250 members of the Society produced, for the first time in Leicester, Handel's *Jephtha*. The following year the Society had another 'first' when it produced, on the fiftieth anniversary of his death, Beethoven's *Engedi*. In March 1877 the Society, which was by now affiliated to Trinity College London, invited Phillippe Sainton to conduct a rehearsal of his wife Charlotte's composition *St Dorothea*. The following Easter, with over two hundred and fifty in the band and chorus, Charles Hancock conducted Mendelssohn's *Elijah* in the presence of his former teacher Sir George Elvey, composer and organist of the Chapel Royal Windsor. Later that year the Society, with a performance of the *Messiah*, raised £68 for the benefit of the survivors of the Abercaine Colliery Disaster.[8]

At the Society's Easter 1880 production of Mendelssohn's *St Paul*, one of the audience was Dr Hayden Keeton, organist of Peterborough Cathedral, who was so impressed with the performance that he invited the Society to sing in the Cathedral the following June. The day in the diocesan capital was made into a gala event with the Midland Railway putting on a cheap excursion train for the 300 singers and 700 supporters who took up the doctor's invitation. Keeton kept his contacts with Leicester, agreeing in 1883 to play with the Society at a concert held for the benefit of the Infirmary.[9]

In 1882, when the Prince of Wales proposed to establish a Royal College of Music as a national institution, people all over the country got together to raise funds for the venture. In Leicester a committee was formed under Thomas Tertius Paget, MP for South Leicestershire. Their first venture was a combined music and drama concert in the Royal Opera House at which the Choral Society played a leading part. With the Mayor, Henry Chambers, giving his patronage to the show (which included Dibdin's *The Waterman*), £87 was raised for the project. Although the other musical societies of the town also held concerts, some were very poorly attended, so that by the end of October, at a public meeting chaired by George Grove, secretary of the Crystal Palace concerts (who was shortly to be knighted prior to becoming director of the College), it was announced that so far Leicester had been able to raise only £600.[10]

In April 1883 eleven young musicians from Leicester sat the College's preliminary entrance exam with three, Miss Josephs (piano), Mr Jackson and Sidney Waddington (composition), being selected to attend the final examination in London. Designed ultimately to promote the latent musical talent of all English speaking countries, 1,588 candidates applied for the 50 scholarships,(25 male and 25 female), of which 35 were free. Of the three Leicester applicants only 14 year old Waddington gained entry to the College, which was inaugurated by the Prince of Wales in May 1883.[11]

From the 1880s with systems of examination under the auspices of the associated boards of the Royal schools of music teachers gained publicity through results. This was in some cases unfair as some pupils, for reasons best known to themselves, moved to new teachers just before the exam. When the newspapers published lists of successful candidates it was the new teacher who was given the praise.

The Orchestral Union

Established in 1874 by Edgar Taylor and Thomas Carter, a viola player in whose school room the Union practised, the Orchestral Union's first conductor was William H. Wale whose song 'Throw open the door in the Morning' was sung to an enthusiastic audience at the Union's concert in April 1877. Catering mainly for the middle classes, in 1879 the Union presented the début of Wale's *Concert Overture in G*, while in 1891 they gave a grand concert in commemoration of the centenary of Mozart's death. The Orchestral Union was disbanded just before the outbreak of World War I.[12]

The New Musical Society

In 1873 a committee was formed with the intention of bringing together the several musical societies of the town into one good and efficient society which would provide an efficient and sufficiently large body of performers able to perform the more difficult and higher class of compositions. Under the direction of George Löhr, Henry Nicholson and Christopher May, the New Music Society gave four concerts a year for an annual subscription of twenty-one shillings.[13] The December 1874 concert, conducted by Löhr, included the pianist and orchestral leader Charles Hallé, who returned in 1875 and 1884.

The March 1875 presentation was *The Creation* with Edith Wynne, Vernon Rigby and Charles Santley taking the leading rôles. The concert, which played to a full house, was not a musical success, the singing being described as at a constant *forte* or *fortissimo* with no *piano* or *pianissimo*. On top of this Rigby altered some of the words and Santley's singing was said to have converted the 'Rolling foaming billows' into a 'sluggish Dutch canal'.[14]

The Society's first concert of 1880 featured the pianist Dr Hans von Bulow, who as a boy had been taught music by Fredrich Wieck, father of Clara Schumann. After studying Law at the University of Leipzig, where he also studied counterpoint under Hauptmann, Bulow went on to the University of Berlin where he supplemented his income by contributing to *Die Abendpost*. A performance of *Lohengrin* at Weimar in 1850 moved him so intensely that he gave up Law and went to Zurich to put himself under the guidance of Wagner. From Switzerland he returned to Weimar to study piano under Liszt before making his first concert tour in 1853. Von Bulow obviously thought himself superior to his English contempories, critizing the Liverpool Philharmonic Orchestra as being well below standard and sneering at William Sterndale Bennett as the 'Miniature Mendelssohn'. It is not recorded what he thought of the Leicester musicians![15]

In 1896 when the Society, led by John Kilby, a beer shop keeper and leader of the Rutland Street Ice Rink band, produced *St Paul*, Arthur Barlow, one of the bass singers, came into criticism from the *Wyvern's* reporter who commented that if Barlow 'could resist the slight tendency to bellow he might make a first rate singer'. Later that year, with a big increase in membership, the Society produced a jubilee performance of *Elijah* under the direction of John Addison Adcock. Henry Nicholson, who had played in the first performance fifty years earlier, played lead flute.[16]

In 1898 the Society, which had an imposing appearance with the sopranos in pink, contraltos in green and the gentlemen in evening dress, produced for the first time in Leicester Frederick Cowen's *Sleeping Beauty*; in 1899 Gounod's *Redemption*; and, in 1900, Sterndale Bennett's *The Woman of Samaria*. By the turn of the century, with the Society's appeal waning, it was decided that in order to survive each member would have to sell at least three shillings worth of tickets for each concert. The Society struggled on before finally succumbing with the outbreak of war in 1914.[17]

One of the mainstays of the Society was John Addison Adcock who, born in Melbourne, Derbyshire, had been a boy chorister before learning to play the cello at the age of 17, making his solo debut in 1866. Four years later he moved to Loughborough where he became a professional musician, teaching violin, viola and cello. Although he was established in Leicester by 1879, he still kept his contacts with Woodgate Chapel, Loughborough where he was choirmaster from 1878 to 1892 when he was appointed to the same post at London Road Chapel, Leicester.

In October 1892 a testimonial concert was held for Adcock's benefit in an attempt to recompense him for all he had lost at his popular Saturday evening concerts, many of which had not met their expenses. Attended by many of the leading townsmen, including the Mayor, Thomas Wright, among those taking part were Henry Ellis; Charles Hancock; Henry Nicholson; the reed trio of William and Frank Rowlett and Thomas Wykes; Miss Russell; Annie Jelley (who left Leicester in the Autumn of 1893, married a Mr Burdett and joined the Royal Albert Hall Choral Society); Alfred Page and Donal McAlpin. The last four were described as 'the best quartet of vocalists the town could raise'.[18]

A man of never-failing geniality whose music was his work as well as his pleasure, in the winter of 1890 Adcock inaugurated a singing competition, the winner of which, soprano Leah Clayton, went on to sing with Miss Alleyn's Shakespeare Company. In December 1895 Adcock organised a choir contest in the Temperance Hall which was judged by Edward Minshall, editor of the *Non-Conformist Musical Journal* and one-time organist of the City Temple. Only six choirs bothered to participate in this poorly-attended concert which was won by the town's Thorpe Street Emmanuel Chapel.[19]

In 1885 Adcock founded the Leicester Amateur Philharmonic Orchestra which met on Monday evenings at the Victoria Coffee House, Granby Street. Comprised of young people,

John Addison Adcock was a promoter of cheap popular Saturday evening concerts in Leicester.
(Wyvern *28 October 1892)*

these gatherings gave many their introduction to orchestral playing, including some who would become household names in the town's musical circles such as: Maude Harding; Annie Johnson; Miss F. Booth (soprano); Master Bastick; Alfred Page (tenor); Donal McAlpin; Walter Waddington (trumpet); Mr J. Johnson; Mr W. Johnson; William Rowlett (cello); Arthur Chapman (clarinet); Miss A. J. Grant (violin); William Armstrong ('our most talented young flautist'); J. Armstrong (cello); Hettie Jones (singer) and Edith Chester (singer). Also taking part was Ernest Gamble who must have been one of the first people in Leicester to play the saxophone, a instrument which was just making its appearance in military bands.[20]

Two of these instrumentalists, Walter Waddington and William Armstrong were members of a band which, under the leadership of the Mansfield Brothers of 4 Clarence Street, used to spend the summers of the 1890s playing annual ten-week seasons on Worthing pier. Other members of the band were Charles, Joseph, Harry and Robert Mansfield; C. L. Burrows, Benjamin Burrows (the father of the Benjamin, who became one of Leicester's foremost twentieth century musicians), J. Vann, B. Gamble and Harry Matthews. These seaside

This caricacature depicts the singer Alfred Page, one of the most popular singers of the town in the 1890s.
(Wyvern 10 March 1893)

bands came into being with the increased importance of the annual seaside holiday which many working people were now able to afford due to the relatively cheap railway travel. These bands attracted people and many resorts vied with each other as to who had the best band. As early as 1876 Bournemouth engaged a band of Italians and from 1892 a twenty-one piece military band.

As well as frequenting the coffee house Adcock's youthful band also gave concerts at such places as the Fosse Football Club, Waterloo Hall and the Medway School. In May 1898 Adcock's production of Farmer's *Christ and His Soldiers* at St Paul's Methodist Church raised seven pounds ten shillings for the Whitwick Colliery Disaster fund, while a few weeks later a benefit at the Opera House for the same purpose raised £50.[21]

The Leicester Octet. Back row: George Barker (violin), William Heighton Matthews (clarinet), Joseph Muston (bass), Harold Wykes (viola). Front row: B.H. Burrows (cello), James Muston (leader), J.W. Bird (bassoon), William Matthews (horn). (Leicester Guardian 19 May 1906)

Another member of the Musical Society was James Muston, a violinist who had started playing when he was five. By the time he was ten he was leading a children's orchestra which had been organised by his father Joseph, a double bass player. Self-taught, except for two lessons from Kienle and three from Benjamin Burrows, by the age of 14 James was an active member of the Orchestral Union, the Philharmonic and the New Musical Society. In 1893 he was appointed organist at St Peter's.

The Philharmonic Society

Founded in 1841 with the intention of giving six concerts a year, the Philharmonic Society opened its first and, as it turned out, last season for forty-three years, in January 1842 with a concert which included Beethoven's *Symphony in C* and Weber's *Freischutz Overture*. Three weeks later the Society held a grand ball in honour of the christening of the Prince of Wales, tickets being seven shillings and sixpence for gentlemen and five shillings for ladies. At the Society's third concert, in April, excerpts from Mozart's *Magic Flute* were played featuring local flautist Henry Nicholson with his brother Alfred on oboe. The Society's sixth and last concert took place in July with the hope of repeating the success of the first season during the following winter. However, in spite of having two hundred and forty subscribers at ten shillings each, the Society had to fold owing to lack of support.

In May 1859 the New Philharmonic Society, which had for the past year been under the training of Henry Nicholson, held its first soirée in the Temperance Hall, which by now was bearing the Royal Arms. On Boxing Day 1861 Nicholson conducted the Society in a performance of the *Messiah*, the concert beginning with the *Dead March in Saul* as a mark of respect to the recently-deceased Prince Albert.[22]

During the twelve years of the existence of the revamped society, with four hundred plus members at its height, performances included such works as *Israel in Egypt*, *Messiah*, *Elijah*, and *The Creation*. One of the members was Richard Charles Allen, an aerated water manufacturer, who played double bass and violin, and sung bass in St Martin's choir.[23]

In July 1886 the Society was re-resurrected, this time by music shop owner James Herbert Marshall who had been a member of the old Harmonic and Philharmonic Societies. Born in 1851 at Zouch Mills near Loughborough, as a boy Marshall had taken violin lessons from John Kilby as well as being a chorister under George Löhr at St Margaret's Church from the age of nine. The first ten years of his working life were spent as a commercial traveller selling pianos, before, in 1882, he opened his 'Marshall's Midland Musical Depot', at 84 Rutland Street, a building which he had personally designed and where he kept a stock of £20,000 worth of pianos and £4,000 worth of violins.[24]

Leicester's representative for the Royal Academy and Royal College of Music, Marshall brought many famous musicians to Leicester, usually at his own expense. Reputedly he once offered Caruso 1,000 guineas to sing in the town but, due to other commitments, a mutually convenient date could not be arranged. Among those who did appear at Marshall's concerts was Nikita,'The American Nightingale'. A very popular singer, at one of her concerts, in a nineteenth century version of 'Beatlemania', the audience stormed the stage, tearing the ribbons off her dress as souvenirs.[25]

Others whom Marshall brought to Leicester include Sarasate, the Italian violinist; Joseph Joachim, a Hungarian who was regarded as the finest living violinist; Emma Albani, a Canadian who had first appeared in London in 1872; Charles Santley; Zelia Trebelli; Antoinette Sterling; Charles Chilley; Ignace Padereswski; Bernhard Stavenhagen; Clara Butt and Ella Russell. In March 1894 Marshall, who kept an album of autographs of all the stars who appeared at his concerts, was to hold Adelina Patti's farewell concert. Sadly, however, the prima donna died two days before the date of the event, which went ahead with the musicians wearing black armbands as signs of mourning.[26]

The Christmas concert of 1892 featured Haydn's *Farewell Symphony* which was performed in the same manner as it had been in 1772 when the composer had conducted it before Prince Esterhazy. Each member of the orchestra had a lighted candle which, as the work approached its end, they extinguished as they left the stage one by one, leaving the conductor to beat time by himself.[27]

In March 1894 the Society produced Mendelssohn's *Elijah* in the Corn Exchange. Built in 1850, in 1858 a concert had been held there with the intention of seeing if the building was suitable for musical meetings. The event proved, however, that the Exchange's acoustics were such as to make it totally unsuitable for musical purposes. The

TEMPERANCE HALL, LEICESTER.

J. HERBERT MARSHALL'S

FOUR GRAND

SUBSCRIPTION CONCERTS

ARTISTES:

MADAME ALBANI,
The World-renowned Prima Donna.

MADAME NORDICA,
Of the Royal Italian Opera, Covent Garden; Metropolitan Opera House, New York; and the leading Opera Houses of Europe and America.

MADAME AMY SHERWIN,
The Australian Prima Donna.

MISS GRACE DAMIAN, The Popular Engl sh Contralto.	**MR. CHARLES CHILLEY,** The Popular Tenor.
MISS DEWS.	**MR. ANDREW BLACK.**
MR. and MRS. HENSCHEL, Dramatic Vocalists,	**MR. BISPHAM.**
	MR. ZOLTAN DOME.

The celebrated MEISTER GLEE SINGERS.
Mr. William Sexton, Mr. Gregory Hast, Mr. W. G. Forington, Mr. Webster Norcross.

HERR JOACHIM, The World-famed Violinist.	**MR. GIBSON,** Viola Popular Concerts, St. James' Hall.
SENOR ARBOS, The eminent Spanish Violinist.	**Mr. WHITEHOUSE,** The well-known Violoncellist.

M. JOSEPH HOFFMAN, Violoncellist to the King of Holland.
MR. F. A. SEWELL. MISS FANNY DAVIES, The eminent Pianist.

Principal Instrumentalists from the Albert Hall, Crystal Palace, Royal Italian Opera, St. James Hall, and Festival Orchestras.

THE PHILHARMONIC SOCIETY (Band and Chorus, 300 Performers.)
Mr. J. Herbert Marshall, Musical Director.   Mr. H. B. Ellis, Hon. Conductor.
Mr. J. S. Collier, Hon. Secretary.

Works selected: "**The Martyr of Antioch**" (*Sir Arthur Sullivan*). Selections from "**Tannhauser**" (*Wagner*), first performance in Leicester. "**Der Freischutz**" (*Weber*)

First Concert, Thursday, October 20th, 1892. | Third Concert, Thursday, February 2nd, 1893.
Second Concert, Thursday, November 17th, 1892. | Fourth Concert, Tuesday, March 7th, 1893.

Subscription for the Four Concerts: Reserved Gallery, 25s. Reserved Body of Hall, 21s. With priority in selection of seats, All Tickets transferable. Plans now open to Subscribers Only at

J. HERBERT MARSHALL'S, MUSIC DEPOT, Rutland Street, Leicester,
Subscribers are requested to Book Seats early, as the Plans must shortly be opened to the Public for the First Concert.

This advertisement, published in the Wyvern *on 30 September 1892, is for Leicester impresario J. Herbert Marshall's 1892–93 season of subscription concerts.*

acoustics must have been improved, for in 1899 the Exchange was the venue for a performance of Gaul's *Holy City*.[28]

Other major works produced by the Society in the last decade of the century include Sullivan's *Martyr of Antioch*; Berlioz's *Faust*; Sullivan's *The Golden Legend*; Parry's *Judith*; Gounod's *Redemption*; Saint Saëns's *Samson and Delila*; Verdi's *Requiem*; Goring Thomas's *The Swan and the Skylark*; and Gounod's *Iren*. Not only was the Society popular with concert-goers, who would follow the music from Novello's vocal scores, but also with the amateur musicians of the town who wished to be members of this prestigious company. In 1894, when the Society advertised for new members, there were sixty applicants for the ten vacancies on offer.[29]

Although subscription tickets cost as much as twenty-five shillings for a series of four concerts, the not so well off were also provided for by the 'Shilling Gallery' where people, mainly skilled workmen, would stand two or three deep at the back of the hall. Not always the most attentive of listeners there were often complaints of talking during the performances.[30]

As well as nationally-known names Marshall, who had attended his first concert as a programme seller, also introduced many local musicians to the concert platform. Among these were Sidney P. Waddington, Colin McAlpin and Lucy Downing.

Sidney P. Waddington

Sidney P. Waddington, son of a local newsagent, passed his Trinity College examinations in 1877. In 1883 he became a Mendelssohn Scholar of the Royal College of Music in 1883 where he spent seven years studying composition and violin. A member of the Royal Italian Opera orchestra, in 1894 his own opera *John Gilpin*, which he had composed especially for the Philharmonic Society, received its public début. Performed to an enthusiastic audience who had come from the surrounding towns with special returns on the Midland Railway, before taking the podium the young composer was presented with a silver baton. Two years later Waddington, who was by now musical director of the Amateur Opera Society of London, had the satisfaction of seeing his work performed at the Crystal Palace. A contributor to musical journals, in 1898, on his return from New York where he had directed a performance of Charles Stanford's opera *Shamus O'Brien*, he was conducting at the Crystal Palace and playing the piano at

Covent Garden. In 1900 he composed his second major work, *Salve Regina*, before, in 1902, going to Australia as an examiner for the Royal Academy and Royal College of Music.[31]

Colin McAlpin

Marshall also played a big part in helping Colin McAlpin's musical career. Born in 1870 McAlpin had shown composing talent from boyhood. His first published work, *The Cuckoo*, appeared when he was but 15, and, while still at Wellingborough School, had produced his own opera, *Robin Hood*. In 1897 McAlpin's first major work, *King Arthur*, was produced in the town.[32]

In 1903, a year after his oratorio *The Prince of Peace* was first performed, McAlpin won a £250 prize for the best opera by a British composer. This work, *The Cross and the Crescent*, was produced at Covent Garden later that same year. Based on Francis Coppée's *Pour la Couronne*, the score received its Leicester début the following February. The shy young composer, who was said to understand the human voice by giving it phrases worth singing, had to be dragged to the stage many times to take bows to the full house which heartily received his work.[33] One of the most powerful and individual composers in the country, writing 22 organ pieces, McAlpin died in Dorking in 1942. His two brothers, Kenneth and Donal, who played a big part in the musical life of St John's, Clarendon Park, were to a lesser degree also involved in the musical life of the town.

Lucy Downing

When, in 1878, Lucy Downing obtained third class honours in her Trinity College exam, little did she know that within twenty years she would be one of the town's foremost composers. Organist at Clarendon Park Congregational Chapel, in 1893 she wrote a cantata *The Ten Virgins* which received its début in that place of worship with Mrs Russell, Annie Jelley and Dr Barlow taking the leading rôles. In 1895 with the title changed to *A Parable in Song or the Wise and Foolish Virgins* it was published by Novello & Co, being available in Leicester from Marshall's shop at two shillings a copy. In December of the same year it was performed, for the benefit of the children's hospital, by the Philharmonic Society, led by J. Betjemann and conducted by Henry Ellis. although not many bothered to attend to hear the work. At this time women composers were almost wholly unknown, the only one of note being Ethel Smyth who had her *Anthony and Cleopatra* produced at the Crystal Palace in 1890.[34]

Other Local Societies

Other societies which came and went in the last fifty years of the nineteenth century included the New Harmonic Society which was established in 1874 under the direction of Elizabeth Hodgkins a piano and singing teacher of 13 Evington Lane; the Secular Choral Union, which was in existence in 1860; the Amateur Instrumental Society, in existence by 1862; and the New Orpheus Society who, in 1865, gave the town its first chance hear Handel's *Samson*; the Anemonic Union, founded in 1855; and the Amateur Music and Drama Society.

LEICESTER MUSICAL SOCIETY,

SIXTH SEASON, 1878-79.

TEMPERANCE HALL, LEICESTER.

THE SECOND CONCERT

WILL TAKE PLACE ON

FRIDAY EVENING, DECEMBER 6th, 1878

ARTISTS:

MADME. EDITH WYNNE.   MISS HELEN D'ALTON.
MR. BARTON McGUCKIN   MR. THURLEY BEALE.

(Solo Violin.)   (Solo Pianist,)

MADME. TÉRESE LIEBE,   HERR CARL WEBER.

(Her first appearance in Leicester).

PLAN ready (for Subscribers only) on Saturday Morning (10 o'clock) November 9th, at DEACON'S Music Warehouse. For Non-Subscribers, Tuesday, November 13th.

Chapter 13

𝄞 *CODA* 𝄞

Concerts

As the nineteenth century drew to a close there were increasing opportunities for the less well-off inhabitants of the town to attend musical events. Because music was being disseminated widely among the working classes by military and brass bands, mass choral singing and street musicians, the poorer people began to agitate for more opportunities to hear good music. Admission to some of these concerts, such as that given by the band of the Coldstream Guards at the Floral Hall in 1899, was as low as threepence a ticket, with programmes one penny each. The YMCA sponsored 'Penny Concerts', while, during the summer months, the members of the Bond Street Chapel, led by A. F. Pollock with his daughter Daisy (singer), Frank Muston (violin) and E. Sullivan (piccolo), gave free Saturday evening open air concerts. A far cry indeed from the cost of musical events held in the town at the beginning of the century![1]

Founded in London in 1877, the Leicester branch of the Kyrle Society was inaugurated in 1881 with the intention of bringing the 'refining and cheering influences of natural and artistic beauty' into the homes and resorts of the poor of the town. This was a time when entertainment, although cheaper than before, was still beyond the reach of the poor whose sole place of entertainment was the local gin-palace. One way the Society tried to achieve its objectives was by its music section which gave free concerts at such venues as the Syston Board School, Thorpe Street School and the Borough Asylum.[2]

At one concert, in April 1881, one of the Society members, Percy Skeffington Smith, sung 'Will-o'-th'-Wisp', a performance which came to the attention of Harry Wall, the representative of the Performing Right Protective Society. Wall's job was to seek out unauthorized public performances and then sue the performer for having caused or

Early twentieth century advertisement of local piano dealer W. H. Russell.

permitted the performance without written permission. Smith was subsequently sued for £4 for breach of copyright.

Smith, who refused to pay, was not the only victim of Wall's avarice, for the following week two other singers were taken to court in London. Wall lost the two cases, the judge saying that as every time the song was sung it was getting a free advertisement, there was no way he could expect to be paid, as the free publicity given to the song was reward enough.[3] Needless to say, Smith heard no more about the matter.

As well as Sunday sacred music concerts in the Floral Hall, in the 1890s, the Saxe-Coburg Street Chapel promoted 'Pleasant Sunday Afternoon' concerts at which local musicians gave free performances of sacred music such as Haydn's *Creation* and Mendelssohn's *Hymn of Praise*. One of the regular singers at these popular musical meetings was Arthur Stork who, in 1903, left Leicester to take up the post of Assistant Inspector of Music for Schools at Bradford.[4]

Another promoter of concerts in the last decade of the nineteenth century was Willibald Richter. Born in Kaslau, Germany, at the age of two he used to 'crow out' the tunes that the street barrel organs played. Young Willi commenced piano lessons when he was five and gave his first public performance, in Munster, when he was eight. Five years later he played before Liszt who, so the story goes, took him in his arms, kissed him and offered to give him lessons. The young man accepted the maestro's offer and went to the Stuttgart Conservatorium where he studied under Professor Lebert and, in his second year, under Liszt himself. After leaving

Willibald Richter, a German by birth, made Leicester his home in the last decade of the nineteenth century. (Wyvern 6 March 1896)

Stuttgart he studied for three more years at the Berlin Hochschule before returning home to become an operatic conductor. In 1881 he was appointed Professor of Music at Uppingham School, where he married one of his private pupils, Carlotta.

In 1887 Richter moved to Leicester where he founded the Leicester and County College of Music at Beaumont House, De Montfort Street. One of his more notable pupils was William Mason, a violinist, who attended the college from 1896-98, and received the highest number of marks of all England in his exams. Lady Rolleston was so impressed with Mason that she raised £100 to send him to a teacher in London.[5]

Richter soon integrated himself into the town's musical circles by producing concerts of chamber music, many of which, no doubt due to the 'highbrow' nature of the music, were poorly attended. Having spent the New Year of 1896 giving recitals in the Casino Assembly Rooms, Biarritz, Richter returned to Leicester where, later that year in the presence of the mayor, James Herbert Marshall, he had to give up playing when damp caused the piano keys to stick. In 1899 he was appointed principal professor of piano at Leeds College of Music. In 1902 he became a British citizen.[6]

Just as the cost of concert tickets come into the reach of more of the population so too had the price of musical instruments. Up to the 1850s pianos cost over a year's pay for a skilled artisan but by 1900, with the real cost halved, there was a piano in 'almost every house'.[7]

Societies

By the end of the nineteenth century Leicester had indeed become a musical town. In 1900, when Sullivan's *Golden Legend* was produced by the Philharmonic Society, for the first time the band was able to consist solely of town musicians playing without the assistance of artists from surrounding counties.[8]

As well as the main musical societies in the town by 1900 there were choirs being formed such as the Wesley Hall Orchestral Band founded by Mr Deacon; the West End Choral Society who gave concerts in the Museum Lecture Hall; and St Leonard's Choral Society which Walter Groocock formed in 1900.[9]

Leicester also 'exported' musical talent such as Lina Wingrave, who had sung soprano in St Stephen's choir before moving to the south of

England to become Music and Drama Critic for the *Worthing Gazette* and *Folkestone Telegraph.* In 1898 she emigrated to Frankfurt, and then to South Africa where she married William Keith of the *Transvaal Advertiser.*[10]

In 1904 Cyrus B. Gamble, a viola player of Halford Street, discovered among a collection of music, which had once belonged to E.W. Thomas, conductor of the Royal Opera House and had been purchased by his late father in 1892, *Rule Britannia,* a lost overture by Richard Wagner which had been written in 1837. This important find, which was to be published in 1908, came to the attention of *Punch* who remarked:[11]

Excoriating! Mr Gamble, the discoverer of Wagner's 'Rule Britannia Overture', has had to pay dearly for his good fortune. Every post brings him applications from batsmen who have failed, asking him if he can discover their lost scores too!

The Municipal Orchestra

In June 1895 the Philharmonic Society, which had just made a loss of £50, expressed the hope of being able to erect a more capacious building than the Temperance Hall and also to form a town orchestra. However, after much discussion it was decided that the town would not be able to afford to support such a venture.[12] Three years later, in 1898, through the efforts of James Marshall and John Smith, the germ of such a band, called the Leicester Permanent Orchestra came into being under the direction of Karl Johannessen.

Norwegian-born Johannessen had come to Leicester in 1896

Karl Johanessen (1870–1904) was a Norwegian-born violinist who lived and worked in Leicester 1896–1899.
(Wyvern 8 December 1900)

to take over from Theodore Kienle, who for three years had been a violin teacher at Richter's school of music. In 1879, aged 9, Johannessen had been admitted to the Stockholm Royal Academy of Music. Young Karl made his debut four years later with the orchestra of the Royal Theatre when he was roused from his sleep at two in the morning when one of the principal players had fallen ill. After practising the part all day, the thirteen year old played in the evening concert before the King. After living in Leicester for three years he moved to Ledbury where he died in 1904 aged 35.[13]

In March 1899 there was an appeal for amateur musicians to join the fourteen professionals who were to form, what was to be the Leicester Municipal Orchestra. This core of professionals consisted of Theodore Kienle and John Kilby (violin), Cyrus B. Gamble (viola), John Addison Adcock (cello), Joseph Muston (bass), Mr Geary (flute), Mr Hewitt (oboe), Walter Waddington (trumpet), Mr Bird (bassoon), Mr Matthews (clarinet), Mr Butler (horn), Harry Matthews and Mr Castle (trombones), and Mr Lant (drums). The first conductor was Henry Ellis who directed the band until 1904 when John Addison Adcock took over.[14]

The first concert by the Municipal Orchestra took place in the Floral Hall in October 1899, included Beethoven's *Prometheus* and Schubert's *Unfinished Symphony*. Although the 18 professionals and 24 amateur players put on a first rate performance, it was felt that this programme was too high class to suit the musical taste of the intended audience, so the next concert, the following February in a less than half-full Temperance Hall, was more light-natured including the overture to the *Magic Flute* and *The Lost Chord*, played as a cornet solo by Walter Waddington.[15]

Not withstanding the greatly improved standard of the orchestra its support did not improve. The 1900 Christmas concert, which included Beethoven's *Symphony in C*, Schubert's overture to *Rosamunde*, Mendlessohn's *Athalie* and German's three dances from *Nell Gwyn* only attracted a few hundred concert-goers. It was noted that although there were many young people playing stringed instruments there were very few in the wind section, children preferring to learn to play the violin or cello rather than the flute, clarinet or oboe.[16] From as early as 1901 there were plans to axe the orchestra but it survived until 1910 when it was disbanded. The reasons given at the time were

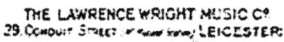

Lawrence Wright, Leicester-born song-writer.

the lack of a large hall and the infrequency of its performances. Three years later the town did get its purpose-built concert hall – the De Montfort Hall.

Lawrence Wright

One of the best known Leicester-born musicians of the early twentieth century was Lawrence Wright. Born in 1888, at 23 Conduit Street, where his father had a music shop, by the time he was 14 he could play five instruments. He had also gained a basic knowledge of printing having worked in a local printing shop. In 1902 he went to Eastbourne to join a concert party where he was paid £2 a week for playing banjo, violin and mandolin as well as singing. The next year he joined a concert party at Mundesley-on-Sea where he had to give his landlady his gold watch to pay for his rent. On his return to Leicester he borrowed £18 and set up a music stall on the Market. He soon became well-known due to his practice of attracting customers by playing tunes on the mandolin. In 1906 he rented a shop at 29 Lower Conduit Street and the Wright Music Company was born with the publication of his first song 'Down by the Stream'. In 1908 Wright wrote 'The Pride of the Force' a memorial march dedicated to Leicester's 24 stone Police Constable John 'Tubby' Stephens who died in April of that year.[17]

Into the twentieth century

Throughout the second half of the nineteenth century the people of the town became more tolerant of each others beliefs, both political and religious. At the beginning of the century the town had been much divided between Anglicans on the one hand and Dissenters on the other. By 1891 differences were being put aside and, in a musical sense, there was a fraternal feeling existing among all the members of the religious community - churchmen, Roman Catholics and dissenters - who were constantly in the habit of assisting each other at their respective places of worship. Along with this the objections to the introduction of instruments in churches were also gradually disappearing, with regular musical masses being performed in Holy Cross Church, organ recitals in the the town's main churches and small orchestral works in the chapels.

With the outbreak of World War I many musical activities in the town were suspended for the duration. The only society that survived was the Philharmonic, indeed it is still in existence and going strong today. The De Montfort Hall is still the city's only purpose-built concert hall, the Temperance Hall, which degenerated into a cinema before being demolished in the 1950s. There is, therefore, very little left in the city to remind us of nineteenth century musical Leicester except the 'Assembly Room', Hotel Street, and the 'New Hall' both of which have escaped the hands of the developers who took away so much of our heritage in the 1950s and 60s. How much of today's Leicester, I wonder, will be still standing at the end of the twenty-first century?

𝄞 CODETTA 1 𝄞

The New Philharmonic Society band members in 1866, as listed in the *Leicester Journal*, 30 Nov 1866.

Violins: Henry Farmer, Thomas Weston, Mr Gibson, Mr Wesley, Christopher Oldershaw, Mr Hayward, Mr Taylor, Mr Foster, John Kilby, Mr Kirkby, Mr Denis, Mr Orchard, Mr Henshaw, John Wesley. Violas: Mr Graham, William Rowlett, Rev John Myers, James Fozzard. Cellos: Mr Selby, Mr Stanyon, Thomas Atkins Wykes, George Inchley. Basses: Thomas Weston. Charles Nicholson, Mr Waring, Joseph Lucas. Flutes: William Nicholson (son of Henry Nicholson junior). Clarinet: Mr Harvey. Trumpet: John Smith. Horns: Frederick Seal, W. Wesley. Trombones: Mr Freestone, Mr Lawrence. Drums: Mr Barnard. Harmonium: George Löhr and William Tertius Rowlett.

CODETTA 2

The members of Philharmonic Society's orchestra in 1897, as listed in *The Wyvern*, 5 November 1897.

Violins: G. H. Betjemann (leader), Theodore Kienle, John Kilby, Richard C. Allen, Arthur Pelham Hanford, C. Mansfield, Jethro Raymond Orgill, Mr Tyler, Richard Mangan, H. A. Marshall. Violas: T. Lawrence, T. Carter, George Tuffley, H. Wykes. Cellos: E. Woodhouse, William Edward Bailey, Mr Durrad, William Rowlett. Basses: J. Hayden, Mr Waud, Joseph Muston, Earnest Albert Gamble. Flutes: H. Hollis, Frederick Seal. Oboes: G. Horton, William Tertius Rowlett. Clarinets: J. Egerton, Frank Rowlett. Bassoons: John Hutchins, Thomas Atkins Wykes. Horns: W. Busby, John Brain, Mr Butler. Trumpets: W. Short, Mr Geary. Trombone: Mr Muller, J. Matt. Tuba: John Castle. Harp: A. Putnam. Tympani: C. Henderson. Bass Drum: Mr Lant.

CODETTA 3

In December 1891 readers of *The Wyvern* were invited to vote for their favourite local musician. The result, published the following January, was:

Henry Nicholson 578 votes.
Henry Bramley Ellis 577 votes.
Joseph Herbert Marshall 548 votes.
Charles Hancock 505 votes.
Alfred Page 186 votes.
Thomas Burnett Laxton 125 votes.
John Alfred Smith 115 votes.
John Addison Adcock 115 votes.

End Notes

Chapter 1

1 O. Deutsch, *Handel A Documentary Biography* p460; Anon, *An Enquiry into the Melancholy Circumstances of Great Britain*.
2 G. A. Chinnery, *Records of the Borough of Leicester 1689–1835*.
3 *Leicester Journal* 21 December 1824.
4 J. Wilshere, *Leicester Towne Waytes*; *Leicester Chronicle* 28 November 1840.
5 *Leicester Chronicle* 20 December 1842.
6 C. Billson, *Leicester Memoirs* p103; E. D. Mackerness, *A Social History of English Music* p89.
7 G. A. Chinnery, *Records of the Borough of Leicester 1689–1835*.
8 J. Thompson, *Leicester in the Eighteenth Century* p45; G. A. Chinnery, *Records of the Borough of Leicester 1689–1835*.
9 St Martin's Church Warden Accounts; MacNutt and Slater, *Leicester Cathedral Organ*.
10 J. Thompson, *Leicester in the Eighteenth Century* pp94–98.
11 *Leicester Journal* 5 June 1762; J. Prophet, *Church Langton and William Hanbury* pp59–60.
12 W. Gardiner, *Music and Friends* vol i pages 3 and 71; H. Thomas, *History of the Great Meeting* p82; *Leicester Journal* 2 January 1801.
13 W. Gardiner, *Music and Friends* vol i p314–315; H. Thomas, *History of the Great Meeting* p57.
14 J. Cradock, *Literary and Musical Memories* vol i p.xxii; *Leicester Journal* 11 September 1771.
15. In 1797 Miss Greatorex seems to have had some unauthorised days off for she was reprimanded by the Corporation, who were paying her annual salary of £10, for neglecting her duties on the days that the Corporation attended civic services at St Martin's. When, in 1800, Miss Greatorex moved to Burton-on-Trent, Sarah Valentine took over, being paid the same civic salary until the demise of the closed corporation in 1835.
16 J. Thompson, *Leicester in the Eighteenth Century* p145–6, 150; W. Gardiner, *Music and Friends* vol iii p156; G. A. Chinnery *Records of the Borough of Leicester*; J. Cradock. *Literary and Musical Memories* vol i p119.

17 J. Cradock, *Literary and Musical Memories* vol i p.xxiv. The penultimate line of the ode is a reference to *Othello* 'the flinty and steel couch of war my thrice-driven bed of down.'(I.iii.227).
18 W. Gardiner, *Music and Friends* vol i pp4–6, 228 vol ii p629; J. Nichols, *History and Antiquities of Leicestershire* vol i p523.
19 W. Gardiner. *Music and Friends* vol i pp16–22.
20 J. Thompson, *Leicester in the Eighteenth Century* p154; W. Gardiner, *Music and Friends* vol iii p7–9; J. Thompson, *Leicester in the Eighteenth Century* p168; N. Temperley, ed., *Music in Britain – The Romantic Age 1800–1914* p135.
21 *Leicester Journal* 8 October 1802; 17 September 1819; 12 September 1822; 10 September 1824.
22 W. Gardiner, *Music and Friends* vol i pp54, 140, 353.
23 W. Gardiner, *Music and Friends* vol i p7. It was William Tilley, the coroner for the county, who, in January 1760, signed the committal to Leicester gaol of Lord Ferrers for the murder of his steward. The earl was subsequently hanged at Tyburn.
24 W. Gardiner, *Music and Friends* vol i p70.
25 A. Temple-Patterson, *Radical Leicester* p66; W. Gardiner, *Music and Friends* vol iii pp128–129. The first recorded organ at St Margaret's is a secondhand one (built by Father Bernard Smith 1629–1708), tuned so that it would not interfere with the bells, installed in 1773. This instrument, which served the church until 1883, was sold to Bishop Street Chapel for £195. The first organist we know of is Ann Valentine who was in office by 1791 and still in post, on a salary of ten pounds, in 1834.
26 W. Gardiner, *Music and Friends* vol i pp112–113; *Leicester Journal* 30 January 1880.
27 W. Gardiner, *Music and Friends* vol iii pp329–340.
28 W. Gardiner, *Music and Friends* vol i p362.
29 W. Gardiner, *Music and Friends* vol i pp33–34; *The New Grove Dictionary of Music and Musicians*.

Chapter 2

1 A. Temple-Patterson, *Radical Leicester* pp89–91.
2 *Leicester Journal* 24 July 1801.
3 *Leicester Journal* 13 Febuary, 16 October 1801, 15 December 1815; C. Billson, *Leicester Memoirs* p109.
4 I. Ellis, *Nineteenth Century Leicester* p188; *Leicester Journal* 6 April 1838.
5 *Leicester Journal* 14 February 1851, 9 December 1859.

6 *Leicester Journal* 19 July 1816.
7 *Leicester Journal* 27 June 1817.
8 J. & T. Spencer, *Leicestershire and Rutland Notes and Queries* p34.
9 *Leicester Journal* 19 January 1827, 25 January 1833.
10 *Leicester Journal* 17 June 1836, 23 January 1846.
11 *Leicester Journal* 7 January 1848; *Leicester Chronicle* 10 March 1849.
12 *Leicester Journal* 4 November 1803, 22 January 1808; 21 July 1809.
13 *Leicester Journal* 22 April 1813; 6 October 1814; 24 January 1817; 2 April 1819.
14 *Leicester Journal* 7 October 1803, 28 January 1820.
15 *Leicester Journal* 31 July 1825; 19 July 1833; 24 January 1834; 22 January 1835.
16 *Leicester Journal* 26 June 1801; 29 July 1808; 6 January 1816; 28 July 1826; 22 January 1831; 14 January 1832.
17 *Leicester Journal* 25 March 1814; 21 April 1820; 31 January, 4 July 1823.
18 *Leicester Journal* 25 September 1846; 24 March 1848; 9 January 26 March 1852, 19 December 1856, 25 December 1857; I. Ellis, *Nineteenth Century Leicester* pp24 and 201.
19 *The Times* 26 March 1862; *Leicester Journal* 2, 23 May 1862; 5 August 1864; 5 June 1874.
20 *Leicester Journal* 13 January 1815, 16 March 1849; T. Combe, *Leicester Directory* 1827.
21 A. Fielding-Johnson, *Glimpses of Ancient Leicester* pp369-70; *Leicester Journal* 10 August 1849.
22 *Leicester Journal* 25 October 1833, 14 February 1834; *The New Grove Dictionary of Music and Musicians.*

Chapter 3
1 *Leicester Journal* 15 July 1803.
2 *Leicester Journal* 13 October, 3 November 1815.
3 *Leicester Journal* 18 August 1826, 28 December 1827.
4 *Leicester Journal* 15 October 1802.
5 *Leicester Journal* 15 April 1813; 9 February 1815.
6 *Leicester Journal* 5 March 1813.
7 *Leicester Journal* 27 January 1814.
8 W. Gardiner, *Music and Friends* vol iii pp488-90; *Leicester Journal* 5 August, 7 October 1814; 30 July 1819; 18 October 1822; 7

February 1823; February 1868.
9 *Leicester Journal* 28 October, 11 November 1814.
10 *Leicester Journal* 30 December 1814; 24 February, 28 April 1815.
11 W. Gardiner, *Music and Friends* vol i p316; *Leicester Journal* 26 November 1819; 24 March 1815.
12 *Leicester Journal* 14 June, 30 August 1822; 30 March, 15 June 1827.
13 *Leicester Journal* 2 March 1827, 21 Nov 1828.
14 *Leicester Journal* 28 April 1815, 12 September 1817.
15 *Leicester Journal* 31 March 1815; W. Gardiner, *Music and Friends* vol ii pp506.
16 *Leicester Journal* 22 Sept 1815, 9 August 1816, 27 January 1826, 18 September 1830; W. Gardiner, *Music and Friends* vol ii pp506–8.
17 *Leicester Journal* 22 March 1816, 21 March 1817; W. Gardiner, *Music and Friends* vol ii p527.
18 *Leicester Journal* 9 September 1836.
19 *Leicester Journal* 17 June 1802; 14 October 1803; C. Billson, *Leicester Memoirs* p119.
20 *Leicester Journal* 29 February 1828; *Leicester Chronicle* 18 April 1829.
21 W. Gardiner, *Music and Friends* vol iii p634; *Leicester Journal* 3 December 1824; *Leicester Journal* 2 December 1825.
22 *Leicester Journal* 28 July, 15 December 1826.
23 *Leicester Chronicle* 9 May 1829, 20 November, 24 December 1830; R. Williams, *The Parish Church of St Helen, Ashby de la Zouch* p11.
24 *Leicester Chronicle* 8 August, 25 September 1830; *Leicester Journal* 10 March 1815.
25 *Leicester Journal* 23 March, 21 June 1827; W. Gardiner. *Music and Friends* vol i p211.
26 *Leicester Journal* 15 June 1827; 20 June 1828.
27 *Leicester Chronicle* 24 January 1829; 4 April 1829; *Leicester Journal* 26 September 1829; 3 April 1830.

Chapter 4

1 *Leicester Journal* 25 December 1807, 14 February 1880; *Leicester Guardian* 16 May 1903.
2 *Leicester Journal* 29 April 1814; 12 May 1826; G.A. Chinnery *Records of the Borough of Leicester*.
3 *Leicester Journal* 18 February 1820; 12 July 1822, 7 December

1823, January 1825; 28 April; 15 December 1826.
4 *Leicester Chronicle* 1 January 1831; *Leicester Journal* 31 December 1831; 9 May 1834.
5 *Leicester Journal* 2 November 1849; 16 April 1852; 15 October 1858.
6 I. Ellis, *Nineteenth Century Leicester* pp172–3.
7 *Leicester Guardian* 16 May 1903; *Leicester Journal* 1 June 1856.
8 *Leicester Journal* 28 March 1862.
9 *Leicester Journal* 23, 30 November 1866.
10 *Wyvern* 15 May, 30 October 1896.
11 *Wyvern* 5 May 1899; *Leicester Guardian* 23 May 1903.
12 *Leicester Journal* 22 November 1822; 22 April 1825.
13 *Leicester Journal* 22 April, 18 November 1825; 17 October 1826; 3 May 1827; 16 May 1828; *Leicester Chronicle* 4 June 1829; 14 September 1830.
14 *Leicester Journal* 31 March 1826; 25 August 1848; Census Returns.
15 *Leicester Journal* 5 November 1852; 20 March 1857; 2 April 1858; 22 June, 23 November 1860. M. Wade-Matthews *Great Glen, the Story of a Leicestershire Village*.
16 *Leicester Journal* 24 January 1817; 28 March, 25 July 1823; 15 July, 5 October, 23 December 1825; 30 June 1826.
17 *Leicester Chronicle* 20 November 1830.
18 *Leicester Journal* 21 July 1826; 14 September 1832; *Leicester Chronicle* 8 October 1831.
19 *Leicester Chronicle* 24 December 1830; *Leicester Journal* 21 February 1834; 24 November 1848. The first recorded use of the word 'hit' used in this context occurs in W. H. Ireland's *Scribbleomania* published in 1815.
20 Leicester Journal 10 December 1852; 18 May 1855; 3 December 1858; 30 April 1869.
21 *Leicester Journal* 5 August 1864.
22 *Leicester Journal* 15 April, 23 September 1814; 18 February 1820; 26 June 1835.
23 *Leicester Journal* 25 October 1878; 31 January 1879; 3 June 1881.
24 *Leicester Journal* 16 January 1880; 26 May 1882; *Saturday Herald* 8 January 1887; *Wyvern* 22 April 1898.
25 *Leicester Journal* 7 July 1882; 24 August 1883; 17 October 1884.
26 *Wyvern* 17 February 1893, 18 February 1898; *Leicester Guardian* 11 August 1900.

27 *Leicester Guardian* 16 February 1901.
28 *Leicester Guardian* 8 October 1904.
29 *Leicester Daily Mercury* 6 January 1880; *Leicester Guardian* 11 November 1899; *Leicester Journal* 12 January 1877.
30 *Leicester Guardian* 8 June 1901.

Chapter 5
1 *Leicester Journal* 6 May 1803: W. Gardiner, *Music and Friends* vol i p372.
2 *The Times* 10 October 1826.
3 Anon. *An Account of the Grand Music Festival held at Leicester* p.7.
4 Anon. *An Account of the Grand Music Festival held at Leicester* p.9.
5 Infirmary Committee Minutes.
6 *Dictionary of National Biography*.
7 W. Gardiner, *Music and Friends* vol i p361. *Dictionary of National Biography*.
8 Infirmary Committee Minutes; *Dictionary of National Biography*.
9 *The New Grove Dictionary of Music and Musicians*.
10 W. Gardiner, *Music and Friends* vol *i* pp8–9, 322; *ii* p528; *iii* p108; *The New Grove Dictionary of Music and Musicians*.
11 M. Wade-Matthews, *The Monuments of the Church of St Martin, Leicester*.
12 W. Gardiner, *Music and Friends* vol *iii* p107
13 Infirmary Committee Minutes.
14 *Leicester Chronicle* 21 April 1827; Infirmary Committee Minutes.
15 *Leicester Journal* 18 August 1827.
16 Infirmary Committee Minutes.
17 Infirmary Committee Minutes; W. Gardiner, *Music and Friends* vol *i* p230.
18 *The New Grove Dictionary of Music and Musicians*; *Leicester Chronicle* 8 September 1827.
19 *Leicester Chronicle* 8 September 1827.
20 Anon. *An Account of the Grand Music Festival held at Leicester* p.12.
21 Infirmary Committee Minutes; *Leicester Chronicle* 8 September 1827.
22 Infirmary Committee Minutes.
23 Infirmary Committee Minutes; Anon. *An Account of the Grand Music Festival held at Leicester* p.47. *Leicester Journal* 15

September 1827.
24 *Leicester Chronicle* 1 September 1827.
25 *Leicester Journal* 31 August 1827.
26 *Leicester Chronicle* 8 September 1827.
27 *Leicester Journal* 7 September 1827.
28 *Leicester Journal* 24 August, 7 September 1827.
29 *Leicester Journal* 31 September 1827; *Leicester Chronicle* 8 September 1827.
30 *Leicester Chronicle* 1 September 1827.
31 Anon. *An Account of the Grand Music Festival held at Leicester* p15.
32 Anon. *An Account of the Grand Music Festival held at Leicester* p19.
33 *Leicester Journal* 7 September 1827.
34 *Leicester Journal* 7 September 1827; Anon. *An Account of the Grand Music Festival held at Leicester* p15.
35 *Leicester Journal* 7, 24 September 1827.
36 Anon. *An Account of the Grand Music Festival held at Leicester* p10.
37 *Leicester Chronicle* 8 September 1827; Anon. *An Account of the Grand Music Festival held at Leicester* pp36, 40.
38 Anon. *An Account of the Grand Music Festival held at Leicester* pp17, 25, 35 and 39.
39 Anon. *An Account of the Grand Music Festival held at Leicester* p21.
40 *Leicester Chronicle* 8 September 1827.
41 *Leicester Chronicle* 8 September 1827.
42 Anon. *An Account of the Grand Music Festival held at Leicester* p46; *Leicester Chronicle* 8 September 1827.
43 *Leicester Journal* 7, 14 September 1827.
44 Infirmary Committee Minutes.

Chapter 6
1 *Leicester Chronicle* 9 October 1830; 15 January, 16 April 1831.
2 *Leicester Chronicle* 24 December 1830; 28 May, 4 June 1831.
3 *Leicester Journal* 16 November 1832; *The New Grove Dictionary of Music and Musicians.*
4 *The New Grove Dictionary of Music and Musicians.*
5 A. Fielding-Johnson, *Glimpses of Ancient Leicester* p368; *Leicester Chronicle* 2 February 1833.
6 *Leicester Chronicle* 5 January 1833; *The New Grove Dictionary of*

Music and Musicians.
7 *Leicester Journal* 29 March, 26 April 13 September, 20 December 1833.
8 *Leicester Journal* 21 February 1834.
9 *Leicester Chronicle* 8 June, 12 October 1833.
10 *Leicester Journal* 6 September 1833; *The New Grove Dictionary of Music and Musicians.*
11 *Leicester Journal* 31 January 1834.
12 *Leicester Journal* 3 January 1834.
13 *Leicester Journal* 17 January 1834; *Leicester Chronicle* 5 April 1845; R. Read, *Modern Leicester* p217 (who mistakenly puts Toone's year of death as 1859).
14 *Leicester Journal* 26 September, 5 December 1834.
15 *Leicester Journal* 13 January, 4 September 1835.
16 *Leicester Journal* 12 December 1835.
17 *Leicester Chronicle* 27 March 1830; 20 February 1836; *Leicester Journal* 26 February, 18 April 1836.
18 *Leicester Journal* 15 April 1835; *Leicester Chronicle* 23 April 1836.
19 *Leicester Journal* 19 September 1834.
20 *Leicester Journal* 11 September 1846; 25 August 1848.
21 *Leicester Chronicle* 30 November 1838.
22 *Leicester Journal* 25 September 1846.
23 *Leicester Journal* 28 March 1851.
24 *Leicester Journal* 17 March 1865; *Punch* March 1851.
25 *Leicester Journal* 2 April 1858; 20 April 1860.
26 *Leicester Journal* 19 January 1827.
27 *Leicester Journal* 10 July 1846.
28 *Leicester Journal* 1 June 1849.
29 *Leicester Journal* 31 August, 21 December 1849; 18 January 1850.
30 *Leicester Journal* 2 July 1847; 9 November 1849; I. Ellis, *Nineteenth Century Leicester* p252.
31 *Leicester Journal* 11 October 1850.
32 *Leicester Journal* 1 November, 6 December 1850.
33 *Leicester Journal* 10 January 1851.
34 Leicester Journal 2 January, 16 January 1852.
35 *Leicester Chronicle* 11 September 1840.
36 *Leicester Journal* 12 July 1850.
37 *Leicester Journal* 13 December 1850.
38 Mary Kirby, *Leaflets from my Life* p30; *Wyvern* 24 September

1897.
39 W. Gardiner, *Music and Friends* Vol ii p594.
40 *Wyvern* 22 January 1897; A. Fielding-Johnson, *Glimpses of Ancient Leicester* pp356/7; *Leicester Journal* 19 December 1823.
41 *Leicester Journal* 21 October 1853.
42 *Leicester Journal* 6 October 1851. *Leicester Journal* 16 October 1857; 26 May 1865.
43 *Leicester Journal* 1 November 1850.
44 *Leicester Journal* 7 October 1853.
45 *Leicester Journal* 15 December 1854.

Chapter 7
1 M. Wade-Matthews, *Grave Matters* p2; *Leicester Journal* 19 December 1851; 19 March, 9 April, 23 April, 28 May, 23 Sept 1852, 23 September 1853.
2 *Leicester Journal* 28 May 1852; 26 August 1853; 16 August 1878; M. Wade-Matthews *Grave Matters* p32.
3 *Leicester Journal* 16, 23 September 1853.
4 *Leicester Journal* 16 September 1853.
5 *Leicester Journal* 9 September 1853.
6 *Leicester Journal* 21 October 1853.
7 *Leicester Journal* 23 December 1853; 2 December 1864. The Leicester Temperance Hall was not alone in suffering from this problem. In London the St James Hall, built in 1858, held concerts of chamber music which were often spoilt by the sound of the Christy Minstrels performing in the adjacent room.
8 *Leicester Journal* 18 December 1868; 29 January 1869. Alfred G. Vance (real name Alfred Peck Stevens) surnamed 'The Great Vance', was a comic impersonator who specialised in Cockney dialect studies and was said to appeal to 'those whom that class of entertainment has always peculiar attraction' came to the town in 1868, 1869, 1870, 1871 and 1876.
9 *Leicester Journal* 9 October 1857.
10 *Leicester Journal* 23 October 1857.
11 *Leicester Journal* 6 November 1857.
12 *Leicester Journal* 12, 26 December 1862.
13 *Leicester Journal* 25 January 1867; 28 April 1882; 9 March 1883; 21 November 1884.
14 *Leicester Journal* 12 May 1865; 6 March, 15, 29 October 1880.
15 *Leicester Journal* 10 September, 12 November 1880; 25 February, 13 May 1881.

16 *Leicester Journal* 29 February 1856, 28 March 1862; *Leicester Chronicle* 1 March 1856.
17 *Leicester Journal* 14 February; 21, 28 March 1862.
18 *Illustrated London News* 15 March 1856; *Leicester Journal* 4, 26 September, 21 November 1856.
19 *Leicester Journal* 19 November 1858.
20 *Leicester Journal* 28 January 1859.
21 *The New Grove Dictionary of Music and Musicians.*
22 *Leicester Journal* 19 March 1852.
23 *Leicester Journal* 4 February 1853.
24 *Leicester Journal* 4 January 1856; 15 October 1875.
25 *Leicester Journal* 3 May 1850; 21 January 1853; 12 June 1857; 5 November 1858; 31 December 1859; 15 October 1869. 26 *Leicester Journal* 5 February 1847; 26 March, 20 August 1858.
27 *Leicester Journal* 29 November 1861.
28 *Leicester Journal* 24 December 1869.
29 *Leicester Journal* 10 October 1862.
30 R. Read *Modern Leicester* p218; *Leicester Journal* 28 October 1864.
31 *Leicester Journal* 18 November 1864.
32 *Leicester Journal* 17 January, 25 April 1873; 4 September 1874; *Wyvern* 18 March 1898.
33 *Leicester Journal* 7 June 1872, 23 November 1883; *Wyvern* January 5 1894.
34 *Leicester Journal* 3 April 1880, 7 April 1882; *Wyvern* 23 October 1896, 19 November 1897.
35 *Leicester Journal* 17 February 1871, 24 November 1876; *Leicester Chronicle* 4 April 1874; *Wyvern* 10 September 1897.
36 *Leicester Journal* 3 November 1876.
37 *Leicester Journal* 10 March 1876; *Wyvern* 9 March 1894.
38 *Leicester Journal* 12 January 1855.
39 *Leicester Journal* 12 December 1856; 22 January 1858.
40 *Leicester Journal* 27 February 1852; 4 December 1874.
41 *Leicester Journal* 21, 28 May 1852.
42 *Punch* vol xxiii p159; *Leicester Journal* 18 March 1853; 26 September 1856.
43 *Leicester Journal* 2 May 1862; 1 January 1875.
44 *Leicester Journal* 2 November 1883; *Wyvern* 2 June 1893.
45 *Leicester Journal* 31 March; 7 July, 25 August, 15 December 1876.

Chapter 8
1 Letter from Mr Nicholson; *Leicester Journal* 4 February 1822; 2 September 1825; A. Fielding-Johnson *Glimpses of Ancient Leicester* p402; *Leicester Chronicle* 14 January 1832.
2 *Leicester Journal* 14 April 1820; 30 May 1823.
3 *Leicester Chronicle* 21 May 1831.
4 *Leicester Journal* 10 July 1846; 11 February, 9 December 1859.
5 *Wyvern* 2 March 1894.
6 *Leicester Journal* 22 July 1853; 30 June 1854; 13 November 1857.
7 *Leicester Journal* 28 October 1859, 15 January 1864.
8 *Wyvern* 27 November 1891; *Leicester Guardian* 22 February 1901.
9 *Wyvern* 27 November 1891; *Leicester Chronicle* 15 March 1845.
10 *Leicester Guardian* 28 March 1903; Letter from Mr Nicholson.
11 *Leicester Journal* 15 May 1846.
12 *Leicester Journal* 13 August 1852; 3 February 1854; 16 March 1855.
13 *Leicester Journal* 10 March 1854; 30 January 1880; *Nottingham Journal* 8 April 1836.
14 *Leicester Journal* 19 January 1855.
15 *Leicester Journal* 4 January 1856; 28 November 1856.
16 *Leicester Journal* 4 February 1859; 16 March 1860.
17 *Leicester Journal* 14 April 1857; *Illustrated London News* 27 June 1857.
18 *Leicester Journal* 16 November 1866; 19 November 1880.
19 *Leicester Journal* 11 September 1857.
20 *Leicester Journal* 11, 24 November 1854; 18 December 1857.
21 *Leicester Journal* 26 June 1846; 28 September 1849; 25 April 1873; *Wyvern* 8 December 1893.
22 *Leicester Journal* 30 April, 11 June 1858.
23 *Leicester Journal* 12 October 1850; 30 November 1866; 27 August 1880.
24 *Leicester Journal* 9 October 1857, 8 May 1858.
25 *Leicester Journal* 18 March, 1 April, 20 May 1859; 19 April 1861.
26 *Wyvern* 27 November 1891; *Leicester Journal* 13 January 1865.
27 *Leicester Journal* 14 June 1867; 17 February 1871.
28 *Leicester Journal* 21 October, 25 November 1870, 24 February 1882.
29 *Leicester Journal* 31 October 1884; 26 January 1872.
30 C. Dickens *Sketches by Boz.*
31 *Leicester Journal* 21 June 1868; 29 September 1876, 1 November 1878.

32 *Leicester Journal* 20 September, 18 October 1861, 19 October 1860.
33 *Leicester Journal* 3 October 1879.
34 *Leicester Journal* 30 March 1860; 16 September 1881; *Wyvern* 25 November 1898.
35 Letter from Mr Nicholson.
36 *Leicester Chronicle* 2 April 1845; *Leicester Journal* 18 January 1850.
37 *Leicester Journal* 25 September, 23 October 1868; *Leicester Guardian* 28 May 1904.
38 Letter from Mr Nicholson.
39 *Leicester Journal* 24 April 1856; 12 March 1858.

Chapter 9
1 *Leicester Journal* 29 October 1858.
2 *Leicester Journal* 25 March 1864; *Wyvern* 2 February 1894.
3 *Leicester Guardian* 15 June 1901; H. and R. Leacroft, *The Theatre in Leicestershire* p63; *The Times* 13 June 1901.
4 *Leicester Journal* 30 April 1869; 17 August; 14 September, 2 November 1877; *Wyvern* 15 October 1897.
5 *Leicester Journal* 11 March, 6 May 1870; 18 February 1876.
6 C. Billson, *Leicester Memoirs* p120; *Leicester Journal* 9 May 1879; 20 August 1880.
7 *Leicester Journal* 7 November 1879.
8 *Leicester Journal* 13 May 1881; 8 December 1882; 6 February 1885.
9 *Wyvern* 17 January 1896.
10 *Leicester Journal* 23 May 1851; 31 December 1852; 26 November 1858.
11 *Leicester Journal* 9 June, 20 October, 5 November 1854.
12 *Leicester Journal* 19 May 1854.
13 *Leicester Journal* 6 January, 24 August 1860.
14 *Leicester Journal* 11 January 1861; 12 October 1866; 14 August 1868.
15 *Leicester Journal* 9 May 1862; 24 November 1865; 1 April 1870.
16 *Leicester Journal* 22 November 1861.
17 *The Times* 19 September 1861; E. Adams, *Great Britain and the American Civil War* vol ii pp6–7; *Leicester Journal* 12 December 1862.
18 *Leicester Journal* 15 March, 3 May 1867; 25 September 1868.
19 *Leicester Journal* 2 February, 9 March, 25 May 1866.

20 *Leicester Journal* 13 October 1871; I. Ellis, *Nineteenth Century Leicester* p88.
21 *Leicester Journal* 24 November 1867.
22 *Leicester Journal* 4, 18 December 1868; 19 March, 8 October 1869.
23 *Leicester Chronicle* 4 April 1874; *Wyvern* 5 November 1897.
24 *Leicester Journal* 30 March 1883; 18 April 1884.
25 *Wyvern* 13 March 1896.

Chapter 10
1 Churchwarden Accounts.
2 M Wade-Matthews. *The Monument of the Church of St Margarets.*
3 *Leicester Journal* 4 August 1826; 21 December 1832; 17 October 1834; 5 June, 7 August 1846.
4 *Leicester Journal* 18 February 1848; 25 April 1851; 15 July 1853;
5 *Leicester Journal* 9 July 1847; 20 January 1860.
6 *Leicester Journal* 31 October 1879.
7 *Leicester Journal* 27 September 1861; 4 October 1867; 18 September 1868.
8 *Leicester Journal* 31 October 1879; *Leicester Guardian* 31 January 1903; 3 March 1900.
9 *Leicester Guardian* 19 December 1903; *Leicester Journal* 15 January 1875; 19 December 1879; 22 September 1882; 8 February 1884; *The Bee* 17 February 1883.
10 *Leicester Journal* 16 February 1872.
11 *Leicester Journal* 20 January 1860; 16 August 1861; 15 December 1871; 10 May 1872.
12 *Leicester Journal* 12 October 1866; 16 November 1871; 10, 31 May, 2 August 1872. 19 September 1873; 12 June 1874; 31 March 1882; *Leicester Guardian* 5 April 1902; *Leicester Daily Mail* 7 February 1874. On leaving Leicester, Crow's teaching practice was taken over by Edward Charles Tompkins of 73 London Road. Tompkins soon after relocated to 20 Friar Lane.
13 *Leicester Journal* 21 October 1870; 10 January 1873; 23 March, 13 July 1866; 30 March 1877; *Leicester Chronicle* 7 March 1874.
14 Letter from Mrs Brown; M. Wade-Matthews *Grave Matters.* The apple-tree is still faring well at 75 Church Street, near the Minster.
15 *Leicester Journal* 25 April 1874.
16 *Leicester Journal* 16 April 1880.
17 *Leicester Journal* 13 August 1875; *Wyvern* 26 February 1892.
18 Letter from Mrs Brown; Leicester Chronicle 30 April 1910.

19 *Leicester Journal* 22 December 1876; *Leicester Guardian* 17 June 1905. Victoria Road is now nominated University Road, the church, on the corner of London Road now being used by the Seventh Day Adventists.
20 *Leicester Chronicle* 16 January 1830, 30 May 1874; *Leicester Journal* 13 December 1867; 21 July 1868; 20 January 1869.
21 *Leicester Journal* 14 January 1870; 28 February, 28 March 1873; *Leicester Guardian* 22 December 1900.
22 *Leicester Journal* 16 June 1871; 12 April 1872; 16 July 1875.
23 *Leicester Journal* 14 April, 15 September 1876; 13 July 1877; 9 September 1881; 31 March 1882.
24 *Leicester Journal* 7 December 1877; 19 September 1884.
25 *Leicester Journal* 28 May, 1 October 1880.
26 *Wyvern* 3 March 1893.
27 *Leicester Guardian* 23, 30 December 1899; *Wyvern* 3 March 1899; LRO Misc 754
28 *Wyvern* 26 March, 9 April 1897; *Leicester Guardian* 28 June 1902.
29 *Wyvern* 15 March 1895, 7 February 1896; *Musical Times* January 1895; *Leicester Guardian* 18 November 1899.
30 *Leicester Guardian* 9 December 1899; 27 August 1904.
31 *Leicester Guardian* 1 July 1905. *Leicester Journal* 2 February 1866; 3 June 1881.
32 W. Gardiner *Music and Friends* vol iii p27; H. Thomas. *History of the Great Meeting* pp85 and 580.
33 *Free Press* 28 August 1909; *Leicester Journal* 24 September 1880.
34 *Wyvern* 2 December 1898.
35 *Leicester Guardian* 11 May 1901; 15 April 1905; C. Aston. *Leicester Polytechnic – Centenary History of the School of Textiles* p4.
36 *Wyvern* 12 April 1895.
37 M. Wade-Matthews. *Grave Matters.*
38 S. Taylor. *S Taylor & Son, Organ builders, New Street Leicester;* *Leicester Journal* 1 October 1880.
39 S. Taylor. *S Taylor & Son, Organ builders, New Street Leicester;* (LRO L681,8166).
40 *Leicester Guardian* 10 February 1900; 6 May 1905.
41 *Wyvern* 24 December 1897; *Leicester Guardian* 27 May 1905.
42 *Leicester Journal* 1 October 1880.
43 *Leicester Journal* 21 April 1882; LRO N/U/179/132/36.
44 T. North. *Church Bells of Leicestershire* pp37–74.

45 J. Thompson. *Leicester in the Eighteenth Century* p148; 'John Martin His Book'.
46 'John Martin His Book'.
47 W. Gardiner. *Music and Friends* vol i p25; 'John Martin His Book'.
48 *Leicester Journal* 3 January 1834; *Leicester Chronicle* 17 March 1832.
49 *Leicester Journal* 28 April 1848; 28 May 1852; 29 December 1854; 9 January 1857.
50 *Leicester Journal* 24 March 1871; 12 April 1872.
51 *Leicester Journal* 22 November 1873.
52 *Leicester Journal* 21 November 1879.
53 *Leicester Journal* 25 June 1880; 12 January 1883.

Chapter 11
1 *Leicester Journal* 16 July 1847.
2 *Leicester Chronicle* 21 July 1843.
3 *Wyvern* 12 February 1892.
4 *Leicester Journal* 21 August 1857, 20 July 1860.
5 *Leicester Journal* 12 April 1861, 15 January 1864.
6 *Leicester Journal* 3 May 1872, 2 June 1876, 26 January 1877; 29 March 1878. Robert Read was an amateur historian who, in 1881, published Modern Leicester. Although some of his dates need verifying the book gives an interesting picture of life in Victorian Leicester.
7 *Leicester Journal* 23 January 1891.
8 *Leicester Journal* 23 January, 30 January 1891.
9 *Leicester Guardian* 1 December 1900, 12 January 1901.
10 *Leicester Journal* 3, 17 June 1853; *Punch* 1851; *Leicester Guardian* 5 July 1902.
11 *Leicester Journal* 1, 8 July 1853.
12 *Leicester Journal* 31 March, 28 April 1854; 8 May 1857.
13 *Leicester Journal* 14 April, 5 May 1854; 11 July 1856.
14 *Leicester Journal* 31 July, 14 August 1857.
15 *Leicester Journal* 5 June 1857, 17 June, 15 July 1859.
16 *Leicester Journal* 16 August 1861, 9 May, 4, 11 July, 15 August 1862.
17 *Leicester Journal* 5 June 1874.
18 I. Ellis. *Nineteenth Century Leicester* p184; *Leicester Journal* 25 July 1856.
19 B. Hall 'On the Performance of Military Bands in the Parks of

London' cited in E. Mackerness. *A Social History of English Music* p186.
20 *Leicester Journal* 8 August, 12 December 1856.
21 *Leicester Journal* 17 July, 7, 14, 21 August 1857; 16 October 1857.
22 *Leicester Daily Mercury* 21 October 1904.
23 *Wyvern* 20 May, 9 June 1893.
24 Park Committee Minutes 21 April 1895; *Wyvern* 1 May, 14 June, 1 August 1895.
25 *Leicester Journal* 27 July, 16 November 1855; 25 April 1856; 21 March 1879; M. Wade-Matthews. *Grave Matters, A Walk Through Welford Road Cemetery, Leicester;* A. Fielding-Johnson. *Glimpses of Ancient Leicester* p369.
26 *Leicester Journal* 12 February, 16 December 1864.
27 *Leicester Journal* 3 June 1864, 17 March, 6 October 1865.
28 *Leicester Journal* 17 May, 21 June, 30 August 1867; A. Fielding-Johnson. *Glimpses of Ancient Leicester* p369.
29 *Leicester Journal* 20 December 1867, 21 March 1879.
30 *Leicester Journal* 7 July 1882.
31 M. Wade-Matthews. *Grave Matters, A Walk Through Welford Road Cemetery, Leicester.*
32 *Wyvern* 10 May 1895.
33 *Leicester Journal* 22 September 1854, 7 January 1870, 1 January, 21 May 1875; *Leicester Chronicle* 4 April 1874.
34 *Leicester Journal* 17 August 1877, 5 March 1884.
35 *Leicester Journal* 25 June 1875; 20 May 1881.
36 *The Bee* 14 October 1882.
37 *Wyvern* 16 June 1899.
38 *Wyvern* 20 July 1894; *Leicester Guardian* 18 November 1899. John Richardson saw it as his duty to help men demobbed from the army find work in his Friar Lane wholesale druggist business. The major formed a works' brass and reed band which, led by his son Hubert, gave popular concerts in the town.
39 *Wyvern* 10 November 1893.
40 *Wyvern* 13 May 1898.
41 *Leicester Guardian* 21 April 1900; 5 December 1903.
42 *Leicester Journal* 19 August 1859.
43 *Leicester Journal* 24 August 1860, 1 July 1864, 6 September 1878.
44 *Leicester Guardian* 6, 21 October 1899.
45 *Leicester Journal* 3 March 1848; 28 July 1858, 9 August 1872.
46 *Leicester Journal* 31 August 1877.

47 *Leicester Guardian* 21 March 1903.
48 Catalogue of the 1897 Leicester Commemorative Exhibition.

Chapter 12
1 *Leicester Journal* 21 September 1866.
2 *Leicester Journal* 20 April 1860; 27 April 1866; 13 May 1870; 15, 22 September 1876.
3 *Leicester Journal* 18 January 1884; *Wyvern* 23 December 1898.
4 *Leicester Journal* 10 October, 5 December 1851; 20 February, 27 August 1852; *Leicester Guardian* 3 September 1904; W. Gardiner *Music and Friends* vol iii p374. The Barrow fossils, are still on display in Leicester's New Walk Museum, while a replica of the pliosaur, or 'Barrow Kipper' is displayed on 'Kipper Island', Barrow-on-Soar.
5 *Leicester Journal* 21 January 1876; *Wyvern* 17 June 1892; *Leicester Guardian* 20 June 1903.
6 *Leicester Journal* 7 April, 26 May 1876.
7 *Leicester Journal* 7 January 1877.
8 *Leicester Journal* 15 September 1876; 9 February, 9 March 1877; 15 March, 18 October 1878.
9 *Leicester Journal* 11 June 1880; 5 October 1883.
10 *Leicester Journal* 12 May, 27 October 1882.
11 *Leicester Journal* 6 April 1883; *Musical Times* 1 June 1883.
12 *Wyvern* 27 November, 11 December 1891; *Leicester Journal* 20 April 1877, 25 April 1879; *Leicester Chronicle* 30 April 1910.
13 *Leicester Journal* 23 May, 11 July 1873; *Leicester Journal* 9 October 1874.
14 *Leicester Journal* 19 March 1875.
15 *Leicester Journal* 26 December 1879.
16 *Wyvern* 24 April, 5 June, 4 December 1896.
17 *Leicester Guardian* 2 December 1899; 19 May 1900.
18 *Wyvern* 24 November 1892.
19 *Wyvern* 30 October 1891, 20 December 1895.
20 *Wyvern* 24 November 1892, 5 April 1895.
21 *Wyvern* 20 May, 24 June 1898.
22 *Leicester Journal* 13 May 1859; 20 Dec 1861.
23 *Leicester Journal* 7 January 1870; I. Ellis *Nineteenth Century Leicester.*
24 *Wyvern* 11 December 1891.
25 *Wyvern* 30 October 1891.
26 *Wyvern* 2 March 1894.

27 *Wyvern* 16 December 1892.
28 *Leicester Journal* 26 November 1858; *Wyvern* 23 March 1894; 13 January 1899.
29 *Leicester Guardian* 6 January 1900; *Wyvern* 12 October 1894.
30 *Wyvern* 17 January 1896, 8 March 1895.
31 *Wyvern* 19 January; 2, 9 February 1894; 6 December 1895, 17 April, 18 December 1896; *Leicester Guardian* 10 November 1900; 28 June 1902.
32 *Wyvern* 22 October 1897; *Leicester Guardian* 13 June 1903.
33 *Leicester Guardian* 26 September 1903, 5 March 1904; *Musical Standard* 1903.
34 *Leicester Journal* 12 July 1878; *Wyvern* 17 March 1893; 15 February; 8 March, 13 December 1895.

Chapter 13
1 *Wyvern* 20 January 1899; *Leicester Guardian* 9 June 1900; 17 February 1906.
2 *Leicester Journal* 4 February, 8 April, 4 November 1881, 14 April 1882.
3 *Leicester Weekly Post* 16 April 1881; *Leicester Journal* 16 June 1882.
4 *Leicester Guardian* 13 June 1903.
5 *Wyvern* 27 May 1898; *Leicester Guardian* 26 May 1900.
6 *Wyvern* 10 January, 11 December 1896; 17 March 1899; *Leicester Guardian* 13 September 1902.
7 *Leicester Guardian* 25 August 1900.
8 *Leicester Guardian* 27 October 1900.
9 *Leicester Guardian* 1, 15 December 1900.
10 *Wyvern* 28 October, 2 December 1898; *Leicester Guardian* 28 May 1904.
11 *Leicester Guardian* 14 May 1904; *Punch* 25 May 1904.
12 *Wyvern* 14 June, 1 Nov 1895.
13 *Wyvern* 2 December 1898.
14 *Wyvern* 3, 10 March 1899; *Leicester Guardian* 14 October 1905.
15 *Leicester Guardian* 21 October 1899, 24 February 1900.
16 *Leicester Guardian* 22 December 1900.
17 L. Wright *Souvenirs for a Century.*

BIBLIOGRAPHY

Newspapers and Periodicals

a) Local
The Bee
Leicester Chronicle
Leicester Daily Mail
Leicester Daily Mercury
Leicester Guardian
Leicester Journal
Leicester Weekly Post
Leicestershire and Rutland Heritage
Nottingham Journal
Saturday Herald
Wyvern

b) National
Bell News and Ringers Record
Free Press
Illustrated London News
Musical Standard
Musical Times
Punch
The Hornet
The Times

Primary Sources
Anon, *An Account of the Grand Music Festival held at Leicester* (Leicester 1828)
Anon, 'Change Ringers Book' (MS notebook, Leicestershire Record Office DE
Catalogue of the Leicester Commemoration Exhibition 1897
Churchwardens Accounts – St Martin's (Leicestershire Record Office)
Churchwardens Accounts – St Margaret's (Leicestershire Record Office)
Martin, John, 'John Martin His Book' (MS notebook, Leicestershire Record Office DE 2641/112)

Leicester Council Park Committee Minutes (Leicestershire Record Office)
Leicester Infirmary Records, (Leicestershire Record Office 13D54 14/1-45)
Chinnery, G A, ed. *Records of the Borough of Leicester 1689-1835* (Leicester University Press 1965)
Combe, Thomas. *Leicester Directory* (Leicester 1827)

Secondary Sources

Anon. *An Enquiry into the Melancholy Circumstances of Great Britain* (c.1775).
Anon. *Leicester Illustrated 1891* (London).
Adams, E. D. *Great Britain and the American Civil War* (Gloucester Mass 1957).
Aston, C E John, ed. *Leicester Polytechnic – Centenary History of the School of Textiles* (Leicester Polytechnic Press 1983).
Billson, Charles James. *Leicester Memoirs* (Leicester 1924).
Cradock, Joseph. *Literary and Musical Memories* vols I-IV (London 1828).
Crutchley, Neil. 'Benjamin Burrows 1891-1966' in *Leicestershire and Rutland Heritage* (Issue 8, Autumn 1990)
Deutsch, Otto. *Handel A Documentary Biography* (1955).
Dickens, Charles. *Sketches by Boz* (London 1834).
Dictionary of National Biography.
Ellis, Isabel C. *Nineteenth Century Leicester* (1935).
Fielding-Johnson, Agnes. *Glimpses of Ancient Leicester* 2nd edition (Leicester 1906).
Foster, Joseph. *Alumni Oxonienses* (London 1891).
Gardiner, William. *Inauguration of the Statue of Beethoven at Bonn* (Leicester 1846).
Gardiner, William. *Music and Friends or Pleasant Recollections of a Dilitante* Volumes I, II (1836) and III (1853).
Grewcock, Craig E. 'The Leicester Mechanics' Institute 1833-70', in *The Adaptation of Change Essays upon the History of 19th Century Leicester and Leicestershire*, ed. Daniel Williams (Leicester 1980).
Kirby, Mary. *Leaflets from my Life* 2nd edition (Leicester 1888)
Leacroft, Helen and Richard, *The Theatre in Leicestershire* (Leicester 1986).
Mackerness, E.D. *A Social History of English Music* (London 1964).
MacNutt and Slater. *Leicester Cathedral Organ* (Leicester 1930).

Medforth, Martin. 'The Valentines of Leicester' in *Musical Times* December 1981.
Mellor, G.J. *The Northern Music Hall*
Morris, Ernest. *The Bells of the Cathedral Church of St Martins Leicester* (unpublished LRO DE1564/404).
Nichols, John. *History and Antiquities of Leicestershire* (London 1795-1815).
North, Thomas. *Church Bells of Leicestershire* (Leicester 1876).
Prophet, John. *Church Langton and William Hanbury* (Sycamore Press 1982).
Read, Robert. *Modern Leicester* (Leicester 1881).
Sadie, S. ed. *The New Grove Dictionary of Music and Musicians* (London 1980).
Soldene, E. *Theatrical and Musical Recollections.*
Spencer, J. & T. *Leicestershire and Rutland Notes and Queries* (Leicester and London 1891).
Spencer, J. & T. *Spencers Illustrated Leicester Almanac,* (Leicester 1880).
Sumner, W. L. 'The Organs of St Margarets Church Leicester' in *The Organ* Vol. XXXVI April 1957.
Syer, Geoffrey. 'Beethoven and William Gardiner' in *Musical Times* May 1987.
Syer, Geoffrey. *The First Performance* (Plover Press 1987).
Talbot, Arthur B. *More or Less-stir* (Leicester 1911).
Taylor, S. *Taylor & Son, Organ builders, New Street Leicester* (Leicester c1915).
Temperley, Nicholas. *Music in Britain – The Romantic Age 1800-1914* (London 1981).
Temple-Patterson, A. *Radical Leicester* (Leicester 1954).
Thomas, Hermann. *History of the Great Meeting* (Leicester 1908).
Thompson, James. *Leicester in the Eighteenth Century* (Leicester 1871).
Venn, J. A. *Alumni Cantabrigienses* (Cambridge 1953).
Wade-Matthews, Max. *Grave Matters, A Walk Through Welford Road Cemetery, Leicester* (Heart of Albion Press 1992).
Wade-Matthews, Max. *The Monuments of the Church of St Margarets Leicester* (Heart of Albion Press 1995).
Wade-Matthews, Max. *The Monuments of the Church of St Martins, Leicester* (Heart of Albion Press 1994).
Wade-Matthews, Max. *The Monuments of the Church of St Mary de Castro Leicester* (Heart of Albion Press 1993).

Wade-Matthews, Max. *The Monuments of St Nicholas Church and All Saints Church Leicester* (Heart of Albion Press 1994).
Williams, Richard H. *The Parish Church of St Helen Ashby de la Zouch* (Ashby de la Zouch 1980).
Wilshere, Jonathan E. O. *Leicester Towne Waytes* (Leicester 1970).
Wilshere, Jonathan E. O. *William Gardiner of Leicester* (Leicester 1970).
Wright, Lawrette. *Souvenirs for a Century 1888–1988* (Layport 1988).

𝄞 INDEX 𝄞

All places, societies, bands, etc. are in Leicester unless otherwise stated.

Abbey Park 174
Adcock, John 89, 110, 115
Addison, John 187, 202
Adelphi Philosophical Society 16
African Opera Troupe 108
Alhambra Music Hall (Belgrave Gate) 109
Allen, Richard 191
Amateur Harmonic Society 123, 137, 149, 182
Amateur Instrumental Society 137, 196
Amateur Musical and Dramatic Society 155, 196
Amateur Philharmonic Orchestra 188
Amateur Vocal Society 145, 182
American Civil War 126, 137
Amphitheatre 85, 86, 117
Anderson, Lucy 83
Anemonic Union 125, 145, 196
Angelus Orchestral 53
Anglo-Viennese Ladies Orchestra 110
Apollo Glee Union 155
Aptommas 125
Armstrong, William 189
Arnold, Thomas 22
Askew, Alice 176
Aspull, George 76
Assembly Room (Haymarket) 2, 5, 6, 7, 8, 27
Assembly Room (Hotel Street) 21–23, 28, 32, 34, 59, 67, 72, 74, 137, 143, 147, 149, 204
Attwood, Thomas 49
Austin, Alfred 50
Austin, Elizabeth 34, 37, 64

Band Of Hope 137, 175
Barker, George 76, 84, 136
Barlow, Arthur 187
Barlow's Commercial Room 28, 40
Barnett, John Francis 128
Barnett, Morris 29
Barrow, William 142, 156, 180
Barthélmon, François 35
Barthélmon, Mary 8
Baschik, Kransky 104
Bass, John 2
Bates, Joah 11, 12
Bath Gardens 11
Beethoven - music first played in England 15–16; Statue in Bonn 16
Belgrave Gate Theatre 109
Belgrave Musical Society 121
Bell founding 157
Bellairs, George 33
Belvoir Castle 114, 163
Bennett, William Sterndale 184, 187
Betjeman, J. 195
Bett, Thomas 158
Biggs, Edward 159
Biggs, John (statue) 181
Bilson, Charles 169

Birch, Charles 176
Birmingham Flute Society 123; Music Festival 37
Bishop, Anna 83; Henry 81, 110
Bithrey, William 48
Blagrove, Henry 38, 99, 103
Blagrove, Richard 34, 38, 121
Blagrove, William 99
Bland, Angelina 26
Bland, C. 38, 39
Bland, Henry 25–26
Blind Institute 110, 136
Bochsa, Nicholas 77, 81
Boulton, William 5
Bowater, Frances 15
Bowling Green (St Peters Lane) 12, 27
Boyce, William 8
Bradgate Park 165
Braham, John 33, 37, 38, 60, 69, 70, 72, 85
Bramley apple 144
Branston, William 93, 99, 119, 136
Brass Bands: Albion 178; Archibald Turner Work's 175; Belgrave 175; Bradgate House Brass Band 126; Caillard Boys' Home 177; Gasworks 168, 177, 181; Great Glen 175; Highfields 168, 178; Hodges & Son Work's 175; Leicester Workhouse 179; Midland Railway 163, 175, 180; Newtown Linford 162, 175, 180; Imperial Prize band *q.v.* Highfields Band; People's Band 169; Police Band 163, 168, 175-177; Rawson's Work's 163; Richardson's Works 177; Saxe Coburg St 175; Temperance and Albion 168; Volunteer Rifle 137, 163, 168, 171, 177; Wesley Temperance 163, 175, 179; Working Men's Club 135
Brass Bands: Contests 179, 180; Leicester Festival 179; Sunday Concerts 169-170
Briggs, William Thorpe 119, 121, 122
British Music Society 44
Brooke, John 15
Brousil family 107
Brown, Samuel 50
Browne, Thomas Chapman 120
Brummel, George 'Beau' 24
Buchanan, John 168
Bunney, Walter 151, 183
Burden, William 51
Burnaby, Rev. Robert 12, 15
Burnaby, Rev. Thomas 15, 22, 33, 34
Burrows, Benjamin 46, 189, 191
Burton, John 173
Butt, Clara 192

Cambridge, Frederick 144
Caradori, Maria 65
Carl Rosa Opera Company 134
Cartwright, Samuel 152
Caruso, Enrico 192
Castle 3, 8, 160
Catlin, Richard 56
Cave, George 173
Change Ringers, Society of 158
Chapels: Bishop St 137, 152; Bond St 44, 197; Carley St 171; Clarendon Park 153, 195; Curzon St 183; Emmanuel 188; Gallowtree

Gate 152; Great Meeting 7, 16, 93, 141, 152, 157; Harvey Lane 184; Humberstone Rd 145,146; London Rd 188; Saxe-Coburg St 199; Victoria Rd 46, 147, 153
Chapman, John 178
Charles Moore Collection 129
Charlestown Opera Troupe 108
Cherubini, Luigi 34
Chiroplast 39
Choral Society 41-42, 78, 90, 102, 147, 183, 185
Christy Minstrels 107
Church Congress 149
Church Langton 6
Churches: All Saints 157; Holy Cross (RC) 37, 156; Holy Trinity 121, 143, 144, 148, 151; St Andrews 143; St George 140, 160, 174; St John's 110, 138, 142, 144, 145, 149; St Leonards 143; St Mark's 142, 160; St Margaret's 7, 8, 15, 22, 42, 59, 66, 69, 121,122, 140, 141, 143, 147, 158, 159, 183, 192; St Martin's 3, 5, 6, 8, 11, 32, 61, 62, 70, 140, 142, 147, 148, 149, 150, 151, 158, 191; St Mary de Castro 33, 42, 44, 46, 127, 138, 142, 144, 145, 159, 160; St Nicholas 51, 141, 142; St Pauls 190; St Peters 151, 191; St Saviours 139
Clarke, John 173, 178, 180
Clementi, Mazio 37
Clock Tower 2, 138
Clowes, Anna Maria 45
Cockpit 22

Coleman, Robert 15
Collins family 89, 107
Coltman, William 50
Combe, Thomas 22, 34, 57, 62, 75
Commemorative Exhibition (1897) 181
concertina 50, 89, 121
Conservative Club 110
Cook Memorial Hall 112
Cook, Annie 112
Cook, Catherine 147
Cook, Thomas 98, 100, 112
Corah & Son's Band 175
Corn Exchange 104, 192
Corpus Christi Gild 3
Cort, Law & Co 48
County College of Music 200
County Rooms *q.v.* Assembly Room
Cox, Robert 55
Cradock, Joseph 8, 62
Cramer, Franz 59
Craven, Richard 146
Cremona Musical Union 107
Cricket Ground (Wharf Street) 67, 97, 114, 135, 165, 180
Crimean War 135, 171
Crotch, William 18
Crow, Edwin John 143–144

Dalby Hall 15
Dancing Masters, Association of 143
Dare, Henry Morgan 137
Davis, French 102, 125
Davis, John 31
De Montfort Hall 203, 204
Deacon Prize 46, 153
Deacon, Adelaide 44
Deacon, Frederick 43

Index

Deacon, John 43
Deacon, Lucy 44, 45
Deacon, Mary Ann 44–46, 89, 91, 96, 99, 129, 121, 124, 146, 150, 154, 163, 182
Deacon, Samuel (senior) 43
Deacon, Samuel (junior) 35, 42-44, 49, 50, 57, 66, 99, 141
Derby Choral Union 150
Dibdin, Charles 18, 49, 126, 185
Discharged Prisoners Aid Association 175
Distin, John 105, 121, 124, 168
Distin's Brass Band Journal 105
Döbler Abbe 15-16, 119
Dobney, Frederick 49, 57
Dobney, Frederick 49
Dodgson, William 55
Downing, Lucy 195
Dragonetti, Domenico 60
Duke of Rutland: Band 26, 81, 114, 117, 119, 128, 162, 163, 165; statue 181

Eames, William 50
Early Closing Association 135
Electric Pianista 110
Ella, Henry 45, 46
Ella, John 29, 31, 35, 39, 82
Ellis, Ethelwyn 146
Ellis, Henry Bramley 144-146, 149, 154, 182, 188, 195, 202
Ellis, Leonard 146
Elvey, Sir George 148, 185
Emmet, Dan 107
Exchange 3, 4, 36

Farmer, Henry 91, 115, 122, 138, 152; John 135
Fèmy, Ambrose 34

Fèmy, François 30, 34, 39, 89
Fèmy, Henry 34
Findley, George 55
Findley, William 55
Flint, William 76
Floral Hall 113, 176, 180, 181, 197, 199
Fosse Football Club 139, 190
Foster, Beatrix 151
Foster, Joseph 151
Foster, Stephen 107
Fowke, Frederick 34, 74
Framework Knitters Relief Fund 114
Freak, Frederick 28
Freer, Dr John 31
Freestone, John 175

Galer, Elliot 123, 131, 133, 173
Gamble, Cyrus 201, 202
Gamble, Ernest 189
Gamble, John 110
Gardiner, Thomas 7, 11, 15, 93
Gardiner, William 2, 15, 16, 29, 34, 35, 37, 39, 41, 57, 59, 61, 62, 64, 73, 74, 75, 87, 93–96, 135
Garrick, David 8, 175
Garrick, James 175
Garrick, Tom 175, 177
Giardini, Felice 8
Gilbert, Frank 178
Gill, Henry 80, 83, 90, 91, 93, 99, 119, 153
Ginn, Henry 102
Gladstone, Thomas 23
Goddard, Henry 117, 138
Goldschmidt, Otto 102
Goodrich, William 184

Gouldburn, Edward 23
Great Washington Lady Troupe 109
Greatorex, Anthony 61
Greatorex, Thomas 61, 74
Gregory, John 6
Groocock, Walter 143, 200
Grove, George 185
Guildhall 2, 3, 4, 15, 76, 176
Gumley Hall 8, 12
Guynemer, Charles 37, 38, 39, 81, 82

Halford, Sir Henry 164
Halle, Charles 125, 186
Hanbury, William 6
Hancock, Charles 45, 148-151, 184, 188
Handscomb, Isaac 39, 78, 82, 93, 141
Hanford, Henry 141
Harbot, Benjamin 50
Harmonic Society 182
Harrison, James 19
Hayes, William 6
Heighton, Musgrave 5
Hewitt, John 39, 57, 95
Hextall's Long Room 27
Heyrick, Robert 49
Hickling Square 97
Hill, Dr John 57, 77
Hodgkins, Elizabeth 196
Hodgson, Thomas 4
Hoffmann's Organophonic Band 112
Holmes, Mr 29
Horn, Charles 49
Hough, Henry 82
Howe, Earl 65
Hudson, Sir Charles 62
Humberstone, Andrew 177

Hungarian Music Company 112
Hymns Ancient And Modern 141

Infantry Volunteers 36
Infirmary 8, 22, 37, 80, 103, 110, 137, 150, 154
Infirmary Ode 8
Inns and public houses:
    Angel 34; Bell 23, 41, 85, 182; Blackamoor Lady 14; Black Horse 101; Cap And Stocking 5; George 27, 28, 41, 44, 68; New Inn 28; New Inn, Newtown Linford 165; Plough 85; Saracen's Head 28; Stag And Pheasant 85; Three Cranes 6, 12, 68; Three Crowns 12, 31, 68; White Hart 27, 28; White Lion 182

Jackson, Enderby 179: J 150
Japanese Tommy 108
Jarvis, Charles 35, 37
Jarvis, Sarah 35, 36, 37, 39, 58, 84
Jelley, Annie 188, 195
Jelley, J. 175
Johannessen, Karl 201
Johnson's Jewellers 28
Johnson, John 22
Jones, Ebenezer 29, 58
Jubilee Singers 139
Jullien, Louis 85–87, 90, 117

Keeton, Dr Hayden 151, 185
Keighley, Thomas 169
Keighley, William 95
Keiserwetter, Mr 65
Kentucky Minstrels 108

Index

Kienle, Theodore 202
Kilby, John 187, 192, 202
King & Co 31
Klee, Joseph 156
Knyvett, Mrs 72
Knyvett, William 62
Kyrle Society 197

Ladies Fund for the Relief of the Poor 23
Lake, George 89
Lancashire Relief Fund 137
Landergan, A. 138
Laurence, Alexander 50
Laxton, Thomas 126
Leamington Quadrille Band 30, 85
Leicester lifeboat 137
Lester, Cecilia 46; Dr H. T. 137
Lilling, Richard 140
Lind, Jenny 102–103
Lindley, George 81
Lindley, Robert 59, 84
Linwood, Mary 24, 36, 57
Liszt, Franz 75, 91, 199
Literary And Philosophical Society 96, 183
Litoff's Quadrille Band 74
Livermoor Minstrels 110
Lockey, Charles 99
Logier, Johann 39
Löhr, Frederick 143
Löhr, George 45, 93, 121, 123, 141, 143, 157, 182, 186, 192
Löhr, Harvey 182
Löhr, Richard 143
London Musical Union 31
Lounde, John 140
Lowe, J.W. 51
Lucas, Charles 98

Madrigal Society 183
Maffre, Joseph 35, 36, 39, 58
Malibran, Maria 78, 80
Mammatt, Edward 40, 78
Manning, John 97
Mansfield, John 22, 57, 74
Mansfield, Robert 189
Mara, Gertrude 11
Mark, Dr 136
Markham, John 179
Marshall's Midland Musical Depot (Rutland St) 51, 192
Marshall, James Herbert 51-55, 134, 191, 200, 201
Martin, Abraham 149
Mason, William 200
Masonic Hall 121, 147
Matthews, Harry 189, 202
Mavius, Charles 39, 40, 42, 46-48, 58, 66, 67, 82, 83, 90, 91, 112
May, Christopher 186
May, Henry 183
McAlpin, Colin 195
McAlpin, Donal 188
McRobie, James 139, 183
Mechanics' Institute 42, 91, 92, 93, 96
Merrylees Virginia Female Christy Minstrels 109
Midland Steam Pianoforte Works 50
Militia Band 11-12, 16, 35, 129, 167, 173
Minstrel Troupes 107–110
Mitford, Capt. 49
Monroe, James 38, 85
Moore, Francis 55
Moore, William 50
Mori, Nicholas 77
Morland, James 147

Morland, John 147–148
Moulds, Arthur 175
Museums: New Walk 143, 183, 200; Newark Houses 73
Music Society 33, 35, 78, 102, 133, 191
Muston, Frank 197
Muston, James 191
Muston, Joseph 191, 202

National Grand Opera 134
National Music Library 31
National Sunday League 169
Nedham, William 68
New Choral Society 183–185
New Hall (Wellington Street) 22, 23, 75, 76, 78, 80, 83, 87, 90, 91, 136, 173, 183, 204
New Musical Society 150, 151, 182, 186, 191
New Orpheus Society 174, 196
New Philharmonic Society 136, 184
Newark Orphanage 135
Newcombe, Robert 158
Newcombe, Thomas 140, 157
Nicholson, Alfred 45, 91, 92, 115, 117, 120, 121, 126–129, 135, 178, 181, 183
Nicholson, Arthur 125
Nicholson, Henry (senior) 23, 26, 58, 61, 75, 89, 114, 141, 162, 165, 166, 168
Nicholson, Henry (junior) 32, 44, 45, 88–92, 98, 99, 102, 105, 111, 114, 115, 117–127, 129, 133, 135, 137, 138, 145, 150, 152, 173, 180, 181, 183, 184, 186, 187, 191
Nicholson, Valentine 99, 115, 122, 129
Nicholson, William 124, 126
Nikita 192
Noble, William 155
Norman, Barak 7
Norton, John 34, 35, 37, 82, 99
Novello, Clara 81, 121

Odames, Samuel 168
Ohrmann, Jonathan 7
Old Confractory 147
Oldershaw, Christopher 93, 96, 99, 119, 163
Oliver, Thomas 77
Opera House, Royal 115, 131, 156, 175, 185, 190, 201
Orchestral Union 104, 152, 153, 186, 191
Orpheus Society 151, 184
Oxford Music Hall 109

Padereswski, I 192
Paganini, Niccolò 75, 78, 80, 114, 117
Paget, Alfred 121, 183, 188, 189
Paget, Thomas 25, 37, 77, 83, 174
Paget, Thomas Tertius 133, 185
Palmer, Caleb 177, 181
Parry, John 83
Parsons, William 38, 85, 149
Partington, George 26–28
Pasta, Guidetta 65, 69
Paton, Mary Ann 65
Patti, Adelina 125, 129, 192
Paul, William 109
Payne, Benjamin 27, 67
Peach, Thomas 34
Penny Concerts 197
People's Dispensary 139

Index

Performing Rights Society 197
Permanent Orchestra 201–202
Petch, William 50
Philharmonic Society 44, 123, 137, 147, 151, 191–195, 200, 201, 204
Phillips, Henry 60
Phillips, John 5
Phonographic Society 53
Piano Forte Magazine 19
Picco 103–104
Plant, Stephen 178
Pohlmann, Johannes 18
Pole, A.T. 51
Pole, James 51
Pole, Thomas 51
Pollock A.F. 197
Pollock, Daisy 197
Porritt, John 146
Porritt, Joshua 102, 145, 157
Powell, Henry 131
Pringle Scholarship 151
Promenade Concerts 118
Prussian Horn Band 80
Ptacek, Francis 164, 166, 168, 171–175
Punch 123, 201

Quilter, Edward 32
Quinn, William 139

Railway 85, 90, 149, 179, 183, 185, 190, 195; Benevolent Institution Orphanage 110; special trains 165
Rainer family 40
Ray, Mr 24
Read, Robert 164
Reeves, Fanny 131, 173
Reeves, Herbert 102
Reeves, Sims 90, 91, 102, 103, 119, 123, 124, 126, 133
Richter, Willibald 199–200
Rigby, Vernon 186
Robertson, Miss 28
Rosa, Carl 132, 134
Rowe, Ranshall 152
Rowlett, Elizabeth 93, 121
Rowlett, Frank 145, 153, 154, 188
Rowlett, William 152, 154, 188, 189
Rowlett, William Tertius 153
Royal College of Music 176
Royal Opera House 115, 131, 156, 175, 185, 190, 201
Royal Theatre (Royal) 37, 38, 59, 85, 89, 102, 112, 131, 134, 135, 164, 175, 178, 181
Russell, Henry 88, 107
Rutland, Duke of: Band 26, 81, 114, 117, 119, 128, 162, 163, 165; statue 181
Rutland Street Ice Rink 187

Sainton, Charlotte 185
Salomon, Johann 16
Salvation Army 170
Sandwich, Earl of 8, 15, 61
Santley Prize 143
Santley, Charles 45, 126, 186
Sax, Adolphe 105
School of Art 164
Schools: Alderman Newtons Green Coat 183; Belgrave 136; Dover Street 144; Medway 190; St Mary's 138; Red Cross Street 90; Stoneygate 29; Syston 197; Thorpe St 197; Uppingham 200; Wyggeston 145
Scott, Mary 147

Scott, Thomas 147
Secular Choral Union 196
Sedan chair 36
Seddon, T. 178
Selby, Thomas 115
serpent 35
Sharpe, Elizabeth 39, 78, 82, 84, 89, 153
Simpkin, Joseph 175
Smallfield, George 119
Smart, Caroline 29
Smart, Charles 29
Smart, Sabrina 29
Smith, Charles Loraine 33, 74
Smith, John 55, 88, 99, 115, 162, 168, 175, 180, 201
Smith, Percy Skeffington 197
Snetzler, John 7, 11, 147
Soldene, Emily 133
Sophie and Annie 106, 135
Sousa, John Philip 117, 181
Southfields College 173
Southwell Minster 144
Spencer, John 50
Spencer, Thomas 50
Spiers, Thomas 51
St John's Ambulance Brigade 139
St Leonard's Choral Society 200
St Margaret's Catch Club 7
St Martin's Musical Society 147
Stafford, John 157
Stephens, Catherine 64, 124
Sternberg, Thomas 47, 48, 58
Stewart, Reuben 143
Stockhausen, Franz 82
Stone, Joseph T. 144
Storace, Nancy 38
Stork, Arthur 199
Sunday School Union 171
Sutton Charity 154

Swiss Female Singers 112
Symphony Orchestra 179
Syston Choral Society 147

Talbot, Arthur 46
Tay Bridge disaster 129
Taylor, Cardinal 156
Taylor, John H. 155
Taylor, Stephen 154, 157
Taylor, Thomas 165
Temperance Hall 45, 75, 97–110, 127, 131, 133, 135, 136, 138, 150, 151, 155, 164, 174, 182, 184, 188, 191, 201, 202
Teray, Mr 28
Theatre, Royal 37, 38, 59, 85, 89, 102, 112, 131, 134, 135, 164, 175, 178, 181
Thomas E.W. 201
Thomas, Victor 46
Thornton Reservoir 100
Tilley, William 12, 18
Toone, Richard 78, 82
town walls 7
Tyrolean Minstrels 112
Tyrrell, Mr 4

University College 46

Valentine, Ann 15
Valentine, Henry 5, 14, 15
Valentine, John 5, 14
Valentine, Mark 5
Vauxhall Gardens 12, 27
Viccars, Samuel 29
Victoria Coffee and Cocoa House 53, 188
Victoria Park 163–164
Vinning, Louisa 104
von Bulow, Hans 187

Waddington, Sidney 185, 194
Waddington, Walter 53, 189, 202
Wagner, Richard 134
Waits 1–2, 43, 175
Waldrom, John 35, 37, 58, 114
Wale, William 145, 186
Wanlip Hall 62
Ward, Cornelius 115
Ward, George 51
Waterloo Hall 149, 190
Watson, Edward 181
Welford Road Cemetery 28, 97, 117, 127, 142, 151, 153, 175
Wesley Hall Orchestra 200
Wesley, John 152
West End Choral Society 200
Weston, C. 99, 115
Weston, Elizabeth 82
Weston, Samuel 26, 41
Weston, Thomas 91, 99, 115, 119, 141, 180, 184
Weston, William 168
Whetstone, Charles 50, 89
Whitwick Colliery disaster 190
Windley, Sybil 146
Windley, Thomas 146
Windram, William 50
Wingrave, Lina 200
Winks, Frederick 97
Winks, Joseph 97
Winterhalder, Joseph 156
Winterton, William 113
Wood, Edward 46
Wood, Henry 49
Wood, Joseph 184
Wood, William 55
Working Mens' Institute 175
Wright, Lawrence 203
Wykes, Elizabeth 99, 141
Wykes, Lewis 153

Wykes, Samuel 82, 84, 88, 141
Wykes, Thomas 145, 153, 188

Yeomanry Cavalry Band 114, 116, 117, 129, 135, 162, 165, 175
YMCA 147, 197

Zerdahalj 135

Also by Max Wade-Matthews
and published by Heart of Albion Press

Great Glen - The Story of a Leicestershire Village

Glen's history can be traced to the Iron Age and the arrival of the Romans. It became a royal estate centre in the Anglo-Saxon era but then faded into relative obscurity, although we know how the rigours of the English Civil War affected Great Glen.

Village life was boosted with the advent of regular coach services in 1760, followed by the mail coach service a quarter of a century later, although these in turn were ousted by the arrival of the railway in 1857.

Max Wade-Matthews well-informed and, at times dramatic, narrative shows how local families and the Church shaped community life during all these times of change. The preoccupations of past generations are shown to be much like those of our own day - such as how to assist the poor and single mothers, how to raise local taxes and fund local road maintenance, together with the tensions between those leading the Church and those teaching the young.

This book will delight anyone curious about the village's history. The information on St Cuthbert's church provides an introduction for visitors, while the information about former residents will assist those interested in 'family tree' research.

A5, 74 pages, 20 b&w photos, 5 line drawings, 6 maps.

£4.95

Also by Max Wade-Matthews
and published by Heart of Albion Press

Grave Matters
A Walk Around Welford Road Cemetery, Leicester

No Gothic horror tale but a guide to the lives of some of the eminent citizens of Leicester who are interred in this Victorian cemetery. A5, 43 pages, 37 photos, 10 line drawings, 1 map, card covers. **£2.95**

The Monuments of the Church of St Mary de Castro, Leicester

A complete transcription of the funeral monuments of this historic church, with brief biographies of many of the more notable persons. A5, card covers, 50 pages, 2 illustrations. **£2.95**

The Monuments of St Martin's Church Leicester

The most extensive of the series, covering the Cathedral's many notable internments.
A5, 76 pages, card covers. **£3.95**

The Monuments of St Nicholas Church and All Saints Church Leicester

Continuing the series of booklets transcribing the monuments of Leicester's city churches with brief biographies of notable internees. A5, 38 pages, card covers. **£2.50**

The Monuments of the Church of St Margaret, Leicester

The last of the series covering Leicester's medieval churches. A5, 56 pages, card covers. **£3.50**

Also available from Heart of Albion Press

Cinema in Leicester 1896–1931

David Williams

If you have enjoyed *Musical Leicester* then you will want to explore the history of Leicester's 'popular culture' by reading *Cinema in Leicester*. Thorough research into the early cinemas of the city with no less than 233 illustrations.

A5, full colour laminated card cover, 260 pages. **£12.95**

The Heart of Albion catalogue contains details of nearly *fifty* books and booklets on Leicestershire local history - and many more titles.

Please phone, write or e-mail for your copy:

Heart of Albion Press
2 Cross Hill Close, Wymeswold
Loughborough, LE12 6UJ, UK

01509 880725

bobtrubs@gmtnet.co.uk

Or visit the on-line catalogue:
http://www.gmtnet.co.uk/indigo/albion/